The Legal Fraternity and the Making of a New South Community, 1848–1882

ᔕᔕᔕ

The Legal Fraternity
and the Making
of a New South Community,
1848–1882

ᔕᔕᔕ

Gail Williams O'Brien

The University of Georgia Press

ATHENS AND LONDON

This publication has been supported by the National Endowment for the Humanities, a federal agency which supports the study of such fields as history, philosophy, literature, and languages.

© 1986 by the University of Georgia Press
Athens, Georgia 30602
Set in Linotron 202 Galliard
The paper in this book meets the guidelines for permanence and durability of the Committee on Production Guidelines for Book Longevity of the Council on Library Resources.
Printed in the United States of America

90 89 88 87 86   5 4 3 2 1

Library of Congress Cataloging in Publication Data

O'Brien, Gail Williams
    The legal fraternity and the making of a new South community, 1848–1882.

    Bibliography: p.
    Includes index.
    1. Community organization—North Carolina—Guilford County—History—19th century. 2. Power (Social Sciences) —History—19th century. 3. Lawyers—North Carolina— Guilford County—History—19th century. 4. North Carolina—Economic conditions. 5. North Carolina— Social conditions. I. Title.
HN79.N82G856   1986   306'.09756   85-28952
ISBN 0-8203-0849-8 (alk. paper)

Contents

∽∙∽∙∽

Tables

*One place comprehended can make us
understand other places better.
Sense of place gives equilibrium;
extended, it is sense of direction too.*

—Eudora Welty, *The Eye of the Storm*

Acknowledgments

ᗡᨵᔿᨵᔿᨵᗞ

Many individuals contributed to the completion of this work. I initially benefited from the advice and assistance of Donald G. Mathews at the University of North Carolina at Chapel Hill. Both the concepts and personal support and encouragement of Samuel P. Hays also proved crucial as I worked with him at the University of Pittsburgh.

Stuart Blumin, Michael Frisch, and Harry Watson offered thoughtful comments on the project, and Paul Escott gave the entire manuscript one of the most careful, sensitive readings that it received. I also owe thanks to James Barrett, William Harris, James Horton, Anthony LaVopa, Steven Vincent, and particularly Joseph Hobbs for their suggestions and support. Elizabeth Suval rendered vital assistance on the regression analysis, and John O'Brien took time during critical stages of his own endeavors to write the point assignment program and to assist in the interpretation of statistics during the early phases of the analysis.

The staffs at Perkins Library at Duke University, the Southern Historical Collection at the University of North Carolina, and the North Carolina Department of Archives and History provided tireless assistance and good humor. Thanks in particular to Frank Gatton, Percy Hines, Dick Lankford, Minnie Peebles, and Richard Shrader. I should like to offer a special word of gratitude to Malcolm Call, who did all he said he would as the manuscript progressed through the review process and who was willing to take some risk with a nontraditional product. Thanks to those who labored tirelessly in the production of the work, Terri Anderson, Trudie Calvert, Ellen Harris, and Annette Smith, as well as to Patricia Gwaltney for her special part. I also appreciate the support of the National Endowment for the Humanities for its role in funding the publication of the book.

This book is dedicated to John, who in many ways made it possible, and to Kelly, who made it worthwhile.

Introduction

ぐんぐんぐん

Compared with the rest of the nation, the South barely held its own in industrial development following the Civil War, but it achieved much in absolute terms. Even in the war decade, manufacturing expanded in striking contrast to agriculture, and industrialization accelerated following the end of Reconstruction and a nationwide economic recession in the mid-1870s. Production of cotton textiles was particularly impressive, with the number of southern spindles almost doubling in the 1880s and more than doubling in the following decade. Capital invested in textiles grew from $22.8 million in 1880 to $123.4 million by the turn of the century.[1]

Nowhere in Dixie was the quickening pace of industrialization more striking than in North Carolina. The poorest southern state in 1860, the Old North State distinguished itself as an industrial leader by 1900, making significant gains in tobacco, furniture, and, most notably, textiles. Doubling the value of textile production between 1860 and 1880, North Carolina then added cotton mills at an average rate of six per year in the last two decades of the nineteenth century.

Did industrialization accelerate in the postwar South because the Civil War catapulted new leaders into power? C. Vann Woodward in his landmark study, *Origins of the New South,* published in 1951, replied that an "industrial evolution" had indeed occurred in the old Confederacy because a planter aristocracy had perished in the ashes of war and new, aggressive, middle-class entrepreneurs rose to take its place. Challenges to Woodward's thesis have appeared in recent years, but a definitive answer, based on existing literature, is complicated by the way scholars have categorized studies of the war and by the disparate approaches to power they have used.

Historians of the South have traditionally regarded the conflict as such a crucial event that they have organized most of their scholarship around it. Studies either end at the commencement of hostilities, focus solely on them, or begin with the Reconstruction or post-Reconstruction eras. Several investigations of the war's impact on the northern economy have suggested a different approach, and two recent monographs traced southern planters from the eve of the struggle through its aftermath.[2] But southern historians have rarely treated the pre- and postwar eras as a single unit. This tendency makes it difficult to assess the extent and nature of long-term political change in the South, just as it impedes an understanding of the war's effects on other aspects of society.

The disparate approaches to power that scholars of the ante- and postbellum periods have used and the divergent conclusions that analysts of the postwar era, in particular, have reached also complicate an assessment of political change. Students of the prewar South concerned themselves primarily with social structure and the composition of the Whig and Democratic parties.[3] A few also investigated public officials.[4] Historians of the postwar era concentrated on the quality of leadership provided during Reconstruction by Republicans and then by Democrats.[5] Several also discussed the social origins of Democratic leaders but disagreed on whether they represented forward-looking middle-class "Redeemers" with few ties to the old regime or backward-looking agrarian "Bourbons" with strong connections to old notables.[6]

A major problem with both the class and party analyses is the lack of a direct link between the individuals under discussion and the exercise of power. The students of social structure assumed that those who controlled most of society's resources exercised most of the power; those who investigated parties attributed authority to party leaders. Neither tested their assumptions by focusing on those who actually held positions of leadership.

Studies that focused on state officials who belonged to a particular party or on state and local officeholders per se confronted the issue of power more directly than those concerned with social structure or the composition of political parties, but they suffered from at least two drawbacks. First, they concerned only political officials and thereby excluded individuals who may have exercised power in other ways. Second, and more important, they described officeholders without regard to the specific social settings in which they operated. Therefore, it was impossible to compare these leaders with the population from which they derived and to understand them in relation to it. Thus if the analysts of social structure are right in their presumption that those at the top of the socioeconomic ladder dominated nineteenth-century southern society, studies of political officials as they have been conducted will not show it, just as studies of socioeconomic arrangements tell us little about political officeholding or participation in other public affairs.

This study analyzes participants in public affairs in a community setting. It begins a decade before the war and concludes fifteen years following it in an effort to determine the patterns of leadership under peaceful conditions and the short- and long-term effects of war on these patterns. It investigates powerholders per se to avoid preconceived notions about the implications of social structure or partisan arrangements for power relationships, and it focuses on a single community to facilitate the comparison of leaders with one another and with the local populace. It also uses a community approach because I believe the nature of nineteenth-century southern society demands local studies.

Unquestionably, a community study is the best way to investigate participants in all aspects of public affairs—economic, social, and cultural as well as political—and to compare leaders and followers. Studies at the local level are also more likely to include leaders from diverse backgrounds than those at wider levels of society, and they are essential in investigations of preindustrial America.

Social theorists interested in the term "community" usually define it in terms of people in social interaction, having one or more common ties, and a firm territorial base.[7] The ideal community meets the basic social needs—production, distribution, consumption, socialization, social control, social participation, and mutual support—and thus constitutes a place where individuals can satisfy their physiological, psychological, and social requirements.[8] As a type of "human whole" where virtually all life-sustaining activities are conducted, a community offers a unique opportunity for assessing the many facets of public leadership.[9]

Because movement at the local level of society is limited, residents concern themselves primarily with affairs related to their daily, personal lives. Individuals acquire knowledge and carry on activities through personal experiences and face-to-face encounters. The primary nature of human interaction at the local level is in contrast to secondary contacts, which occur over wider geographic areas such as states or nations.[10]

The variation between local communities built on primary relationships and larger social units constructed on secondary contacts gives rise to different social institutions, perceptions, and mechanisms of decision making. An individual who exercises power at the local level represents smaller constituencies and thinks in more specific terms than one who operates in a wider geographic framework. Different outlooks and abilities are required, and it is possible that persons from more heterogeneous backgrounds may wield more influence at the local level of society than at the state, regional, or national levels. To campaign over a broad geographic area requires considerable financial resources and leisure time, but the possession of an ability to remember constituents' names, a warm, firm hand-shake, and a reputation for personal integrity may suffice at the community level.[11]

The local level of society is not only intrinsically different from wider levels, but it also represented the most important echelon in preindustrial America. The significance of preindustrial communities derived from their capacity to satisfy most social and individual needs. This autonomy in turn made community leaders very powerful, but the growth of cities, the expansion of professions, the development of better methods of communication and transportation, and the acceleration of industry all promoted an upward shift in decision making. Local officials lost the undivided attention of constituents who developed secondary ties that broadened their contacts and perspectives, and they were bypassed as state leaders assumed greater responsibility for projects such as road construction. They were rendered increasingly impotent as absentee ownership of industrial enterprises occurred.[12] In contrast, local leaders remained preeminent in places characterized by limited industry and few cities. Not surprisingly, scholars have long regarded decentralization and particularism as important features of the nineteenth-century South.

Thus it is essential to investigate power arrangements in the nineteenth-century South in a community setting because this approach facilitates the analysis of complex political phenomena, focuses on the arena where decision makers had the greatest capacity to affect the lives of a large number of people, and enhances the possibility of identifying powerholders from diverse backgrounds. If large slaveholders exercised power at the local level of southern society, where they constituted a definite minority and where the acquisition of power was not as dependent on affluence as at wider levels, they must have been very important. Even if one argues that power lay ultimately with farmers and that they chose to use their collective influence to elevate planters to positions of authority, the discovery that large landowners held power would reveal a great deal about the values and attitudes of southern farmers and the basic ground rules under which the nineteenth-century South operated.

Although the nature of nineteenth-century southern society mandates studies of power at the local level, this unit of analysis presents certain practical problems for the contemporary researcher. First, because the inhabitants often moved within a limited geographic area and frequently interacted on a face-to-face basis, the "paper trail" is potentially less voluminous than that at wider levels of society. Additionally, the boundaries of communities are more abstruse than those of states or nations. Fortunately, in this particular investigation, lengthy visits by local legislators to the state and national capitals and prolonged absences from home necessitated by the war provided far more written communications than might otherwise have been the case. Too, the nineteenth-century practice of using local newspaper editors as secretaries of organizations and meetings resulted in detailed press coverage of local affairs. Committee members and delegates were usually enumerated along with important officers.

In the determination of community boundaries, southern counties came closer to the theoretical definition of a community than did neighborhoods or towns. Most counties included a small town, usually the county seat, and outlying farms.[13] The town or village served as a marketing and service center for local farmers and as the place where legal business was transacted. Political parties, schools, newspapers, and voluntary associations were also organized along county lines. Hence the nineteenth-century southern county constitutes a very appropriate unit for investigation. It meets the theoretical requirements of a community, and it offers a body of public, official documents that deal with the same issues and involve the same people as private, institutional records and individual papers.

A North Carolina piedmont county seemed a likely choice for analysis because the Tar Heel State had become the South's acknowledged industrial leader by 1900 and almost all of this development had occurred in the state's thirty-four piedmont counties.[14] Initially, it might seem inappropriate to focus on North Carolina, one of the poorest southern states before the war, and particularly on the piedmont, a region populated almost exclusively by small farmers before the conflict, but it was necessary to deal with an area where industrialization accelerated following the war to maximize the chances of discovering middle-class entrepreneurs or any other newcomers in positions of authority. Additionally, more people lived in the piedmont than in the coastal plain throughout the nineteenth century, at least in North Carolina, so that any study concerned with power arrangements that affected the most southerners would have to focus on that area.[15]

Using three major approaches to power, I identified individuals in positions of influence in the north-central North Carolina piedmont county of Guilford within two years of and including four census years, 1848, 1849, *1850* (census year), 1851, and 1852; 1858, 1859, *1860*, 1861, and 1862; 1868, 1869, *1870*, 1871, and 1872; and 1878, 1879, *1880*, 1881, and 1882. The identification of leaders in these four five-year spans of time constituted the first step in the development of a technique for measuring power, and it demonstrated the routes to influence in Guilford County and the war's effects on these routes. The investigation of avenues to power also underscored the "southern" qualities of this uplands community. The development of a technique for measuring power was essential because I wanted to assess the relative influence of various minorities such as planters within the county.

Once powerholders were identified and their relative influence in the community assessed, I compared them in a variety of ways. I looked, for example, to see whether the size of the four power groups increased or decreased over time relative to the larger community, whether leaders were achieving influence in the same ways, and to what extent the same individuals appeared in successive groups. I also categorized leaders in each group as high, medium, or low on the basis of their power scores and compared the personal characteristics of individuals in each category through time. Manuscript census returns provided most of the personal information. In all, I analyzed more than eighteen hundred participants in public affairs.

Designed meticulously to assess change, the study discovered considerable stability in power relationships. Elite control remained intact, caution and conservatism continued to characterize social and political relations, and economic progressivism prevailed after the conflict as before. Certainly, the war changed many aspects of life. In the political arena, the conflict and its aftermath produced a discordant two-party system that was in striking contrast to the partisan consensus that had previously existed. But most noticeably, considerable continuity prevailed.

In large part, stability persisted through the war era because of the growing importance of a strategic group within the county's elite—local attorneys. The multifaceted planter-businessman-attorney became noticeable on the eve of the war, and the influence of that group grew steadily throughout the postwar years. This trend, which occurred in much of the upper South, had important implications for Virginia, Tennessee, and, most notably, North Carolina.

Because this work considers both the war's impact on power arrangements and the role of attorneys in maintaining continuity, it is divided into two parts. Part I, "Power and Permanence," explains the selection of Guilford as a unit of study, investigates the routes to power and the war's effects on them, and examines statistically the impact of the war on leadership patterns. Particularly, it underscores a stability in power relationships that bitter Reconstruction politics belied.

Part II, "The Bar as a Strategic Elite," explores the role played by lawyers in building an economic consensus before the war and in maintaining it, despite partisan differences, following the conflict. It shows that in the darkest days of Reconstruction, attorneys never ceased interrelating socially or professionally and that they never floundered in their quest for economic development. At the same time, most lawyers, influenced by a variety of local and personal factors, avoided the party of black suffrage and local autonomy. Thus members of the bar were just as responsible for the limited democracy that characterized the upper South as they were for the economic gains it made.

Part I involves the constant interplay of theory and empirical evidence as it develops a paradigm for assessing political change. Part II, in turn, relies on more traditional historical methods as it explores the implications of the findings presented in Part I. The second segment could not have existed without the first, and both were essential if the investigation were to move beyond the current, incisive literature on southern social structure and partisan conflict. Above all, I hope that the combination of approaches reveals the complexity of the human experience while facilitating a better understanding of it.

PART I

Power and Permanence

1. *The Setting*

⪼⪻⪼⪻

Situated in the north-central piedmont of North Carolina, Guilford County possessed several attributes that made it attractive for investigation. In addition to abundant written records, including lengthy runs of Republican newspapers, Guilford had potential for crises, socioeconomic characteristics similar to other antebellum piedmont communities, and an industrial surge that commenced in the mid-1880s—the same time industrialization accelerated in other parts of the piedmont South.[1] The potential for crises was an important criterion of the community under investigation because leaders are sometimes so powerful that in the absence of stressful situations they can operate entirely "behind the scenes."[2] A remnant of Quakers and a number of Wesleyan Methodists, both of whom opposed slavery at a time when it was expanding within the community, assured open confrontations and the public appearance of leaders in Guilford County.

As in most North Carolina communities, settlers arrived in Guilford "secondhand" from other colonies. Especially, they traveled from Pennsylvania, down the great Philadelphia Wagon Road, between the years 1740 and 1775. They moved as families, establishing their own distinctive places of worship, and their names persisted among the annals of leadership. To eastern Guilford came members of the German Lutheran and German Reformed churches such as the Albrechts (Albrights), Brouns (Browns), Klaps (Clapps), Emigs (Amicks), Fausts (Fousts), Kaubs (Cobbs), and Weiricks (Wyricks). Temporarily submerging their religious differences in the face of frontier realities, these families united in the mid-1740s to build a log structure known as Fridans Church and, by 1770, another house of worship called first Der Klapp Kirche in recognition of the strenuous efforts of the Clapp family in establishing it and, later, Brick Church. By the time Brick Church was constructed, schismatic differences had become affordable, and Low's Lutheran was completed three years later. Coble's Lutheran followed Lowe's in 1812.

To southern and, more particularly, western Guilford came English Quakers bearing such names as Armfield, Beeson, Blair, Coffin, Gardner, Hodgin, Hunt, Pugh, Mendenhall, Starbuck, Welborn, and Worth. They established meeting houses at their frontier settlement of New Garden and later, at Deep River and Centre. Filling in the center of the county were Ulster Scots Presbyterians, whose ranks included the Caldwells, Dennys, Donnells, Gorrells, Lindsays, McAdoos, McMickels (McMichaels), and Weatherlys. The young Reverend David Caldwell proved astute enough to serve both Buffalo (Old Style) and Alamance (New Light) churches and to add to the family's income by establishing a classical school known as Log College. Log College alumni included a number of lawyers, judges, ministers, and physicians and no less than five state governors. Reverend Eli W. Caruthers, another prominent Guilford divine, followed Caldwell as pastor of Buffalo Church. By the early 1820s, through the encouragement of Reverend William D. Paisley, members of the Buffalo congregation who had moved to the county seat of Greensboro founded First Presbyterian Church, the home of a congregation described, even today, as "Greensboro's most prestigious."[3] Along with Paisley, other prominent ministers of this church during the nineteenth century included John A. Gretter and Jacob Henry Smith. Both immigrated from Virginia, with Gretter following Paisley and Smith taking over in 1859, when his predecessor, also named Smith, was driven from the community as a result of a dispute involving Smith's preaching of a tract on infant salvation.[4]

Although many of the early family names persisted among Guilford notables, the community lost much of its religious diversity by the middle of the nineteenth century because of an influx of Methodists and the emigration of many Quakers. Methodists established a church in Greensboro about 1829, and by midcentury, Methodist accommodations were far larger than those of any other single religious denomination. With twenty-four churches and a combined seating capacity of more than fifty-six hundred in 1850, Methodists had almost twice the accommodations of their closest rivals, the Quakers and Presbyterians, although the value of Presbyterian church property, with only four churches, was slightly higher than that of Methodists and much higher than that of Quakers. The German churches by this time possessed a combined seating capacity only half the size of that of the Presbyterians and Quakers and church property with value comparable to that of the Friends. A few Wesleyan Methodists organized churches in Guilford and surrounding counties in the fall and winter of 1847–48 in opposition to the proslavery stance of the Methodist Episcopal church, South, and about forty members petitioned the Allegheny conference in Ohio to send a minister. Small Baptist and Christian churches completed the religious establishments before the war.[5] The growing presence of the Methodist Episcopal church, South, was emphasized by the construction of a large church on West Market Street in Greensboro in 1851. This church was located near a "Methodist colony" created by community leaders and Reverends Peter Doub, S. D. Bumpass, and N. H. D. Wilson, and a well-known Methodist layman, Peter Adams.[6]

The decline of Quakerism in Guilford was related to the antislavery stance of the Friends. Although some Quakers continued in the nineteenth century to own slaves, many had never done so and a considerable number freed their chattels around the time of the American Revolution. As hostility toward antislavery advocates accelerated, approximately four hundred Quaker families emigrated around 1830. By 1850, all Protestant churches combined, excluding Friends, outnumbered Quakers almost five to one. Friends had only one-third of the total church accommodations in the community and one-ninth the church wealth.

Although the role of Quakers was decidedly less important by midcentury than it had been earlier, the Quaker legacy contributed to antislavery and antiwar sentiments among Guilford residents, not all of whom were Friends. Antislavery tensions climaxed in the trial of a former Quaker and Wesleyan Methodist minister, Daniel Worth, in 1859, and antiwar feelings were manifested in Unionist sentiment, which persisted among a stubborn minority throughout the war and resulted in a number of residents either hiding out "in the bushes" or fleeing northward to avoid conscription. The differences of opinion regarding troop procurement ultimately broke the Whig political consensus that characterized the antebellum community and thereby caused one of the most enduring effects of the war.

More important than the potential for conflicts or an abundance of sources, the socioeconomic characteristics of Guilford and the industrial direction that it took after the war made this county attractive for investigation. Guilford differed from other North Carolina piedmont counties only in that it was more successful in procuring roads and railroads than many, and it ardently embraced Whiggery longer than some (see Chapters 2 and 7).

Like most southern communities, Guilford was overwhelmingly agrarian with a growing slave population before the war, and it remained decidedly rural long after the conflict ended. Its leaders, similar to their counterparts in the rest of the landlocked piedmont, eagerly sought better means of transportation, ostensibly to facilitate the marketing of agricultural products. Several hamlets emerged along the county's expanding transportation arteries, but only the county seat town of Greensboro grew to any size before the war, and Greensboro's population did not begin to expand significantly until late in the nineteenth century. Hampered by the war and an agricultural depression, the growth of Greensboro and the county's second largest village, High Point, awaited the arrival of a new railroad and an industrial surge that began in the mid-1880s.[7]

The assumptions in this study about Guilford County as a rural community were no longer relevant and the indices for measuring power were no longer valid for Guilford during the period when industrialism accelerated in the last decade and a half of the nineteenth century, so the investigation ceased. The changes that began to develop in the mid-1880s were therefore important for two reasons. They figured prominently in the selection of the county for investigation, and they determined the timing of the conclusion of the work.

Throughout the years covered by the study, the composition of Guilford's work force underscored its agricultural orientation. Among employed workers in 1880, 69 percent were engaged in agriculture, and the proportion before the war was at least as high. The classification of agricultural workers by census enumerators as unskilled laborers rather than farmers made precise figures impossible to determine, but agrarians in 1860 probably represented about 80 percent of the county's work force (see Table 1).[8] Table 1 also shows that the business element of the community grew and that the proportion of artisans declined very slightly between 1860 and 1880. The percentage of professionals, like that of government officials, changed little over time.

A few copper mines operated in the community before the war, but very little manufacturing took place. A cotton mill, constructed in the 1830s, was relocated outside the county in 1850 because wood was scarce

TABLE I.

Percentage of Employed Workers by Occupation[a]

Year	Agriculture	Business	Professional	Government Officials	Artisans	Laborers
1860	38.4 (1,566)	4.4 (180)	3.0 (123)	0.3 (11)	8.5 (347)	45.4 (1,851)
1880	69.0 (5,359)	5.9 (461)	2.7 (209)	0.4 (33)	7.5 (582)	14.5 (1,127)

Source: Figures and percentages were derived from a hand count by the researcher of occupations listed in the population schedules of the Eighth and Tenth Censuses of the United States, 1860 and 1880: Guilford County, North Carolina; originals in NCDAH.

[a]Absolute numbers are in parentheses. For the specific jobs assigned to various occupational categories, see Appendix 1.

and no railroads existed to bring coal.[9] At midcentury, industry outside the home employed 159 hands and was capitalized at $89,625, with the largest establishment employing only 8 people. Efforts were launched in the 1870s to make Greensboro a center for tobacco manufacturing and, in the 1880s, for iron and steel production, but through the early 1880s, industry remained small in scale, serving primarily a local clientele.

A large number of Guilford agrarians owned no land, and the vast majority of the landowners operated small to medium-sized farms. That many agricultural workers were not landowners was suggested by the sizable proportion of the work force who were categorized in 1860 as laborers and in 1880, as agricultural workers. Landowners were usually designated as farmers. The limited scope of economic endeavors in the community outside of farming also suggested that most unskilled workers were engaged in agriculture. Finally, the discovery, demonstrated in Table 2, that almost 50 percent of the household heads before the war and over 50 percent after the conflict possessed no real property buttressed the idea that many agrarians owned no land. One can only speculate about work arrangements between farm owners and laborers before the war. Some of the unskilled workers may have been herdsmen who had few ties with owners, but it seems clear that a good number of day laborers, cash renters, or sharecroppers existed in the county long before the abolition of slavery and the alleged beginning of the sharecropping system. Among landowning farmers, only 2.5 percent (thirty-eight individuals) possessed farms in 1860 of five hundred acres or more, and just under 51 percent held one hundred acres or less.[10]

Largely subsistence farmers at midcentury, most grew grains and some cotton. A few also produced wool and a larger number, dairy products. Commercial nurseries and orchards were operated on a limited basis. When a railroad line was extended to the community in 1856 and another added during the war, many farmers began to shift from grain to tobacco cultivation. Between 1850 and 1880, wheat production increased less than 5 percent and the production of rye, oats, and corn fell by roughly 25 percent, but tobacco production shot up from 1,900 pounds in 1850 to 422,716 pounds in 1880.[11]

The increasingly commercial nature of Guilford agriculture was reflected in a 6 percent expansion in the slave population between 1850 and 1860. In contrast, both the white and free black populations declined slightly during this decade. By 1860, slaves constituted approximately 16 percent and free blacks 3 percent of the county's total population of 20,056. In 1870, as well as 1880, Afro-Americans composed 28 percent of the population.

As the antebellum slave population expanded, slaveownership grew more concentrated with slaveholders declining from 20 percent of the total households in 1850 (607) to 12 percent in 1860 (481).[12] As the number of slaveowners shrunk, small slaveholders, those who possessed between one and four slaves, declined as a percentage of the total, and medium (five to nineteen slaves) and large (twenty or more) slaveowners increased. Thus, as fewer Guilford residents came to own slaves in the 1850s, those who did have them were likely to possess larger holdings than was the case at the outset of the decade. Even so, in this community, as in other piedmont counties, slaveholdings rarely reached the very large sizes that they did in communities with easy access to transportation facilities. Of the eighteen slaveholders in the large category in 1850, only one owned more than fifty slaves. By 1860, forty slaveholders made up the large category; one possessed more than fifty slaves and another more than one hundred. Hence the term "large slaveholder" as it applied to this community meant the possession of a much smaller aggregation of slaves than was the case in the coastal regions of the South.

Aware of the relationship between economic growth and the ability to market their products, Guilford leaders aggressively sought better methods of transportation. Like their counterparts in the rest of North Carolina's hinterland, they urged a variety of transportation schemes and strongly supported the commercially oriented Whig party.

A few hamlets developed at the junctures of Guilford's transportation arteries, but only Greensboro achieved any size before the war. Established in 1808 in the center of Guilford to serve as the county seat, Greensboro contained about fifteen hundred inhabitants at midcentury, and its economy was closely tied to the marketing of cereals and fruits. Largely serving a local clientele, its businessmen counted among their number ten times as many merchants as High Point, the next largest village, as well as patent medicine dealers, druggists, and a jeweler. Other business establishments included taverns and inns, along with a couple of insurance companies. Like other southern county seats, Greensboro served both political-administrative and economic functions. The location of most of the business activity of the town in the vicinity of the courthouse underscored this duality of purpose.[13]

For Greensboro, as for the rest of the county, economic activity slowed considerably during the war decade, although the town experienced a revival sooner than the countryside. Taken as a whole, the assessed value of the county's land rose roughly $1 million during the 1850s and then declined about $240,000 in the 1860s.[14] Even more indicative of the hard times of the war years, real property was distributed among households almost exactly the same in 1870 as in 1850 despite a temporary upward shift in the number of households with $500 or more in real property in 1860. As demonstrated in Table 2, the percentage of propertyowners in every category above $500 expanded between 1850 and 1860 and declined between 1860 and 1870.[15] Concomitantly, both absolutely and relatively, more household heads held no property in 1870 than at any other time. This situation resulted both from the loss of land by farmers who were unable to meet tax payments and from the introduction of former slaves, the vast majority of whom owned no real property in 1870, into the economic structure.

Similar trends characterized the distribution of personal property in the community between 1860 and 1870, although because there were no personal property assessments in 1850, it was impossible to determine if 1870 levels were comparable to those at midcentury. The decline for personal propertyowners was even sharper than for real ones in the war decade with 15 percent holding property valued above $2,000 in 1860 and 2 percent in the same category in 1870. The loss of slaves was the primary reason for this steep decline.

Twenty years after the conflict, economic indicators were mixed with rural areas continuing in a depressed state but Greensboro showing signs of recovery. As in the 1850s, the arrival of a railroad, this time the Cape Fear and Yadkin Valley, stimulated the revival. In 1879, D. Frank Caldwell, one of the town's most independent and cantankerous politicians, gloomily reported, "'Honesty, Honor, & Credit banished from the land not to return in own day!! Cannot sell the best property in the land to anybody for anything.'"[16] To make matters worse, deep snow and a "wood famine" beset the county in 1880, and one-third of the population was reportedly

TABLE 2.
Percentage of Households by Property Valuations[a]

Year	0	$1–499	$500–1,999	$2,000–3,999	$4,000 and Above
1850	48.6 (1,482)	22.1 (672)	23.7 (722)	3.6 (110)	2.0 (62)
1860	42.3 (1,271)	11.5 (344)	26.0 (781)	12.3 (368)	8.0 (241)
1870	52.8 (2,169)	15.4 (633)	23.4 (960)	5.6 (231)	2.8 (116)

Source: As was done in classifying employed workers by occupation, the categorization of household heads by their real property was accomplished by a hand count, using the Seventh, Eighth, and Ninth censuses of the United States, 1850, 1860, and 1870: Guilford County, North Carolina, Population Schedules; originals in NCDAH.

[a]Absolute numbers are in parentheses.

out of work.[17] Three years later, farm prices continued low, and one observer described land "so poor in some places that it almost makes one shed tears to ride over it."[18] The lack of prosperity became especially obvious when conditions in Guilford were compared with those in the northern state of Indiana: "We like this country much better than old N.C. we can have plenty to eat and wear and when we want to go any place we can have a horse and buggy to go with and don't have to walk like we did there."[19]

Despite rural poverty, a Greensboro resident who was reluctant to leave the town in 1879 because he had hardly a dollar to take with him after his debts were settled believed prospects for the community were "excellent." His optimism was spurred by the prospect of new railroads, which would give the town "an impetus it is already beginning to feel."[20] Although the resident, carpetbagger Albion Tourgée, departed, his instincts were correct. From a village of 2,105 in 1880, Greensboro grew by the turn of the century to a bustling town of 10,035 with thousands more clustered in mill villages around its periphery.[21] Just ten years after Tourgée's assessment, a former Republican colleague happily reported: "Greensboro is improving and is being improved greatly. Gas, water, electric lights, paved side-walk both sides of street from depot to the Courthouse, sewer in centre of street, and street from depot to C.H. paved with Belgian blocks are among the changes."[22]

Industrial expansion that followed the arrival of the Cape Fear and Yadkin Valley Railroad in 1884 explained Greensboro's growth. From eleven small "manufactories" with a combined capitalization of $59,000 and a work force of 202 in 1879, industrial establishments reached seventy-nine by the turn of the century. There were more than fifteen hundred workers, and the firms were valued at almost $2 million.[23]

Did the expansion at the end of the century result from a change in leadership during the war? A scholar who focused on the growth of Greensboro as a New South city detected an interest in industrialization from the outset of his study in 1870, but, like his predecessors, he assumed that this interest represented a new phenomenon.[24] He left unexplored the question of whether a planter aristocracy perished in the holocaust of the 1860s or, indeed, if such a group had ever prevailed over the multitude of small farmers who toiled from "can see to can't see" in North Carolina's uplands. To what extent were power arrangements disrupted and old, familiar alliances broken by the exigencies of war? This is the issue addressed in this study.

The investigation focuses on a piedmont county because it was in the southern piedmont that industrialization accelerated following the war. It explores power arrangements in Guilford County because this community represented a prototype of the "New South." Largely agrarian with an expanding slave population before the war, Guilford experienced accelerated urbanization and industrialization late in the nineteenth century. If middle-class entrepreneurs rose to power anywhere in the South as a result of the war, it should have happened in this community.

2. The Institutional Road to Power

಄ೲ಄ೲ಄

Power is the capacity of an individual to affect the lives of others. One can observe opportunities for exercising power and the effects of it but rarely the action itself. This study focuses on opportunities for wielding power or influence in the public arena.[1] It is not concerned with private domination such as that of a master over his slaves, a husband over his wife, or parents over their children. It assesses opportunities in both institutional and extrainstitutional settings. Institutions include ongoing political, economic, and social arrangements, whereas extrainstitutional affairs encompass short-term commemorations, celebrations, and decisions or crises that took place outside of institutional boundaries.[2]

The study carefully assesses opportunities for exercising authority in the public arena for two reasons. First, it is important to illustrate how one might have acquired influence in antebellum Guilford and how the opportunity structure changed as a result of the war. Second, it is the first step in the creation of a method for measuring an individual's influence within the community. This procedure, described at the outset of Chapter 4, involved the ranking into high and low categories of institutions, organizations within institutions, and positions within organizations, as well as commemorations, crises, and roles within them. Generally, activities that offered the opportunity to influence large numbers of people were assigned a high ranking, and those that affected a small proportion of the populace were rated low. After the ranking operation, points were assigned to each category so that an individual's participation in public affairs could be described numerically.

Procedures for measuring power were designed, not to impose a rigid, mechanistic quality on the data, but to assess the relative importance of various groups of individuals within the community. In a society where large planters were few in number, the discovery that this social group constituted a low proportion of powerholders and that farmers were a high percentage would have revealed only that more farmers than planters were present in the county, and that information was available from the outset of the study. Only a means of assessing an individual's influence numerically made it possible to perceive the role played in public affairs by small categories of persons, and, unfortunately, even this technique did not permit statistical tests for extremely small numbers of individuals such as female and black powerholders.

In searching for persons who were afforded or who seized opportunities for wielding influence, the study identified participants in public affairs within two years of and including each of four census years. Thus the investigation included community leaders in the years 1848–52, 1858–62, 1868–72, and 1878–82. Use of these five-year segments of time increased the likelihood that manuscript census data related to individual powerholders reflected their socioeconomic status during the time they were influential. The segmentation also made it possible to compare the characteristics of groups of leaders before and after the war.

In gathering information about the activities of community leaders, samples, rather than the entire population, were used only three times. These instances occurred when complete coverage was not available for all individuals in all four time periods, and samples were taken to avoid biasing the power groups in favor of those persons whose names happened to be available.[3]

Among the various institutions in Guilford County, political participation offered the best chance of influencing a large number of people. Persons holding public offices with responsibility for levying and collecting taxes were in an especially strong position to affect many county residents. In contrast, economic and social organizations did not touch nearly as large a portion of the populace. Railroad companies were certainly important to commercial farmers, but only a small, though growing, portion of the community engaged in commercial agriculture. Similarly, even the most popular voluntary association included only a small segment of the population, for Guilford remained, throughout the years of the study, a community of independent farmers integrated socially into the system largely to the degree they themselves chose.

The remainder of this chapter focuses on the political institution, with attention given to both public offices and partisan affairs, and on the social and economic institutions. This description demonstrates the road to power via institutional arrangements and the way the war affected this route. Also, in conjunction with the following chapter, it lays the foundation for describing influence numerically, discussed at the beginning of Chapter 4.

Political Institution

Within the political institution, those who held important public offices had a greater opportunity to touch directly the lives of large numbers of people than did those who occupied minor positions or who participated in partisan affairs. A party leader might influence the selection of a particular candidate or become a candidate himself and thereby impress his philosophy upon others, but the occupant of a public office was in an especially strong position to impose his will on, or invoke sanctions against, others.

Public Offices. Important public officials in prewar Guilford included members of the three levels of the state court system: magistrates or justices of the peace, the County Court made up of selected magistrates, and the Superior Court judge, along with the Finance Committee, which also consisted of selected justices, and a small number of elected officials. The inauguration of a new state constitution in 1868 and the abolition of the old court system, greatly reduced the power of magistrates, although they regained much of it with constitutional revision in the mid-1870s. In lieu of magistrates and the antebellum Finance Committee, county commissioners and a county treasurer emerged as powerful figures in the postwar years. Elected officials themselves, the commissioners and treasurer were joined as significant postbellum officeholders by a popularly chosen sheriff, state legislators, a congressional representative, and a Superior Court clerk.

County magistrates were the prewar officials who performed the major administrative, judicial, and legislative functions in North Carolina counties. Generally, they were charged with preserving the peace, performing marriage rites, and doing whatever was necessary to execute their varied duties. A single magistrate or one acting in conjunction with another justice constituted the bottom rung of the antebellum North Carolina court system. Thus not only did a magistrate have jurisdiction over civil actions up to $100, but he also had the power to levy a large number of penalties and forfeitures. Moreover, his criminal jurisdiction included such powers as the summary trial and punishment of slaves for trivial offenses, the examination and detention of felons and suspects, and the collection of their testimony. In addition to these powers, a justice might order apprentices, question the mother of bastard children, take evidence for the court of equity, administer oaths, and change private roads. Two justices might perform actions such as committing persons to the state insane asylum or discharging insolvent debtors.

Unfortunately, it was difficult to know the variety of actions taken by individual Guilford magistrates because their records were either ill-kept or ill-preserved, but they did serve in militia captain's districts as tax listers or assessors, as well as the heads of trios who supervised legislative and gubernatorial elections.[4] Additionally, they listed individuals over the age of twenty-one suitable for jury duty. Collectively Guilford justices chose from their own ranks five members who constituted the second rung of the North Carolina court system called the Special Court, County Court, or Court of Pleas and Quarter Sessions. Usually about fifty magistrates performed this task.

Once selected, justices of the Special Court served four terms during the year, February, May, August, and November. Grand and petit juries were selected by the court for the February and November terms at which time judicial duties were performed. In addition to dealing with civil actions in which penalties ranged up to $100, they also handled criminal cases that did not involve death or dismemberment. The Revised Code of 1855 gave them authority over sixty-two different misdemeanors.

Nonjudicial actions performed either by the Court of Pleas and Quarter Sessions acting alone or in conjunction with other magistrates included levying county taxes, exempting certain people from payment of poll taxes, maintaining the courthouse and jails, binding of apprentices, issuing licenses to peddlers and retailers of liquor, levying fines in bastardy cases, and determining the location of roads and bridges and letting contracts for them.[5]

Not surprisingly, as the most important administrators in the county, local magistrates initially handled affairs related to defense when North Carolina seceded from the Union in May 1861. At the request of the state assembly, forty Guilford justices unanimously agreed to a $50,000 appropriation for volunteers to defend the home soil, although they proved reluctant to spend it, even for local military companies.[6] Similarly, when confronted with a shortage of salt in 1862, the magistrates agreed to supply it at cost, but never free of charge, to needy civilians.[7] The justices also appointed relief commissioners, who distributed the salt and furnished other provisions to wives and children of volunteers. In August 1862, the families of conscripts were added to the list of those receiving county aid.[8] Aid was never sufficient, however, even in the early stages of war, and deprivation helped fuel disaffection with the war effort.

Besides constituting the first level of appeal during serious crises such as war and appointing temporary officials like the relief commissioners, the County Court also handled less dire problems and named temporary committees such as one to build a new courthouse. Additionally, the Court of Pleas and Quarter Sessions selected many more permanent officials.

The Special Court assigned responsibilities both to other magistrates and to private citizens. Of all its appointees, only the Finance Committee performed duties that had a significant impact on the community as a whole. This group received and disbursed county funds. Magistrates appointed by the County Court as poor wardens dispensed funds to the poor, but the money was given to them by the Finance Committee. Justices also served on the Orphan's Court. Appointed officials who were not magistrates and who performed limited duties included the superintendents of each of the sixty-five school districts; the examiner of applicants to teach in public schools; the superintendents of public roads, of the county poor, and of public health; and overseers of the poor, road overseers, deputy sheriffs, constables, patrols, patrol checkers, and the county auctioneer, revenue deputy, ranger, surveyor, solicitor, coroner, and standard keeper.

The third rung of the North Carolina court system, above the justices of the peace and the Court of Pleas and Quarter Sessions, was the Superior Court. The Superior Court judge had original jurisdiction in civil cases involving more than $100 as well as concurrent jurisdiction with the County Court in civil cases, jurisdiction in all criminal cases, and original jurisdiction in all felonies. Additionally, this court acted as a court of equity, and the judge appointed the clerk and master of equity, who served a four-year term. In comparison with the County Court, however, the administrative duties of the Superior Court were few.[9] One involved the appointment of attorneys for persons suing as paupers and for those emancipating slaves over fifty years of age when the master could prove meritorious service. Superior Court judges were required to hold court in each county, but a judge served several counties in a particular district. Before the adoption of a new constitution in 1868, Superior Court judges were appointed to office for life by the legislature; after 1868, they were elected by popular vote for six-year terms.

In addition to the Superior Court, the County Court, and individual justices, a militia court also convened annually. Its activities were restricted largely to hearing appeals from militia captains concerning individual fines for militia duty infractions such as absence or tardiness. The militia court also mustered people out of the militia who were past the age of thirty-five. Like the militia court, militia officers had little authority in the community by midcentury. Their position had at one time been honorific as well as functional, but the luster had dimmed considerably by 1850.

Of the prewar popularly elected officials, the sheriff, state legislators, and congressional representative performed duties that had the greatest impact countywide. The sheriff was the chief peacekeeping officer, but much of his power derived from his role as tax collector and from his independence of the County Court. State legislators not only introduced and effected legislation pertaining to their home communities, they also recommended magistrates who were subsequently appointed by the governor. Although congressional representatives represented more than one county, they participated in legislative matters that both affected local citizens and were of concern to them.

A new state constitution, adopted in the spring of 1868, transferred the administrative duties of the Court of Pleas and Quarter Sessions to a popularly elected board of five county commissioners and created a township system modeled along the lines of one in Pennsylvania. Township boundaries followed those of the old tax districts, with each township administered by a board of trustees composed of a clerk, who was treasurer, and two justices. These officers were popularly elected and served two-year terms. They handled taxes, finances, and local projects within their townships and were accountable to the county commissioners. Also, under the new plan, the judicial authority of the old County Court was redistributed, with some duties going to the justices but many into the hands of the Superior Court judge and the clerk of the Superior Court. Thus in administrative and judicial matters, magistrates were reduced to petty officials with a few township duties.

Like antebellum magistrates, postwar commissioners administered work on roads and bridges. They also received petitions for special elections such as one on prohibition authorized by a state local option law, appointed jurors, assessors, registrars, and pollholders in special elections, set polling places, established tax rates and verified the sheriff's report on collection, issued necessary licenses like those for the sale of liquor, and authorized payments to citizens such as the poor, jurors, and county officials.[10] Commissioners had the power to declare elections null and void and did so in August 1869 in six Guilford townships, although in making appointments in September in lieu of those disqualified, the commissioners appointed the same individuals who had been chosen in the August election.[11]

In addition to township officers and county commissioners, the county treasurer, surveyor, register of deeds, clerk of the Superior Court, sheriff, and coroner were also popularly elected under the new constitution. The clerk of the Superior Court served four years, but the remainder were in office for two-year terms. The sheriff continued his important job as tax collector, and the county treasurer received and disbursed county funds, acting in a capacity similar to that of the old Finance Committee. The clerk of the Superior Court, in addition to keeping court records, took over several important functions including probating wills and deeds, appointing executors, and binding apprentices.

With constitutional revision in 1875 the state General Assembly was given authority to change any part of the county government section of the 1868 constitution, Article VII, with the exception of those portions that limited the taxing and debt-contracting power of municipal corporations. After 1876, then, a number of changes occurred that affected the responsibilities of public officials. First, the powers of the justices were broadened. The Board of County Commissioners was retained as an administrative body but was chosen for two-year terms by majority vote of the justices. Commissioners were to meet jointly with the justices and obtain their consent before levying taxes, purchasing realty, removing public buildings, constructing or repairing bridges costing more than $500, borrowing money, or changing township boundaries. The magistrates also got control over election machinery, the establishment of voting precincts, and appointment of registrars and judges. Moreover, if the justices deemed it necessary, they could abolish the position of county treasurer, and his duties would be assumed by the sheriff. In a second change from 1868, justices were to be chosen by the state legislature rather than by popular election. There were three for each township plus an additional one for every one thousand people in cities and towns. Their term of office was six years with vacancies filled by the governor or the clerk of the Superior Court.[12]

In actuality, after 1877 Guilford commissioners, chosen by their peers to carry on administrative and judicial duties, functioned much the same as the prewar County Court. Additionally, they assumed the role of Board of Education for a time, with the register of deeds as clerk and the county treasurer as treasurer of school funds. Acting in this capacity, they recommended school books to teachers, based on suggestions by the state Board of Education; confirmed school sites surveyed by appointees; approved mergers of schools; divided the county into school districts and appointed school committees for each district; distributed school funds on the basis of school district population; and in joint session with the magistrates, chose the superintendent of public instruction. The position of county treasurer, unthreatened by Guilford justices, also retained its early postwar vitality. Postwar justices and commissioners were no more willing than their predecessors, however, to enlarge their domain to include welfare responsibilities. In fact, postbellum authorities were not ready to go as far as those who provided salt at cost during the war.[13]

In summary, offices with important powers and duties in prewar Guilford included magistrate, members of the County Court and Finance Committee, sheriff, state legislator, congressional representative, and Superior Court judge. With the constitution of 1868, the Finance Committee and County Court disappeared, magistrates' powers were greatly reduced, county commissioners and the county treasurer emerged as important officials, the sheriff, state legislator, and congressional representative retained about the same authority, and the clerk of the Superior Court assumed new duties. Then, as a result of constitutional revision in the mid-1870s, much of the magistrates' power was restored.

Partisan Activities. Political parties were active in Guilford throughout the period encompassed by this study, but before the war, the county was so heavily dominated by Whiggery that Whig labels persisted long after the national party was moribund. Candidates for state legislative seats and the sheriff's office were labeled Whig by the press as late as 1860, although most of these aspirants participated in an American party convention in Greensboro in 1856 and supported the Bell-Everett National Union ticket in 1860.[14] Whig sentiment remained so strong among postwar Conservatives that they found it very difficult to accept the label Democrat, even though they regarded this party as the only alternative to the Republican party. In 1869 the *Patriot*'s editor suggested that both the names Democrat and Republican were so objectionable to Guilford citizens that a name such as Constitutional Liberal party should be adopted. At one point, he urged a Consolidation party for electing local officials, but ultimately he worked diligently to convince Guilford voters that the postbellum Conservative Democratic party in no way resembled the prewar Democratic party. Indeed, he claimed the suggestion that the new Conservative Democratic party and the old familiar Democratic one were the same was a Republican political trick.[15]

Always weak in antebellum Guilford, the Democratic party was virtually destroyed in 1862, when former Whig Zebulon B. Vance trounced his Democratic opponent, but the election of 1864 brought an extraordinarily close vote with Vance barely edging the so-called "peace candidate," William W. Holden (see Table 3).[16] More significant for local politics, former Democrat Robert P. Dick, the perennial underdog in prewar elections, handily defeated the old Whig senate favorite, Ralph Gorrell. Similarly, peace candidates D. Frank Caldwell, Abraham Clapp, and Abner S. Holton all scored victories for state House seats over their Conservative opponents. Unlike Dick, Caldwell and Clapp were former Whigs, however, and Holton had not been involved in partisan activities before the war. The coalition of Dick, Caldwell, and Clapp underscored the fluidity of politics at this time and demonstrated that the lines between the old and new parties were not always direct.

Table 3 also shows that the 1864 election represented a watershed in Guilford partisan politics. The winners scored exceedingly small margins

TABLE 3.
Votes in Guilford County in Gubernatorial Races, 1848–1880

Year	Whig	Conservative/Democrat	Republican
1848	1,567	442	
1850	1,772	526	
1852	1,524	480	
1854	1,615	528	
1856	2,059	571	
1858	1,819	409	
1860	2,137	457	
1862	1,977	74	
1864		1,209	896 [Peace party]
1866		882	438
1868		1,479	1,739
1872		1,849	1,831
1876		2,264	1,968
1880		2,251	2,248

Source: John L. Cheney, Jr., ed., *North Carolina Government, 1585–1974: A Narrative and Statistical History* (Winston-Salem: Hunter Publishing Co., 1975).

of victory thereafter, especially in 1872 and 1880, when eighteen and three votes, respectively, marked the difference between winner and loser. Voter turnout increased as election outcomes grew closer and as black males were enfranchised in 1868.[17]

As election results became closer, party leaders encouraged widespread participation in partisan activities, and they formalized and publicized party structure. Before the war, both Democrats and Whigs held conventions at the county, district, state, and national levels, but little activity occurred within smaller jurisdictions such as townships or militia captain's districts. The exceptions were Whig political clubs such as the Scott and Graham Club organized in 1852 to mobilize support for the upcoming presidential election. In contrast, an 1872 organizational chart of the Republican party indicated a state Executive Committee of eleven members chosen by the president of the state convention, a Congressional District Committee composed of one member from each county in the district named by the Congressional District Convention, a county Executive Committee consisting of one member from each township selected by the county convention, and a committee of five from each township picked by residents of the township. Two alterations were made in this plan in 1880.

First, each congressional district sent a delegate, along with two nominated by the state convention-at-large, to form the state Executive Committee rather than having them appointed by the state convention president. Second, townships were to choose three delegates and three alternates to attend the county convention rather than the former committee of five. According to a *New North State* account, regular delegates from fourteen of the county's eighteen townships were present at the county convention in 1880, and individuals from the remaining four counties were present and permitted to vote. A committee of one from each township was then appointed to form a Committee on Permanent Organization. After the county convention adjourned, executive committees of the townships chose the County Executive Committee.[18]

The postbellum Democratic organization was structured similarly to the Republican, and it contained at least one feature of the prewar Whig party. Like Republicans, Democrats were organized at the state, district, county, and township levels. In 1872, county activities were guided by a County Executive Committee of twenty-six members, a Central Executive Committee of seven, and a Township Executive Committee of three from each of the eighteen townships.[19] Delegates to the state and district conventions were appointed at the county convention by the chairman, although it was not unusual for a resolution to be offered stating that any Democrat who wished to attend might be a delegate.[20] Democrats also formed local political clubs that functioned during presidential campaigns. They located in Greensboro and adopted names such as the Seymour-Blair Club in 1868, the Greensboro Conservative Club in 1872, and the Hancock-Jarvis Central Club in 1880.[21]

Also, as in the case of Republicans, participation by Democrats in party activities after the war appeared extensive, although all of the following figures were reported in the Democratic press. Present at meetings in Jefferson, Jamestown, and Fentress townships in 1880 were 70, 33, and 35 individuals, respectively; almost all of the townships held meetings to select delegates to the county convention in 1870, which was attended by more than 200 persons. At a meeting to choose candidates for municipal offices in 1872, 15 people from each ward composed the nominating committee alone, and the Hancock-Jarvis Central Club enrolled 176 members at its initial meeting in 1880. Lists of delegates to the state convention included 5 delegates from each township or 90 individuals in 1878 and 180 in 1872.[22]

Party activities were thus carried on at five levels: township, county, district, state, and national, with political clubs sporadically cropping up in the town of Greensboro. Gubernatorial conventions were sometimes held in addition to regular state conventions, and both judicial and congressional district conventions occasionally met. Campaign rallies were staged at all echelons of political activity.

Social Institution

The social institution consisted of community associations of a permanent nature which theoretically facilitated the socialization process. These included educational, professional, and religious organizations, as well as those designed primarily to promote social interaction or achieve some desired social goal. Private schools and literary clubs made up the educational groups, but public schools were excluded because they constituted a part of the officeholding category in the political institution. Professional organizations were oriented toward teaching, medicine, or agriculture. Religious associations included not only various Protestant churches and the Society of Friends but also groups such as Bible and Sunday School societies. Associations that primarily met social needs included fraternal orders, annual committees to celebrate the Fourth of July, and Grange chapters. Those planned to achieve a social goal involved temperance, fire, and monument companies.

Enthusiasm was greatest in the antebellum years for fraternal orders and temperance and monument associations; Grange chapters flourished in the postwar years. Odd Fellows and Masonic chapters were especially popular throughout the county. Minutes of each of their meetings were solicitously reported in the local press along with lengthy accounts of the brothers' participation in the funerals of fellow members. They also marched in full regalia in celebrations such as the groundbreaking ceremonies for the North Carolina Railroad in Guilford in 1851.[23]

A temperance society was organized in the county in 1822, and by 1844 temperance forces were powerful enough to persuade the County Court not to grant any requests for retail liquor licenses, although the state Supreme Court eventually determined that a county court did not have the power to prohibit entirely the granting of such permits.[24] As temperance forces gained momentum generally in North Carolina at midcentury and a state organization formed, local chapters flourished. The Guilford Sons of Temperance, formed in August 1847, saw its membership grow fivefold within a year, and the latter figure trebled in the next year. Another chapter, organized in January 1851, also tripled in twelve months. Affiliated loosely with a state organization, the latter chapter sent six delegates to a statewide meeting the year it formed.[25]

Yet despite the rapid growth of temperance associations, not everyone in the county was of like mind on the issue. One observer, who classified temperance proponents as the "clear headed reflecting class," acknowledged that no person could be elected on that question alone in Guilford. In fact, he admitted that it would be difficult to know which side to take in some parts of the county. Ann Wiley underscored the differences of opinion in a letter to her son and the longtime administrator of the common school system in North Carolina, Calvin H. Wiley. She said the issue "is . . . causeing a mity excitement here. Some is almost ready to fight."[26]

Temperance proponents gathered enough momentum in 1854 to draft a resolution at a Fourth of July courthouse meeting urging the legislature to disallow the licensing of the sale of liquor in all counties except those that voted expressly to permit it. This resolution was sent to all Guilford legislative candidates with a request that they respond to it, but interest had begun to wane. In 1855, three taverns existed in the county, and before the war six more retailers were licensed.[27]

At the close of the conflict, while U.S. soldiers were in Greensboro, the town Board of Commissioners enacted vigorous ordinances curbing the retailing of liquor. These actions resulted, however, not from pressure by temperance groups but from efforts to defuse possible confrontations between citizens and soldiers. Ultimately, Provisional Mayor William L. Scott was forced to appeal through North Carolina Governor William W. Holden to military authorities to stop army sutlers from selling to citizens as well as officers, but once the soldiers departed, the town ordinances were repealed.

Temperance activity was thus confined before the war largely to the formation of local chapters that had loose ties to a state organization. Membership in these associations grew rapidly and declined about as quickly. In contrast, when the temperance issue became the prohibition controversy in the late 1870s, participation spilled out of organized channels. Political campaigns focused on the question, racial and party lines blurred before it, and women became involved in greater numbers than in most public debates.[28]

One additional type of social organization prominent in antebellum Guilford was the monument association. The primary purpose of these organizations was to raise money for the construction of a specific memorial. The Mount Vernon Association solicited funds for the Washington Monument, and the Greensboro Monument Association strove to erect a

memorial to revolutionary war hero Nathanael Greene. Community interest in the latter organization was captured through a series of four lectures in the fall of 1859 by notable North Carolinians, including Guilford's
own Reverend Eli W. Caruthers.[29]

Similar to the fraternal orders in camaraderie and mutual support but
with an economic thrust, several local Grange chapters thrived in the
county in the 1870s. In 1873 the Patrons of Husbandry numbered five chapters with another forming. At the initial meeting of one chapter, so many
prospective members showed up that they exceeded the charter limit of
thirty.[30] Several chapters envisioned a joint stock cooperative store, but
little came of their ambitious plans.[31] By the end of the decade the Grange
in Guilford, as in the rest of the nation, had fallen into disarray. In 1879
local editor James W. Albright reported to state agriculturalist Leonidas L.
Polk that the county organization was "nearly dead."[32]

Economic Institution

Although six roads crisscrossed Guilford by 1820 and the world's longest
plank road passed through the southwestern corner of the community by
the 1840s, marketing remained slow and inefficient, so agitation for rail
service constituted one of the major concerns of prewar leaders. The acquisition of a railroad involved not only the procurement of a charter and
financial assistance from the state legislature but also fundraising efforts by
private citizens. In all of these activities Guilford promoters played a very
prominent role (see Chapter 5).

Especially at midcentury, attention focused on the North Carolina Railroad. When finally completed just five years before the hostilities commenced, this line linked Greensboro to the Wilmington-Weldon Railroad
in eastern North Carolina; to Petersburg, Virginia, via the Raleigh and
Gaston Railroad; and directly to Charlotte, North Carolina, in the southwestern part of the state.

A very short road would also have joined Greensboro to the Danville-
Richmond Railroad, but the rivalry of eastern legislators and the hostility
of Democrats to any plans of the newly formed American party (mainly
Whigs) thwarted such efforts before the war. The line eventually was built
as an emergency war measure through the efforts of President Jefferson
Davis.

Railroad concerns in the immediate postbellum years centered on the
fate of the North Carolina Railroad and the construction of new lines from
Guilford west to Salem (Northwestern North Carolina Railroad) and

south to Cheraw, South Carolina (Central). Of less interest was the Western Railroad, which was to have run from Fayetteville in southeastern North Carolina to Greensboro, and a Virginia project involving the Lynchburg and Danville Railroad. In the late 1870s and early 1880s, local railroad enthusiasts concentrated on the Cape Fear and Yadkin Valley Railroad. With the arrival of this line in 1884, sixteen of Guilford's eighteen townships were penetrated by at least one railroad.[33]

In addition to the rail companies, a number of banks, along with a unique insurance company before the war and several savings and loan associations following the conflict, contributed to the development of Guilford's economy. The role played by these organizations in the accumulation of capital was important, for Guilford, like other developing societies, experienced a constant shortage of cash. In comparison to these firms, the Guilford Co-operative Business Company formed in 1869 and a tobacco association founded in 1872 had limited impact.[34]

At midcentury, a branch of the Bank of the Cape Fear was the only bank in Greensboro. Opening its doors in 1851, this bank was managed by Jesse H. Lindsay, a prominent figure in Guilford banking for over three decades. In 1869, Lindsay, Julius A. Gray, and Eugene Morehead, former Governor John M. Morehead's brother-in-law, son-in-law, and son, replaced the Greensboro branch of the Bank of Cape Fear with the Bank of Greensboro. Six years later, this same trio, along with several others, spearheaded a drive to raise $100,000 to establish a national bank. The following year, the Bank of Greensboro was replaced by the National Bank of Greensboro.[35]

Banking establishments in which Lindsay was not involved included the Farmers Bank, founded two years before the war by Cyrus P. Mendenhall and William A. Caldwell and liquidated at the close of the conflict, and the Citizens Bank, of which little is known except that it was chartered by the state legislature in 1871.[36] The Farmers Bank may have closed its doors in part because it was adversely affected by the war. The state of North Carolina borrowed heavily from the Bank of North Carolina and the Cape Fear, especially in 1861, and possibly from the Farmers Bank as well, but an important factor in the liquidation of Farmers was Mendenhall's desire to use the profits from his bank stock to make investments in Baltimore, Maryland, where he believed money could be made quickly. Mendenhall, an attorney who speculated in land and invested in mines and factories, rarely missed a lucrative venture.

A much more serious financial collapse during the postwar era than the closing of Mendenhall's Farmers Bank was the demise of Wilson & Shober in 1878. According to the local press, this firm, which may have operated without a state or federal charter, sustained some of the largest enterprises in the county for a number of years. The *Patriot* attributed the failure of Wilson & Shober to the reluctance of the owners to press the firm's claims, but the depression that affected much of the nation in the 1870s and the hard times it produced locally more realistically explain the bank's failure.[37]

The precarious nature of Guilford banks as well as their limited number encouraged local entrepreneurs to experiment with other means of raising capital. One of the most important of these ventures before the war was the Greensboro Mutual Life Insurance and Trust Company, which was incorporated in 1852 and unique for the broad investment and capital-generation powers included in its charter. Greensboro Mutual Life, the third life insurance company to be chartered by the North Carolina legislature, was permitted to use funds accruing from insurance premiums not only for granting and selling annuities and endowments in trust but also to buy stock in any chartered or incorporated bank and to purchase stocks or bonds in any chartered or incorporated canal, bridge, navigation, or road company. Additionally, it could hold money in trust, pay interest on it, and issue certificates on the basis of it. Other insurance companies had engaged in this practice, but Greensboro Mutual was the first to have it specified as acceptable in its charter.[38]

Following the war, three savings and loan associations supplanted the insurance company as a means of generating capital. These included Greensboro, founded in 1870, Mechanics in 1872, and Guilford in 1875. These organizations tried to attract a large number of small investors through inducements such as the option of purchasing stock on the installment plan and low monthly payments.[39]

Institutions in Guilford included public offices, the most important of which were usually filled through state appointments; political parties, which grew intensely competitive after 1862; voluntary associations, which performed certain social functions and involved citizens to the degree they themselves chose; and a limited number of economic organizations, designed especially to improve transportation and raise capital.

War and Reconstruction had little impact on these institutions. One seemingly important effect, the replacement of lifelong appointed justices of the peace with popularly elected county commissioners, proved of short duration because much of the power of the magistrates was restored and their selection removed from the local populace with constitutional revision in the mid-1870s. Grange chapters, which flourished following the war, declined in strength as temperance forces had before them when the wider state and national movements floundered. Railroad promotion remained high on the agenda of Guilford leaders after the war as before, and several lines joined the North Carolina Railroad as part of a growing rail complex in the county. A shortage of capital also continued to plague the economy in the post- as in the prewar eras, and powerholders supported several savings and loan associations in place of an antebellum life insurance company as a means of generating cash.

The most durable effect of the war on institutional arrangements was the creation of a strong two-party system. With antebellum Democrats virtually destroyed as a minority party in 1862, the electorate realigned and sharply divided in the following months, never again to achieve during the years covered by this study the consensus it exhibited just two years before the watershed election of 1864. Faced with an almost evenly divided electorate, Democrats and Republicans expanded and formalized party structure in the late 1860s and thereby created a host of new leadership opportunities. Hotly contested elections and the enfranchisement of black men ensured a high level of participation on both sides.

To understand how the war led to the development of bipartisan politics, it is necessary to turn to a series of crises or decisions that preceded it, as well as to the conflict itself. The county's extrainstitutional crises, along with celebrations and commemorations that were also episodic in nature, form the basis of the following chapter and complete the survey of various avenues to power in nineteenth-century Guilford County.

3. The Road to Power through Commemorations and Crises

∽⊶∽⊶∽

There were two routes to power in addition to institutional arrangements. First, an individual might command so much respect or deference that his opinions outweighed those of others or his advice or assistance was specifically sought. Although subtle influence of this nature was difficult to discern in a society whose participants were long dead and interviews impossible, it was assumed that deference could be equated with public esteem and that persons held in high public esteem would become evident in community affairs that were, by their very nature, honorific and prestigious. An examination of three individuals who frequently occupied honorific positions in celebrations and commemorations supported this contention (see Appendix 2). One could also acquire power by participating in the resolution of crises or decisions that arose outside of existing institutions.

Although prestigious and decision-making affairs were similar in that they were episodic as well as extrainstitutional in nature, far fewer people participated in celebrations than in crises. Differences in participation rates stemmed from the perceived import of the episodes. Issues such as abolitionism and secession engendered far more excitement and produced far higher levels of involvement than did a memorial service for the "Great Compromiser," Henry Clay.

Prestigious Affairs

Commemorations, as compared to celebrations, included a very limited segment of the community. The local bar association arranged commemorative events upon the death of a notable Guilford citizen, usually an attorney. The only outsiders eulogized were the nationally renowned Whig Henry Clay, Guilford native and former resident Governor Jonathan Worth, and President James A. Garfield. Local nonattorneys who were memorialized included Jamestown merchant, railroad promoter, and magistrate Jonathan W. Fields and merchant-farmer and brother of John A. Gilmer, Joseph W. Gilmer. Only the ceremony for Clay attracted a large crowd.

Along with the commemoration for Clay, two celebrations elicited a sizable community response. These were the dedication of a monument in the Alamance churchyard to Captain Arthur Forbis, a casualty of the revolutionary Battle of Guilford, and a tribute to the battle spearheaded by the Centennial Association. The Alamance celebration, which took place on the Fourth of July 1860, involved several volunteer military companies including the Guilford Grays, the first military unit within the county to organize.[1] The Centennial Association was established in the spring of 1880 in a series of well-attended meetings; its Executive Committee alone consisted of thirty people.[2]

Decisive Episodes

Extensive involvement in decision making occurred when the community actively supported an issue, as in the case of pre- and postwar railroads and the war in its early months, and when the issue was controversial such as abolitionism, the war in the latter stages, a proposed convention to revise the constitution of 1868, and prohibition. Secession was also very important because its outcome affected most of the community by plunging it into the holocaust of war. Certainly all of these crises did not involve the same number of people. The war penetrated virtually every household in the community, whereas prohibition affected a limited segment of the population. But compared with a series of lesser decisions, these issues— railroad promotion, abolitionism, secession, war, constitutional revision, and prohibition—generated considerable excitement and organized activity.[3]

Antebellum decisions that did not evoke a large-scale community response included efforts to deal with a smallpox scare, a public display of Union sentiment, and consideration of improvements to the Yadkin River. Postwar decisions that were limited in scope involved the procurement of pardons for involvement in the war or removal of disabilities (1865 and 1868), an "a-political Indignation Meeting" encouraged by Democrats to express resentment over alleged aspersions cast at southern women by the Republican *Standard* (1868), opposition to the extension of the term for state legislators (1870), attempts to organize a fire department (1872), and efforts to secure a congressional appropriation for a public building in Greensboro (1881).[4] With the exception of the smallpox scare and disabilities, all of these minor decisions were made at a single meeting expressing support for or opposition to the particular issue. To combat smallpox, patrols were formed in each neighborhood to enforce a quarantine and every person was encouraged to secure a vaccination.

The problem of removing disabilities surfaced during presidential Reconstruction in 1865 and congressional Reconstruction in 1868. In the first instance, special classes of individuals who were not covered in the president's blanket pardon at the war's conclusion had to secure a special dispensation. Interest in obtaining a pardon at this time stemmed not only from the desire for the restoration of political rights but also from the need to transact legal business and protect one's property. During congressional Reconstruction, the removal of disabilities usually concerned aspirants for public office who were barred from assuming a position under the congressional acts of 1867.

In both 1865 and 1868, individuals usually acted in their own behalf or in support of another person. An organized effort to secure pardons occurred only when Albion Tourgée served on a committee that asked Congress to remove the disabilities of individuals in several counties, fifteen of whom were from Guilford.

The rest of this chapter deals with the major crises that beset the community between 1848 and the end of the war, with the exception of railroad promotion, which is discussed in greater detail in Chapter 5. Together, these extrainstitutional conflicts suggest a community in the throes of deep division and change. Because two-party politics emerged as the most visible effect of these decisions, this level of analysis implies that dramatic political change occurred as a result of the war. Additionally, beyond the broad issue of change, the controversy over slavery underscores the "southern" tendencies of the vast majority of Guilford residents; disagreements that arose during the secession period and expanded in the midst of war show how differences of opinion ultimately crystallized into a durable two-party system.

Abolitionism. A Whig county with a Quaker remnant in an increasingly Democratic state, antebellum Guilford was frequently charged with opposition to slavery.[5] Unquestionably, many of these charges were politically motivated, but they contained an element of truth. Historically, certain residents, some but not all of whom were Quaker in religious orientation, had favored the manumission of slaves. William Swaim, who edited the *Patriot* from 1829 to 1835, was aggressive in his stand against slavery, and under his direction the paper was regarded as the unofficial organ of the North Carolina Manumission Society. Richard Mendenhall of Jamestown was heavily involved with the emigration of slaves to "Hayti" in the mid-1820s, and his brother George C. and George's second wife, Delphinia, relocated a number of slaves in the North.[6] Guilford was also reputedly a stop on the underground railroad at midcentury.[7]

Yet despite a legacy of antislavery sentiment, the county as a whole did not fit the image of the abolitionist enclave pictured by the Democratic press. As demonstrated in Chapter 1, the slave population expanded in the decade before the war, although slaveownership was becoming increasingly concentrated. Also, the press misconstrued the position of leading Whigs regarding slavery. Before opposing the proslavery Lecompton constitution for Kansas, John Gilmer was careful to consult Jonathan Worth to make sure no one in his area was especially agitated over the issue, and he sought privately a congressional act that would make it a felony for a territorial governor or legislature to damage or impair slave property. His major concern throughout the 1850s lay in countering extremism on both sides, which he saw threatening the Union. The *Patriot* supported Gilmer's stance on the Lecompton constitution, not from any positive inclination toward abolitionism but on the grounds that Kansas residents did not want it and, if a proslavery document could be forced on them, an antislavery one could be applied to a proslavery people.[8]

Many Whigs, like D. F. Caldwell's father, Thomas, grounded their Unionism in the belief that attempted secession would result in the eradication of slavery; others, such as Calvin Wiley, belatedly pointed out the evils of slavery in a last-ditch effort to save the institution, not to abolish it.[9] Some, like Reverend J. Henry Smith, could defend the institution passionately although freeing their own bondsmen.[10]

Among Quakers, attitudes and practices concerning enslavement were equally varied, especially since many of those who were most ardent in their abolitionist views had emigrated from North Carolina to Indiana in the 1830s. George and Delphinia Mendenhall gradually emancipated their slaves, and George's nephew, Nereus Mendenhall, privately disapproved of the fugitive slave law, but Cyrus, Nereus's brother, had amassed forty-eight slaves by 1860, reflected in a personal property valuation of $96,000.[11]

Thus, although a few Friends continued to strive toward emancipation even as the state became increasingly hostile toward such an activity, others acquiesced in the buying and selling of bondsmen, and many others were reluctant participants in the institution. As a group, however, their presence contributed to a climate of opinion that allowed antislavery sentiments to be expressed. Yet at the same time, the increasingly commercial orientation of the community, which was given impetus by the completion of the North Carolina Railroad in 1856, made the institution of slavery more attractive. Hence the stage was set for explosive confrontations that could easily escalate into the threat, and sometimes the perpetration, of mob violence. The catalyst in each instance was the dissemination of antislavery literature by Wesleyan Methodist ministers, not by Quakers, although the latter, especially George C. Mendenhall, defended the Wesleyans.

Wesleyan Methodist churches had been organized in Guilford, Alamance, and Montgomery counties in the fall and winter of 1847–48 in opposition to the stance on slavery of the Methodist Episcopal church, South. In response to a petition by about forty Guilford Wesleyan Methodists, the Allegheny Conference of the Wesleyan Methodist church in Ohio sent Adam Crooks, who arrived on October 23, 1847. Two years later Jesse McBride joined him. This young, mild-mannered pair aroused the ire of many people, not only because they opposed slavery but also because they preached the full range of Wesleyan Methodist dogma, condemning both the consumption of liquor and membership in secret organizations. Especially galling was their effectiveness at winning converts. Sentiment against them did not crystallize, however, until the *Standard* described a report issued at a meeting of antislavery associations in New York in 1850, which indicated that a Wesleyan Methodist minister had been effectively campaigning against slavery in several North Carolina counties, including Guilford. At this point, McBride and then Crooks were arrested and tried in Forsyth Superior Court.[12] A trio of attorneys, including John Gilmer, prosecuted the two. It was said that no lawyer ought to defend them, but George Mendenhall and James T. Morehead, brother of former Governor John M. Morehead, did so, and Mendenhall, in particular, took the opportunity to denounce slavery, using material gathered for him in part by his nephew Nereus.[13]

When Crooks was acquitted and McBride released on bond, rumblings and the threat of mob violence accelerated, especially against McBride, in Guilford as well as surrounding counties. On April 20, 1851, a large crowd gathered at Isaac Potter's Grove near Jamestown in southwestern Guilford, where McBride was scheduled to speak. Although no violence occurred, several men appeared from Greensboro who were reportedly armed, and considerable excitement ensued. A call was then made for a gathering in

Greensboro at the next court so that Guilford citizens could determine a means to "protect themselves from abolitionism."[14]

Tension continued to mount on both sides in anticipation of the Greensboro meeting. Some Wesleyans placed posters around the community, deprecating the course their opponents were following, and suggested that "sooner or later it would bring upon them the displeasure of the Almighty."[15] About this time, a man named Ballard, against whom a grand jury had failed to find a true bill in the previous term of court, was indicted a second time for circulating a pamphlet similar to the one used by McBride in Forsyth County.[16]

Spokespersons at the Greensboro meeting, held a month after the one at Jamestown, apparently divided along party lines. Whig Nereus Mendenhall reported that "Caldwell, Gilmer, and Wiley [all Whigs] spoke for law and order—though they first denounced the Wesleyans in no uncertain terms." Democrats Robert Dick, James McLean, and Edwards evidently spoke in favor of driving Crooks and McBride from the community because, in Mendenhall's eyes, they "spoke for the mob." After some confusion, a vote was taken and a resolution passed setting up a committee to visit the two Wesleyans and direct them to leave the county or "abide the consequences."[17]

A "committee" of one hundred men turned its attention on McBride, forcing him to give bond that he would leave the state and not send incendiary letters or publications. At this point, McBride was still reluctant to depart, but after talking at length with a member of the mob and gaining assurances that his bondholders would be released, he agreed to their demands. Six days later, he left for Ohio.

Once McBride fled the state, attention turned to Adam Crooks and another Wesleyan minister, J. C. Bacon. This time, bloodshed was not avoided. In July 1851, Crooks arrived in Jamestown but fled when he learned that a number of Greensboro residents intended to arrest him. John Gilmer reported that the county was infuriated at Crooks's escape and that thousands planned to assemble at his next scheduled speech at Union, four miles south of Jamestown. Tensions ran high, as one observer reported: "There seems to be much excitement in Guilford in regard to the Wesleyans. Some are determined to suppress them—others to defend them even at the risk of life."[18]

At the Union meeting, "large numbers of both parties" appeared, "all armed thirsting for battle." Neither Crooks nor Bacon showed up, but a member of Crooks's party was badly wounded, possibly mortally, by a man from Forsyth County. At this assemblage, attended by people from

Guilford, Rockingham, Forsyth, Randolph, and Davidson counties, resolutions were drawn up to continue efforts to expel Crooks and Bacon from the county, whether peaceably or forcibly. A reward of $100 was offered for either one taken in the state after August 5. At this point, George Mendenhall interceded and advised Crooks to depart. Both left, with Bacon returning to Virginia.

Once Crooks and Bacon departed, the excitement in Guilford abated, but seven years later the *Patriot* lamented that slavery agitation was again swallowing up every other issue and worried that Democrats were using abolitionism to win converts.[19] To make matters worse, another explosion was on the horizon, this time involving Daniel Worth, an elderly first cousin of Jonathan Worth, who returned to his native Guilford from Indiana in 1857 as a Wesleyan Methodist missionary.

The son of stalwart Quakers, the twenty-seven-year-old Worth had accompanied his parents from North Carolina to Indiana in the spring of 1822. Nine years later, he abandoned the religion of his family and joined the Methodist Episcopal church. By the early 1840s, he was disillusioned with the latter institution because of its stand on slavery. (Worth had become the first president of the first antislavery society in Indiana in 1840.) Thus he became instrumental in organizing the Wesleyan Methodist church in his adopted state in 1842. He subsequently served for a few years as pastor of several churches in Ohio and was briefly involved in antislavery activities in Kentucky. In 1856, he returned to Indiana as the newly elected president of the Indiana Conference of the Wesleyan Methodist church. His tenure as president was tumultuous for Worth was quickly embroiled with younger members of the conference who were lax in regard to the Wesleyan ban on membership in secret organizations. Worth was the apparent loser in the controversy, for he was sent by his conference as a missionary to his native state even though he was sixty-two years of age and would have to cover a very large circuit. En route to North Carolina, Worth stopped off at the annual American Missionary Association meeting in Ohio, where he was supplied with copies of Hinton Rowan Helper's *The Impending Crisis in the South* and other antislavery literature.[20]

Arriving in North Carolina in the fall of 1857, Worth quickly attracted attention with his sermons. Early in 1858 he was attacked in an article in the *North Carolina Presbyterian,* but no action was taken to inhibit him. A year following its first assault and shortly after the Harpers Ferry–John Brown affair, the *North Carolina Presbyterian* again attacked Worth. The secular press, especially the *Standard,* then took up the cry, and on December 22, 1859, while visiting at the home of a Greensboro relative, Hiram C. Worth, the Wesleyan reverend learned that several warrants had been issued for his arrest. At this point Worth sent for the sheriff and was remanded to the Greensboro jail. Bail was impossible although several people volunteered to come to his aid because, according to an act passed in 1830, the circulation of incendiary material constituted a capital offense. Two days after his arrest, Worth appeared before Justices Jed Lindsay, Joab Hiatt, and Peter Adams. The prisoner refused counsel and chose instead to read from Helper's book. After fifteen or so witnesses testified that Worth's sermons and the book he circulated were incendiary, the preacher was bound over for the spring term of the Guilford Superior Court. Bail was set at $5,000 and immediately posted by two Guilford residents, George W. Bowman and David Hodgin. The court then demanded an additional $5,000 to ensure Worth's good behavior. This time Bowman and Hodgin did not come forward, perhaps because they did not have the funds.[21]

Before his trial in Greensboro, Worth was taken from jail and tried in nearby Randolph County for circulation of incendiary material. In both the Guilford and Randolph cases the judge, prosecuting attorneys, and defense lawyers, like the accused, were the same. At Asheboro in Randolph County, Prosecutor Levi Scott, armed with a twenty-page indictment, opened with the ominous remark that if the jury failed to convict Worth, "The darkness of midnight would be lighted up with our burning buildings to see the massacred bodies of our wives and children, and that the sun would rise ere long upon the dead bodies of slave-holders with their throats cut."[22] The prosecution then introduced a number of witnesses who testified that Worth had sold them copies of Helper's book. The defense offered no witnesses, but Guilford attorney Ralph Gorrell argued for two hours that the statute under which Worth was tried was too stringent, and James T. Morehead closed with an "impassioned plea" on behalf of Worth. After deliberating for four and one-half hours, the jury rendered a verdict of guilty and Worth was sentenced to twelve months in jail, although a whipping was omitted. Fearing certain conviction in Greensboro after the Asheboro verdict, Gorrell explored with Lewis Tappan, a prominent figure in the American Missionary Association, the possibility of new evidence or a different approach in the upcoming trial, but Tappan eschewed all responsibility in the matter. He never mentioned the antislavery literature the society had given Worth before he left for North Carolina.[23]

At the trial held in Greensboro on April 27, two witnesses, including George W. Bowman, were summoned by the prosecution to testify that Worth had sold copies of Helper's book. Gorrell argued that the North Carolina incendiary literature statute specified a written or printed paper or pamphlet and that Helper's book was neither of these, but the judge overruled this technicality, and it took the jury only fifteen minutes to render a verdict of guilty. Worth was then sentenced to the Guilford County jail for twelve months, but he was quickly released on $1,000 bail on the condition that he appear at the fall term of court. George W. Bowman, one of the five individuals who posted bail for Worth, was the only prewar powerholder to do so.[24]

As the editor of the *Greensboro Times* accurately predicted, Worth fled northward, arriving in New York on May 5, just one week after his conviction in Greensboro. There he immediately started a campaign to repay his bondholders. By August, Worth had secured the necessary funds, which included a $50 donation from Hinton Rowan Helper himself.[25] Subsequently, Worth returned to Indiana a hero, although J. D. Winslow, a Quaker and former resident of Guilford, qualified this view by noting that though "Carolina people" in Winslow's community of Fair Mount, Indiana, generally sympathized with Worth and felt that he had been treated unjustly, they would "much rather he had not come away until it was tried out. They think that he is not quite the pluck that he represented himself to be."[26]

Morehead and Gorrell dutifully carried the case to the North Carolina Supreme Court, where they argued again that Helper's book did not constitute a paper or pamphlet and that selling the book to one person did not constitute circulation of incendiary material. Furthermore, they reasoned that to be within the law, the book would have had to have been distributed to a slave or free Negro. Although the court upheld the Guilford decision, the general opinion seemed to be that the defense attorneys had done all they could on Worth's behalf. Shortly after visiting Worth in jail after the Asheboro trial, Worth's cousin and later governor, Jonathan Worth, commented, "He was most ably defended by Hon. Jas. T. Morehead, who owns a very large number of slaves. He speaks in the warmest terms of approbation of the efforts of Mr. Morehead."[27]

In the wake of Worth's convictions, the state pushed on with two additional indictments for the circulation of Helper's book, one against Guilford powerholder Jesse Wheeler. Wheeler, a nonslaveholding farmer who owned property that placed him among the top third of the propertyholders in Guilford, participated in Whig politics at the county and district levels at midcentury and served as county surveyor, president of the Guilford Temperance Society, a delegate to a railroad convention in Salisbury, North Carolina, and a member of a committee to secure legislation desired by the Guilford Teachers Association. He was also a magistrate and electionholder (the term used to describe a poll worker) in 1850, as in

1860, and a tax lister and census taker as well. Yet despite his impressive credentials, Wheeler, who submitted to the charge of circulating Helper's book, was forced to leave the state before the February 1861 term of court.[28]

Thus, in the face of abolitionist charges, the best that voices of moderation like those of Gilmer, Gorrell, Mendenhall, and Morehead could achieve in Guilford in the decade before the war was the restriction of mob violence. Certainly, it was no small feat to see that proper legal procedures were carried out in view of the intense emotions generated as outsiders like Crooks, McBride, and Bacon arrived to promote their unpopular cause, but the conviction of an elderly minister like Worth with whom the community had tenuous ties and the hounding out of the county of a resident as reputable as Jesse Wheeler had more sinister overtones. "Nobody here will countenance the circulation of a book denouncing slaveholders as worse than thieves, murderers, etc.," Jonathan Worth explained, and Governor Vance recalled in retrospect, "The boldest among us did not dare to say a word against any part of the system."[29] North Carolina, like the rest of the South, had become extremely intolerant of critics of the "peculiar institution" by the 1850s; Guilford County proved no exception.

Secession. Despite the growing hostility toward slavery's critics in Guilford as in other southern communities, most in the county did not turn readily to secession as a solution to the problem. Instead, the vast majority managed to support both slavery and the Union, even after Lincoln's election in November 1860. Disunion was a Democratic issue advocated by political extremists eager to consolidate their power, as leaders described it, and Guilford remained, at least in sentiment if not in nomenclature, an overwhelmingly Whig county. It would take more than the election of a "black Republican" to break the political consensus in this community. Thus, unlike the controversy over abolitionism, secession generated little divisiveness. With the exception of a few prominent Democrats, most people in the county, regardless of their views on slavery, were of like mind on this issue until Lincoln's call for troops in April of 1861.

Options for Unionists in the 1850s were narrowing, however, with the demise of the national Whig party, sectionalism plaguing Democrats, and the rise of the completely northern-based Republican party. In February 1861, Guilford voters gave a resounding "no" to a state convention to consider secession, but though the county reported lopsided totals of 2,771 opposed and 113 in favor, the vote statewide was a slim victory for anti-secessionists, with 46,603 votes cast against a convention and 46,409 in favor.[30] Guilford's decision appeared vindicated early in March, when

John M. Morehead returned from a peace conference in Baltimore and announced that he believed the compromise reached there would be adopted by Congress, but hopes were dashed when Lincoln decided to supply Fort Sumter. Gilmer in particular had warned Lincoln against "coercion." He had worked on a plan for the evacuation of federal fortifications, and, like many in the county, he regarded the president's action as "tyrannical."

The change in attitude among many Guilford leaders between the pre— and post–Fort Sumter days was underscored by the responses of Gilmer and William L. Scott. In March 1861, Scott had "prayed that the Union and Constitution and that blessed flag might be forever honored and perpetuated"; by late May, he was organizing a military company that would fight in the first battle of Bull Run. Gilmer, who had offered such an impassioned plea for Union in January 1861 that there was " 'scarcely an eye in the House of Representatives not filled with tears,' " felt by the fall of 1861 "a sort of shame" that he had labored to save the nation. He blamed the North entirely for the commencement of hostilities. "The fiendish stubborness of the Northern people creates with me regret that I even spent any of my time in addressing what I supposed were worth them—reason & understanding," he wrote. "There remains but one thing to do with these fanatics now, & that is to whip a little sense into them and an indescribable quantity of foolishness out of them."[31]

Yet if many leaders closed ranks once it became clear that secession was coming, not all of the powerholders and their followers joined them. Although the *Times* attributed a low turnout at the May secession election to the demands of farm work and similarity in points of view, rumblings of discontent in Centre township belied the notion of harmony. Branch N. Smith, a forty-five-year-old farmer, reported to Ralph Gorrell's son, legislator Julius L. Gorrell, about the time of the election in May that when he sent handbills to neighbors requesting that they attend a meeting in their school district to form a patrol or Home Guard, four or five propertyowners responded that they were Union men, or "Lincoln men." None came to the gathering, and, though attendance was large enough for Smith to term it "a good company," most were of "the other stripe." The individuals who chose not to participate in the assemblage eschewed the idea of a patrol, saying that people must "keep on the good side of the Negroes and there will be no danger from them." Furthermore, they indicated, they did not intend to participate in a Home Guard to protect the homes of those who went to fight against the Union. Consequently, Smith concluded that others would not leave their homes to fight for the Confederacy "in the midst of such a class of fanatics as these."[32]

Smith and some of the "best citizens" of the vicinity, along with several residents of Deep River, all of whom were slaveholders, wanted to oust Andrew C. Murrow as postmaster, and they wanted legislator Gorrell to approach the governor about the matter. Murrow, a thirty-nine-year-old nonslaveholding farmer with property that placed him in the top 21 percent of the owners in the community, had allegedly been "intimate friends" with Daniel Worth, and Smith contended that Worth and Murrow continued to correspond after Worth fled the state. The action that Murrow took which most infuriated Smith and his cronies, however, involved the handling of publications as they arrived at the post office. According to Smith, if publications arrived from a "northern press," Murrow tried to form a club [for subscriptions], but publications from "southern presses" were used for "wrapping paper."[33]

Thus the harmony with which Guilford residents had initially approached the secession question cracked in the spring of 1861. Although most people would support the war effort, the disagreement symbolized by affairs in Centre was never dispelled. It necessitated the formation of a Vigilance Association at the outset of the war, surfaced frequently in efforts to procure troops, and became institutionalized in postwar partisan arrangements. Secession, then, had a special meaning for this community. Not only did it bring war and its attendant deprivations and losses, but it also constituted the first step in the destruction of the political consensus that characterized the antebellum society.

Because harmony prevailed for so long in regard to the secession question, little organizational activity surrounded it. Just before the election in August 1860, a Guilford Union Club was formed, and a rally was held in High Point. These activities probably contributed to Guilford's overwhelming Unionist vote in this gubernatorial election, the largest given by any county in the state. Similarly, a "Mass Union Meeting" chaired by former Governor Morehead occurred just before the presidential election in November 1860.

Considerably more activity characterized the selection of delegates for the proposed convention to consider secession in February 1861. Local meetings were held to select delegates for a county meeting, which in turn chose delegates for the proposed convention. Simultaneously, a group in Jamestown nominated Robert P. Dick as a candidate for a delegate's seat although Dick declined to run. In the subsequent election, he received 547 "complimentary votes," the *Times* noted, because of his strong Unionist stance, but the delegates who were chosen and would have attended had a convention been approved were Whig Unionists Ralph Gorrell, Cyrus P. Mendenhall, and James T. Morehead, Sr.[34] In contrast to the selection of delegates in February, no organizational activity was reported in preparation for the May convention vote. Many had acquiesced to the secessionist tide by that time; others obviously found silence the best course of action. War had settled the issue.

War. The war constituted an extended, penetrating crisis that touched virtually every household in the community. Those who remained at home, particularly persons residing in Greensboro, were caught up in a flurry of organizational activities in the spring of 1861, which was followed by considerable "dullness," as residents phrased it, by the fall. For many, shortages and deprivation prevailed within a surprisingly short time, and personal losses through disease and battles were ever-present. Speculation at home and in the army rendered scarcities even more aggravating, and the "volunteering spirit," never very strong, waned quickly. Desertions from the army accelerated, and attempts to secure exemptions grew frequent as conditions deteriorated. Everyone's desire for peace intensified in March 1865, when the worst battle in North Carolina's history raged at Bentonville and the wounded and dying poured into Greensboro and High Point. Following the battle, defeat was unmistakable as several state officials fled from Raleigh to Greensboro. Jefferson Davis and his entourage also sojourned briefly in the community in their flight southward from Richmond, and they were followed by Governor Vance. These visits marked the end of the war but not of uncertainty and disarray.

The war was an especially important crisis in this investigation because it resulted in numerous mobilization efforts, which provided many leadership opportunities, and it intensified the cleavages among the citizenry that had emerged with abolitionism and secession. The war's unquenchable thirst for manpower, accompanied by deprivation and speculation at home and in the army, alienated many citizens. Differences of opinion regarding North Carolina's course in the war effort found political expression in a peace movement headed by *Raleigh Standard* editor William W. Holden, which commenced in the summer of 1863 and continued through the election of 1864. By the latter date, a majority of Guilford voters were willing to endorse all of the peace candidates for the state legislature, although they remained unwilling to support Holden's candidacy for governor. Far larger numbers of leaders, in comparison, remained committed to Conservative candidates for the legislature as well as to Vance.

Perhaps because secession was so long opposed in Guilford and the community's loyalty frequently questioned by outsiders and certainly because the conduct of the war was viewed initially as the county's responsibility, organizational activities in the spring of 1861 were numerous. One of the largest assemblages of women ever held in the county adopted resolutions to do everything possible to supply local troops with food and clothing, and the town of Greensboro was divided into four districts, with one woman appointed in each district to see that provisions were supplied.[35] Meanwhile, local magistrates were taking action to fund the soldiers and provide some relief for their families, and Guilford teachers were caught up in the war-related problem of what to do about a textbook shortage because most school books were written and published in the North. Calvin Wiley chaired a meeting in Raleigh to consider this issue, and J. D. Campbell, a teacher at Guilford's Edgeworth Female Seminary, served as secretary and a member of the correspondence committee. Aside from Wiley, the most active role assumed by a Guilford resident was that played by Professor Richard Sterling, president of Edgeworth. Sterling chaired the English Textbook Committee, served on the Natural Science Committee, and discussed the objectives of the meeting itself.[36]

To provide for the protection of those at home, a Home Guard and a Vigilance Association were created in the spring and summer of 1861. The Home Guard, authorized by the state legislature, was supposed to consist of every male over the age of forty-five, although as demonstrated by the opposition in Centre, not all were enthusiastic about participating.[37] In contrast to the Home Guard, which was formed to protect the county against invading armies, the Vigilance Association was to safeguard the community from enemies residing within its borders. As the *Patriot* explained, Guilford counted among its number people who were opposed to "Southern institutions" and who might be a problem if the northern army invaded the interior of the state. In creating the organization, the county was divided into four sections, and at least thirty of the "prudest and most reliable men" were appointed in each district. Any five of the members could hold meetings in school districts, militia captain's districts, or simply in populous neighborhoods to ascertain the sentiment of the citizens living there. If an individual chose not to attend one of these meetings, the committee could visit his home. Furthermore, if the person refused to supply information when the committee arrived at his house, the committee could submit his name to the chairman of the association. Similarly, the name of any person who refused to sign a paper indicating support for "Southern institutions" would be turned over to the association's chairman. Finally, if an individual spoke against "Southern institutions" to the extent that five committee members determined the statements treasonable, the person could be arrested. The association was also empowered to detain transients and inquire into their business.[38]

After initial mention of the formation of the Vigilance Association, nothing further was reported about its activities. The extent to which it used its far-reaching powers is unclear. Its major impact may have been psychological, for it could have stifled dissent before blood was spilled in the war and thus at a time when disagreement was most propitious.

In addition to efforts to mobilize to protect the home front, local volunteer military companies were formed, and in May, when a bill authorizing the training of ten thousand troops lay before the state legislature, Greensboro offered herself as a troop drill center. The Guilford Grays, a company of about fifty men, had formed in February 1860 as the Guilford Guards and were at Fort Macon by late April 1861. By the latter date, the press claimed that another company of twenty-eight men was organizing. Ninety "Dixie Boys," formed by Captain William L. Scott, became a fighting unit in late May. With four additional companies reputedly being created, the *Patriot* boasted that Guilford would soon have about one thousand volunteers in Confederate ranks, but the combined total of the Guilford Grays and Dixie Boys appears closer to the actual number in uniform.[39]

Initially, the frenzied preparations for war, the optimism of local volunteers, and the excitement generated by the crowds who thronged into Greensboro to see the soldiers depart gave the appearance of unity and enthusiasm, but even during the early months of the crisis, local attorney James R. McLean noted that "volunteering is *still* at a low ebb in this county" and that battle and disease, shortages, and inflated prices quickly took their toll, even among the enthused.[40] To complicate matters, typhoid broke out among the Dixie Boys and Guilford Grays, as well as in Greensboro, in the summer and fall of 1861. By the time Scott's company participated in the battle of Bull Run, many were ill. In addition to typhoid, several soldiers contracted measles. In November Scott described his regiment as "sorely and dreadfully afflicted," noting that about seventy-seven men from his own company were ill and on one day thirteen corpses lay in their camp.[41]

At home, trade slackened as goods became unavailable and two stores relocated in Richmond. Coffee was scarce and expensive as early as October of 1861, and by November not more than half the county had salt, a very important commodity in the preservation of foodstuffs. By the end of the year, woolen goods were difficult to find and high-priced, and leather was so expensive and scarce that many parents could not supply their children with shoes for the winter. As McLean summarized the situation just seven months after North Carolina left the Union, "To the town-people and especially the poor, times are awful."[42]

High prices and shortages were aggravated by the distilling of the corn crop into liquor and by speculation, an activity that plagued citizens and soldiers alike. McLean noted a relationship between the price of corn and the amount being distilled, and merchant James Sloan wished the railroads would carry the stills to the seacoast to make "salt in place of corn."[43] Thirty-year-old Newton D. Woody, a rural merchant and miller, resisted the temptation to deal in liquor but thought if he had set up a still he could have made a fortune. Alexander McPherson, a friend of Woody's and one of Scott's Dixie Boys, linked the distillation of corn with speculation and cowardice, commenting at one point to Woody, "I hope to god that the draft will take some of those Stillers & speckleaters & the cowrdes of yong men & put them facing the Yankees."[44] Although Sheriff Caleb Boon never associated "stilling" with speculation, his comments particularly demonstrated the frustration engendered by intentional gouging: "— you have never seen so mutch speculation going on in all your life as there is since this war has commenced . . . the men that Prayed for this war—if they Payed at all—they are here getting rich—while you & my son & others are doing the fighting—its hard and its unfair."[45] Similarly, McPherson described "men here in the army a making a fortune off of the por solyers tha ar a grabing at every dime that tha can git."[46]

The "distress" growing out of hard times, as McLean feared, caused "a reactionary feeling against the war" and took its toll on "the spirit of volunteering."[47] Rarely was there hesitancy over supplying the soldiers, but concern over a "draft" heightened when more men had to be procured in February 1862. Resistance ultimately collapsed because a "great number" volunteered their services but not before considerable tension ensued. As James McLean's wife, Nancy, explained it: "The Gilford people have been terrible frighten over a draft that came last week. We did not know but what we would have fighting in our midst, to hear the talk of men that was agoing to resist the draft. But I believe their better judgement prevailed, and a great number have volunteered and left but few to be drafted."[48]

Whether more than the threat of a draft was needed at this early stage of the war to promote volunteering is unclear, but other means were used during the conflict, for P. S. Benbow of Oak Ridge Township explained two years after the war's conclusion that "those in authority" went to great lengths to get persons to bear arms. These lengths included, according to Benbow, men being "whipped, suspended by their thumbs, grazed by bayonets, and marched about with a log on their backs."[49]

As the war dragged on and the Confederacy suffered devastating losses at Vicksburg and Gettysburg in July 1863, discouragement mounted and gloom deepened. In the fall of that year, after being out of battle for a while, the Guilford Grays stumbled upon some Yankees lying behind a railroad embankment and were overpowered. By this time, the Grays, who had once numbered sixty strong, were reduced to nineteen sorely tested individuals. In July 1864, they numbered eight.[50]

As the number of battle deaths accelerated and times at home worsened, desertion, once a cause for embarrassment, became more widespread and acceptable, and those who had managed to avoid conscription found the task increasingly difficult. In December 1863, the Confederate Congress enacted legislation prohibiting the further use of substitutes, and in January 1864, those who had previously furnished them were no longer exempted. A more comprehensive act passed in February repealed all earlier laws related to exemptions and provided for the enrollment of free blacks to work on fortifications and perform other noncombat operations. Slaves were to be used in a similar capacity, though not more than twenty thousand were to be employed and their owners were to be compensated for their use. Still, even with these stringent measures, a report on the operation of conscription from January 1 to April 1, 1864, indicated that the supply of men was nearly exhausted. Zealous conscript officers then accelerated their search, enrolling both older individuals and some members of religious sects, including Friends, although the February legislation specifically exempted those who had been previously dismissed on religious grounds and who had paid the necessary tax.[51]

At this point a few individuals, such as forty-nine-year-old D. Frank Caldwell, managed to avoid military service by running for public office, and others with Quaker ties, such as Newton D. Woody, fled to northern states to wait out the war. Many, including Caldwell, also joined the peace movement, which had sprung to life in North Carolina in July 1863 after the Vicksburg and Gettysburg defeats.

Before the election of 1864, more than one hundred peace meetings were held in approximately forty North Carolina counties. These local assemblages denounced the war and urged the Confederate government to sue for peace, but the major thrust of their complaints was toward the Confederate government. Irritated by numerous Confederate policies such as alleged discrimination against North Carolinians in appointments to high civil and military positions, the unwillingness of the Confederacy to provide adequately for North Carolina's defense against the Federal army in the east, and its impressment of private property as well as conscription, peace meeting participants roundly criticized the government in Richmond. Yet Governor Vance himself had been highly critical of the Confederate government. The issue that differentiated Vance supporters from "peace men" was the proposal of a peace convention. According to this plan, North Carolina would try to get representatives from other southern states to meet and propose terms under which they could end the war. Whether peace men were willing for North Carolina to secede from the Confederacy and propose terms to the Union on its own if other southern states would not send representatives to a convention was unclear.[52]

As part of this effort, a peace meeting was held in Greensboro just a few days before W. W. Holden announced his candidacy for governor on February 10. This meeting, chaired by James A. Long, an ardent Whig who had delivered remarks of approval at the meeting three years earlier which offered Greensboro as a troop drill center, was, like others around the state, highly critical of the Confederate government. The Committee to Prepare Business, which was named and chaired by Robert P. Dick, proclaimed that the law-abiding, loyal attendees were concerned about their civil rights, especially the right of habeas corpus, and that they feared the extension of conscription would endanger the sovereignty of North Carolina.

Nothing epitomized more the divisiveness that afflicted war-torn Guilford than this meeting. Mary Watson Smith, wife of the Reverend J. Henry Smith, noted that "by ten o'clock the town was thronged and the court house jammed to its utmost capacity," and James Long commented that the "commodius Court House was filled to overflowing, while hundreds could not gain admittance." The large turnout stemmed in part from the deep concern of many citizens about Confederate policies; others were present because they were anxious to see that the resolutions passed were not publicized as the sentiment of Greensboro or Guilford. Mrs. Smith reported that some were in favor of going into the meeting and opposing the resolutions; others wished to bring a regiment from Raleigh to prevent the meeting entirely; neither of these solutions, however, secured the endorsement of all opponents. A rumor that Holden was going to be present at the meeting undoubtedly enhanced the size of the crowd and spurred the hostility of some of those loyal to the Confederacy. Many thought the *Standard* editor would never go home alive, according to Smith.[53]

The meeting was disrupted by "boys" or "young men" in the gallery who greeted Dick's attempt to speak and Long's effort to secure order "with hisses, whistling cursing and other disorder," as Long phrased it. Smith commented that eggs, camp meeting hymns, and abusive epithets met D. F. Caldwell when he tried to replace Dick at the podium.[54] In retrospect, Calvin Wiley concluded that anyone who denied loyalty to the Confederacy and went to the meeting as "an avowed Union man" was "courting martyrdom." All a prudent man could hope for was "to prevent extravagance."[55]

The rancor exhibited at the peace meeting continued into the ensuing election. Caldwell believed that printers suppressed his circular announcing himself as a peace candidate, and he noted that a conscript officer followed him with a band of soldiers as he canvassed. Twice he was mobbed by this band and "other ruffins" and twice prevented from speaking. "If you but new the ods I had to contend against and all the circumstances you would be constrained to confess that it is a miracal that I am now in the land of the living," Caldwell later commented.[56]

Yet despite the difficulties faced by Caldwell, he, along with the other members of the local peace ticket, scored victories in 1864, and with this close election, differences of opinion over troop procurement and the Confederacy's continued participation in the war found political expression. Although the Republican party did not form until three years after the war's conclusion and leaders did not move automatically from a particular faction in 1864 to a given party in 1868, strong political divisions existed among the electorate by 1864. Reconstruction attempts intensified these divisions, and ultimately leaders were forced to choose sides.

Thus, whether one assesses the impact of the war on local institutions or in terms of extrainstitutional decisions, the result seems to be the same. Apparently, military conflict caused considerable change in Guilford County, particularly in the realm of politics. A statistical analysis revealed decidedly different implications, however, and it is to this level of investigation that we now turn as we continue our exploration of the war's effects on power arrangements.

4. War, Continuity, and the Rise of Attorneys: A Statistical Analysis

The public affairs described in the preceding two chapters provided a basis for the development of a procedure for measuring an individual's influence within the community during each of the four five-year periods under investigation.[1] First, all of the institutions, organizations, and positions, as well as the commemorations, celebrations, and decisions, along with their attendant roles, were classified into high and low categories. Next, points were assigned to each category. This step made it possible to describe numerically an individual's involvement in a single capacity within an institution or episodic affair. A person's total involvement in the public arena could then be assessed by summing the scores of each individual activity. If someone participated in only one capacity in a single community affair, the addition of points was unnecessary. In addition to total power scores, subtotals were derived for individual powerholders in all of the various categories described in Chapters 2 and 3, that is, public office, partisan affairs, political institution, social institution, economic institution, prestigious activities, and decisive affairs. For a detailed explanation of the ranking and point assignment procedures, see Appendix 3.

The use of five-year spans for the collection of information and the assignment of points resulted in the construction of four groups of powerholders clustered around each of the four census years, 1850, 1860, 1870, and 1880. The determination of four groups of powerholders made it possible to compare those who were influential before and after the war in several ways. Comparisons were made between the proportion of actual to potential powerholders in each successive time period, between the way powerholders clustered based on their power scores, and in the way they earned their power. Most important, the construction of a point assignment procedure and the derivation of power scores permitted statistical tests between power and the various socioeconomic data collected from the census manuscripts about each powerholder.[2] These tests indicated the attributes associated with significant influence in the Guilford community before and after the war and the extent to which the conflict altered these characteristics. Unfortunately, so few blacks and women participated in the predominantly white male power structure that statistical tests related to power and race and power and gender could not be performed. Only limited conclusions about changes in the makeup of these groups could be drawn.[3] (See Chapter 7 for a discussion of black participation in postwar politics and Appendix 4 for comments on the location of leaders in the censuses.)

Regardless of the way powerholders were compared before and after the war, the most striking and frequent discovery was stability in power arrangements. Some expansion in the number of individuals who participated in public affairs occurred between 1850 and 1880. The 1860 group of powerholders grew 12 percent over its predecessor in 1850, the 1870 group was 11 percent larger than the 1860 group, and the 1880 group outdistanced the 1870 powerholders by 7 percent. These rates of growth exceeded those of the general population, but if one assumed that all whites and free blacks had access to power, the proportion of actual to potential powerholders remained at a stubborn 3 percent in all four periods. If, on a more realistic note, one excluded women and children, along with slaves in the prewar era, that is, if one excluded about 80 percent of the population in all four census years, the proportion of actual to potential powerholders grew from 12 percent in 1850 to 13 percent in 1860 to 15 percent in 1870 and 1880. Although these figures compare favorably with those cited for two antebellum northern communities, Kingston, New York, and Cinncinati, Ohio, regardless of whether one chooses the high figures of 12 to 15 percent or the lower figure of 3 percent, the most noticeable feature of the size of the power groups in relation to the larger population was the consistency in the ratios. If institutional leaders alone had constituted the focus of this investigation, the uniformity in the ratios might not have been very surprising because the number of official positions could have varied little over time, but the inclusion of participants in extrainstitutional affairs raised the possibility that institutional and extrainstitutional leaders were synonymous.[4]

The "natural" clustering of power scores resulted in three distinct levels or categories: low (1–4 points), medium (5–19 points), and high (20 points or more).[5] The clustering consistently produced pyramid-shaped power structures with the size of the top group diminishing slightly (from 10 percent to 5 percent) between 1850 and 1870. In turn, the proportion of medium powerholders expanded over the long term (from 33 percent to 39 percent), and that of low scorers remained about the same. Interestingly, the pyramid-shaped structures resemble those discovered by sociologists, who used a reputational approach to power and differ from the ones found by political scientists, who used a decision-making approach in examining power.[6] This was the case, although more individuals in this study scored points through the decision-making than the prestige category.

Some powerholders appeared in more than one power group. Indeed, twenty-seven people were in all four, and of these twenty-seven, ten were high powerholders at least once. These ten included four persons who earned high scores once, three individuals who scored high twice, two people who scored high three times, and one person, D. Frank Caldwell, who was a high powerholder in all four periods. (See Appendix 5 for a list of the individuals who scored 20 points or more, along with their power scores.) Generally, the proportion of persons appearing in successive power groups was consistent, with 31 percent of the 1860 power group having been powerholders in 1850 and 25 percent of the 1870 group having appeared in the 1860 group. Similarly, 31 percent of the 1880 power group were powerholders in 1870. Thus during the war decade, the proportion of repeaters was only 6 percent less than during the ten years preceding the conflict and the ten years following it.

A much more dramatic decrease occurred, however, if only high powerholders were considered. Of the high powerholders in 1860 (twenty-eight individuals), 46 percent had been in that position in 1850. In comparison, of the twenty-seven high powerholders in 1870, only 19 percent had also been high powerholders in 1860; 31 percent of the twenty-six high powerholders in 1880 were in that group in 1870. The drop in the proportion of high powerholders who scored 20 or more points in the previous power group from 46 percent in 1860 to 19 percent in 1870 was in part attributable to the war, but the conflict was not the complete explanation. James McLean, who died in 1870 at the age of only forty-eight, was reported by the Guilford Bar Association to have succumbed because the war broke his health as well as his fortune. Worry over financial losses resulting from the conflict may also have hastened the death of John Gilmer, who described himself in 1865, three years before his death, as "nearly ruined by the war & now having to work harder than ever."[7] But Gilmer, who was sixty-three when he died, also described himself in the same communication as "getting older"; his colleague, John M. Morehead, was seventy at the time of his death in 1866. Similarly, Jonathan W. Fields, David P. Weir, Michael S. Sherwood, and James A. Long, large powerholders in 1860 like Morehead, expired during the war decade from causes unrelated to the conflict. Thus 21 percent of the influential individuals died of natural causes in the 1860s.

Just as stability characterized the proportion of actual to potential powerholders, the shape of the power structures, and the percentage of individuals who appeared in successive power groups from 1850 through 1880, uniformity also prevailed in the average power scores of the leaders and in the way they achieved their influence. Total power scores averaged 8 in 1850 and 6 in the remaining periods. The high average in 1850 was largely attributable to 113 points scored during the 1848–52 period by John A. Gilmer. In comparison, the maximum earned for 1860, 1870, and 1880, respectively, was 50 by Robert P. Dick, 69 by Ralph Gorrell, and 52 by James W. Albright. Gilmer's unusually high score resulted from his very active involvement in railroad promotion, coupled with a leading role in a less important decision, the display of Union sentiment. As a state senator and a participant in several other official positions, he also garnered 23 points in the political institution as well as a smattering of points in all other categories. These scores, along with 79 points in decision making, gave him the high of 113.

Most low powerholders achieved their influence by serving in public offices. Averaging just above a point in this category in 1850, 1860, and 1870 and just under a point in 1880, the overwhelming majority occupied positions such as poll- or electionholder. Their average scores increased slightly for partisan activities following the war (from 0.13 in 1860 to 0.80 in 1880), but neither in this category nor any other did they average higher than 1 at any time covered by the study.

Medium powerholders attained higher means in public officeholding and partisan activities than did low-level leaders, and they also averaged above a point in decision making (from a low of 1.26 in 1850 to a high of 2.08 in 1870). Most noticeably, their involvement in public offices lessened after the conflict (from a high of 7.08 in 1860 to a low of 2.77 in 1880), and their participation in partisan affairs quickened, averaging 0.89 and 0.75 in 1850 and 1860, respectively, and 2.52 and 3.17 in 1870 and 1880.

Like medium powerholders, high powerholders lessened their participation in official positions and accelerated their involvement in partisan affairs following the war, but unlike their medium counterparts, they did not sustain their early postwar level of involvement in party politics into the 1880s (see Table 4). Instead, they fell back to a rate comparable to their prewar level, although that mean was higher than any achieved by other leaders. Table 4 also reflects the high participation rate of influential notables in the Centennial Association in 1880 as their prestigious affairs' score rose to its highest level during that time span.[8]

TABLE 4.

Mean Scores of High Powerholders

			Point Categories			
Year	Public Office	Partisan Affairs	Social Organizations	Economic Organizations	Prestigious Affairs	Decision Making
1850	11.19	4.68	2.42	1.97	1.03	17.65
1860	13.25	4.29	2.93	0.96	0.57	7.21
1870	4.48	13.15	1.33	2.48	1.07	15.56
1880	6.04	5.27	1.77	1.23	5.42	10.08

Source: Guilford County data base.

Especially striking in Table 4 was the high mean score of influential leaders in decision making, particularly in 1850 and 1870, and their relatively low average in 1860. Obviously, the war made no permanent difference in their participation in this arena, but it appeared to have a transitory effect. Closer examination indicated just as many crises between 1858 and 1862 as at any other time, but railroad promotion was quiescent during these years in comparison to 1850 and 1870, and secession engendered few organizational efforts. Even more important, many matters related to the war were handled within existing institutions. As noted in Chapter 2, magistrates initially assumed the task of financing the conflict as well as responsibilities such as the procurement of salt and other relief measures. Apparently, then, the onslaught of war encumbered existing institutions with so many additional duties that powerholders had little time and probably little inclination, at least in the early stages of the conflict, to become embroiled in extrainstitutional decisions. They resumed their very active participation in decision making, especially in railroad promotion, after the conflict ended, and this involvement, coupled with relatively high scores in public offices and partisan affairs, largely accounted for their considerable influence within the community.

Up to this point, the statistical evidence weighs heavily on the side of stability in power arrangements through the war years, but crucial questions remain. Were planters in power before the conflict and ousted afterward? Did middle-class entrepreneurs get an opportunity to exercise influence before and after the holocaust of war? To answer these questions, several types of analyses were conducted. Multiple regression tests were used to assess the relative contribution of each of the social indicators such as age, occupation, and propertyholdings to the variation in power scores. Descriptive statistics such as means and ranges were calculated for continuous variables like age and property for all powerholders, as well as for low, medium, and high leaders. Power was cross-tabulated with each of the nominal variables such as occupation and place of birth.[9]

The analyses indicated that the greatest difference between power-holders and the rest of the community was their wealth in the form of real and personal property and slaves. They resembled the general populace in their place of birth, occupation, and location of residence within the county. High powerholders, in particular, differed from other leaders in age and place of birth in 1870 and occupation and residence in all four periods. The only enduring change was the occupations of large power-holders. The vast majority of these leaders did not engage in farming as a primary occupation at any time during the study, but businessmen, who were almost a majority at midcentury, declined, and professionals, primarily attorneys, rose as a proportion of high powerholders. As this change happened, real property became less important in its relative contribution to the variation in power scores, and occupation became more important. This meant that being a nonfarmer became very significant in the amount of power one might achieve as attorneys replaced businessmen as the preeminent nonfarm group. The replacement of businessmen by lawyers in the running of public activities and the decline in the importance of real property and the rise in the significance of occupation in explaining the amount of power one might achieve reflected both increasing specialization within the community and altered conditions resulting from the war.

In a community where almost half of the households in 1850 and 1860 and slightly over half in 1870 owned no real property and where 69 percent in 1860 and 83 percent in 1870 possessed personal property valued at less than $500, the most striking feature of the power groups was their relative wealth (see Table 5). The dollar value of the real property of the average powerholder increased about twofold between 1850 and 1860 and then re-

TABLE 5.
Mean Property- and Slaveholdings
of All Powerholders

	Real	Personal	Slaves
1850	$2,070	NA	4
1860	$4,226	$8,139	4
1870	$2,567	$1,350	—

Source: Guilford County data base.

turned almost to the 1850 level in 1870. The increase in property values was in part attributable to expansion in the size of farms as the free population declined and the number of farms in the community decreased from 1,668 to 1,503 between 1850 and 1860, while the average farm size increased from 224 to 251 acres. The arrival of the North Carolina Railroad four years before the 1860 census also enhanced the value of real estate, as more crops, most notably tobacco, were raised for export. The war and its disruption of production and trade then took its toll, reflected in much lower land values in 1870, although one historian also attributed the decline in property values to soil depletion and poor farming techniques practiced decades before the conflict.[10] Yet even with an economic setback, the average powerholder remained considerably wealthier than most Guilford citizens. As demonstrated in Table 2 in Chapter 1, in conjunction with Table 5, the average powerholder in 1850 owned more real property than 95 percent of the county's households, more than 92 percent in 1860, and more than 91 percent in 1870.

Similar conditions existed for personal property with the average powerholder among the top 10 percent of the households in 1860 and the top 17 percent in 1870. The dramatic decline in personal property values between 1860 and 1870, seen in Table 5, occurred primarily because slaves, who were freed by the war without compensation to their owners, were counted as personal property before the conflict, but losses also stemmed from the required repudiation of the state debt. This issue was particularly sensitive both to supporters of the Confederacy who held North Carolina bonds and to wartime Unionists who favored repudiation.

The ownership of four slaves by the average powerholder, observed in Table 5, does not appear very large until one considers that 80 percent of the households in 1850 and 88 percent in 1860 owned no slaves. The consistency in the averages also screened a decline in the proportion of the power groups in the 1850s who owned slaves. In 1850 49 percent of the powerholders did not own slaves; in 1860 the proportion of the power group who were nonslaveholders increased to 59 percent. Because the percentage of the powerholders who owned slaves declined but the average number of slaves per powerholder remained constant, it was clear that the slaveholdings of some powerholders were expanding while they were declining for others. Investigation of the number of slaves owned by leaders with varying amounts of power indicated that the average number of slaves owned by medium powerholders increased from four to six between 1850 and 1860, while the average number possessed by low powerholders declined from three to two during the same period. Among high powerholders, the average slaveholdings remained a constant twelve.

Just as high powerholders possessed more slaves than medium, and medium leaders owned more than low scorers, power and property were related in a similar direction. Table 6 clearly demonstrates that, relatively, high powerholders were very large propertyowners indeed, and that, despite lower property values in 1870 than in 1860, they were hardly on equal terms with the general populace or even with other leaders, although medium leaders made significant strides in comparison to high ones in the 1850s. Personal property values among medium and low powerholders declined the most precipitously during the 1860s, resulting from a concentration of capital in slaves by these groups. More diversification characterized the personal propertyholdings of high powerholders, with store inventories of large merchants playing an important role.

If the wealth of Guilford leaders set them apart from the rest of the community, they had the same origins, occupations, and residences within the county as most of the citizens. Ranging from a low of 88 percent of the 1850 power group to a high of 92 percent of the power groups in 1860 and 1870, the leaders were North Carolina natives. Similarly, the primary occupation of the majority, ranging from 55 percent in 1850 to 68 percent in 1870, was agriculture. Although the point might well be made that farming without land or with holdings valued at less than $500, the situation for

TABLE 6.
Mean Propertyholdings of Low,
Medium, and High Powerholders
(in dollars)

Powerholders	Real	Personal
1850		
High	7,436	NA
Medium	1,804	NA
Low	1,320	NA
1860		
High	10,850	26,055
Medium	6,115	12,861
Low	2,743	4,300
1870		
High	7,069	4,532
Medium	3,637	1,881
Low	1,495	734

Source: Guilford County data base.

the vast majority of Guilford farmers, was quite different from managing a farm valued at $2,000 or above, the average amount for powerholders, nevertheless, most of the agrarian powerholders probably shared a world view similar to that of other county inhabitants, especially concerning the intrinsic value of land. This occurred not only because leaders engaged in tasks common to all farmers but also because they lived on their land rather than in town. Among all powerholders, 71 percent lived outside of Greensboro in 1870 and 73 percent in 1880.

In comparison to powerholders generally, medium powerholders were somewhat less likely to be engaged in agriculture, and low powerholders were slightly more apt to be farmers. Correspondingly, medium powerholders were a little less likely to live outside Greensboro and low powerholders somewhat more likely to live in rural areas than all the powerholders combined. The percentages of low and medium leaders born in North Carolina were almost identical to the averages for all powerholders.

In contrast to low and medium leaders, high powerholders were usually Greensboro dwellers (at rates of 74 percent in 1870 and 62 percent in 1880) who did not engage primarily in agriculture, although their ownership of substantial amounts of real property, kinship ties, and the rural atmosphere of Greensboro ameliorated their distance from rural dwellers. They were just as apt to be North Carolina natives as other leaders in 1850, but their ranks included a slightly smaller proportion of natives in other years, especially in 1870, when the proportion of influential persons born in the Old North State dipped to 78 percent. The decline in the number of North Carolina natives among leaders with significant influence resulted largely from another phenomenon that affected high powerholders immediately following the war—the emergence into their ranks in larger numbers than usual of professionals and businessmen who were under forty years of age. The average age for large leaders had ranged from a low of forty-seven years in 1850 to a high of fifty-one in 1860, but the influx of twelve men under forty in 1870, as compared to six in 1850 and three in 1860, decreased the average age of high powerholders to forty-five. The decline was only temporary, however, as only three men under forty were high powerholders in 1880, and the average age rose to forty-nine.

The influx of young businessmen and professionals into the ranks of high powerholders resulted from the vacuum created at the top by the deaths of several notables in the 1860s and from the war itself. The war was important, not because battles took their toll on large powerholders, for most were too old to serve in the army, but because it encouraged mobility among young people and a number of these migrants chose to settle in

Greensboro. Out of the dozen who rose to the top in influence, nine were either native sons of Guilford who had left for a while and were returning to their home turf or newcomers to the community. Only James T. Morehead, Jr., John Gilmer, Jr., and James W. Albright had spent their lives in Guilford; Morehead and Gilmer had been away for educational purposes, and all three men had served in the Confederate army.

Whether native or nonnative, virtually all of these young powerholders resided in Greensboro, pursuing careers outside of agriculture, and they were wealthy. Certainly, a number of them were adversely affected by the war as were other powerholders. James W. Albright went bankrupt in 1868, and attorney-banker Charles E. Shober was forced to borrow from his second wife, Nannie Hundley. Similarly, John Gilmer, Jr., held much less property than his father had before the war. Attorney-editor Patrick F. Duffy also appeared on shaky financial ground in the late 1870s, but if some young leaders seemed in financial straits after the war, their apparent predicament was relative to their prewar situation. With real estate worth $6,000, John Gilmer, Jr., was certainly wealthier than the vast majority of other Guilford citizens. Even Albright's holdings of $3,700 in 1870 made him richer than 91 percent of the households in the community, and Charles E. Shober was the fourth largest taxpayer in the county in 1869. Similarly, the youthful entrepreneur, DeWitt Clinton Benbow, was the largest taxpayer in the community at this time, and James T. Morehead, Jr., paid the largest tax of any attorney.[11] Already a bankowner, Julius A. Gray raised an additional $20,000 in 1871 when he sold a plantation of 1,250 acres in his native Randolph County. Newcomers Duffy and John N. Staples listed no real property in Guilford, but Albion W. Tourgée owned $15,000 in real estate in 1870 and attorney Thomas B. Keogh, $3,000. Indeed, an average real property valuation of $7,575 and an average personal property of $6,770 placed young notables slightly ahead of other high powerholders in real propertyownership and well ahead in personal property. Thus the young leaders who surfaced in 1870 experienced some financial dislocation from the war and some a few years later from the depression of the mid-1870s, but they were not poor relative to the rest of the community or in comparison to other influential powerholders.

The wealthy young attorneys and businessmen who seized high power in 1870 persisted tenaciously in their role in 1880. Six of the twelve continued as large powerholders in 1880, four became medium leaders, and one a low powerholder. Only Tourgée, who was active in county affairs until his departure in 1879 but was gone before the 1880 census was conducted, was excluded from the 1880 power group. Hence the war contributed to the emergence of young men in positions of influence in larger numbers than occurred before or after 1870. Once entrenched, half continued as important leaders a decade later, but no comparable flood of youngsters appeared in the latter years. In the decade of the 1860s, a generation of notables had expired, and war, by encouraging geographical mobility, had produced new, young faces in their ranks, but once the process was completed, the relationship between age and power looked much as it had in 1850 and 1860 with men in their thirties underrepresented among large powerholders and middle-aged individuals typical.

The one enduring change to occur between 1850 and 1880 was the gradual decline of businessmen and the rise of professionals in the exercise of significant power. As seen in Table 7, 42 percent of the high powerholders in 1850 were businessmen (13 people); in comparison, only 23 percent (6 businessmen) were present among the high power group in 1880.[12] Professionals, in contrast, rose from 26 percent of the high powerholders in 1850 to 48 percent in 1870 and then declined slightly to their 1860 level of 39 percent. Individuals whose primary occupation was farming were never as likely as nonfarmers to wield significant influence in this overwhelmingly agricultural society, although their chances improved considerably between 1870 and 1880. (see Table 7). For a list of specific jobs that make up the occupational categories, see Appendix 1.

The businessmen who prevailed among large powerholders in 1850 were overwhelmingly merchants (eight out of thirteen). In comparison, only two of the eight businessmen in 1860, two of seven in 1870, and three of six in 1880 were retailers. The businessmen of 1850 also included two stage contractors, an innkeeper, a printer-editor, and textile manufacturer Morehead. These influential businessmen owned somewhat less real property and slaves than farmers and considerably less than professionals, if the very wealthy manufacturer-attorney-planter Morehead is excluded from the calculations (see Table 8).[13]

In 1860, even with the exclusion of manufacturer-turned-attorney John

TABLE 7.
Percentage of High Powerholders by Occupation

Year	Agriculture	Business	Professional	Other
1850	26 (8)	42 (13)	26 (8)	6 (2)
1860	32 (9)	29 (8)	39 (11)	0
1870	22 (6)	26 (7)	48 (13)	4 (1)
1880	31 (8)	23 (6)	39 (10)	8 (2)

Source: Guilford County data base.

TABLE 8.
Wealth of High Powerholders by Occupation

	Agriculture	Business	Professional
Real Property (mean in dollars)			
1850	4,875	3,225	8,975
1860	7,867	5,663	12,070
1870	5,450	12,700	4,712
Personal Property (mean in dollars)			
1850	NA	NA	NA
1860	21,050	15,418	28,775
1870	1,805	11,033	2,616
Slaves (mean in numbers)			
1850	12	4	21
1860	6	9	18
1870	—	—	—

Source: Guilford County data base.

M. Morehead from the ranks of professionals, as was done for businessmen in 1850, the professionals, who had become preponderant among large powerholders by this time, were significantly more wealthy in property and slaves than were farmers or businessmen. The size of their holdings suggested that these high powerholders were engaged in agriculture as well as other occupational endeavors because they outdistanced even the agrarians in the value of their land and slaves in 1850 and 1860 (see Table 8). Their situation was enhanced dramatically in the 1850s by the completion of the North Carolina Railroad. They benefited both from the ownership of rail stock and the increased opportunities for marketing their crops that the rails brought. Attorneys such as John A. Gilmer, Ralph Gorrell, and Cyrus P. Mendenhall saw their wealth accumulate almost exponentially. Gilmer, the wealthiest in 1850 with $20,000 in real estate and twenty-five slaves, procured by 1860 $30,000 in real property and at least fifty-three slaves. Along with his rail stock and other personal property, this resulted in an evaluation of $77,000. Similarly, Ralph Gorrell increased his real property from $6,000 in 1850 to $19,000 in 1860. But the most dramatic rise in wealth was exhibited by Cyrus P. Mendenhall. From $1,200 in real property and no slaves in 1850, Mendenhall accumulated land valued at $40,000 and forty-eight slaves in 1860, with a personal property evaluation of $96,000 in the latter year. As William L. Scott's father easily detected, "Siras [sic] has rose up here and got rich."[14]

The dramatic rise in wealth for professionals in the 1850s was followed by an even more precipitous decline in the 1860s as their average real propertyholdings plunged below those of both farmers and businessmen and ranked next to the lowest in personal property, just slightly ahead of farmers (see Table 8). The real propertyholdings of businessmen rose between 1860 and 1870 as three wealthy individuals emerged in their ranks in the latter year who had not been there in the prewar years: merchant D. W. C. Benbow, with real property valued at $35,200, who returned from Fayetteville to Guilford in 1862; druggist Alexander P. Eckel, with real property valued at $20,000, who had achieved only limited influence as mayor of unincorporated Greensboro and as a salt procurer in the 1858–62 era; and Julius A. Gray, also with $20,000 in real estate, who had arrived in the community in the 1850s but who did not emerge as a powerholder until the postwar years. In comparison to the real estate of Benbow, Eckel, and Gray, the largest holdings of businessmen before the war were the $12,000 of entrepreneur Peter Adams and the $10,000 and $8,000, respectively, of merchants James Sloan and Jonathan W. Fields. Businessmen, then, as a group, tended to be wealthier in real estate after the war than before, but professionals sustained sharp losses.

The decline for professionals in value of real property resulted in part from a decrease in the size of fortunes of individual families whose members were high powerholders before and after the war and from the influx into the ranks of influential leaders of a few young men who did not own land in Guilford or who did not own real estate at all. In comparison to real property worth $19,000 in 1860, Ralph Gorrell reported an evaluation of $10,000 in 1870. Similarly, John Gilmer, Jr., indicated real estate of $6,000, in comparison to his father's $30,000 before the war. Junius I. Scales and John N. Staples were youthful newcomers among influential professionals for whom no propertyholdings were listed in the 1870 census. Scales probably still owned his father-in-law's estate in Alamance County, and Staples may have had land in Virginia, but their unreported real estate holdings, along with a similar situation for Patrick F. Duffy, had an adverse effect on the average real property of professionals revealed in Table 8.[15]

Professionals sustained sharper losses in personal property than businessmen during the war decade because, like agrarians, they held much of their personal property in slaves. The war also rendered other types of personal property held by professionals such as rail and bank stock virtually worthless. In contrast, the merchants who persisted among high powerholders in 1860 had their personal property tied up in store inventories rather than slaves, so their losses were not nearly as steep as those of professionals and farmers. Before the war, for example, James Sloan possessed $45,000 in personal property but only eight slaves, and Jonathan W. Fields owned $12,000 in personal property and no slaves. Similarly, after the conflict, merchants D. W. C. Benbow and Jed Lindsay reported personal property valued respectively at $31,330 and $18,000. Although the merchants themselves were not the same individuals before and after the war, the main source of their personal property, store inventories, was identical.

The professionals whose wealth fluctuated so dramatically in the 1850s and 1860s were increasingly attorneys. From 63 percent of the professionals in 1850 (five individuals) to 85 percent in 1870 (eleven persons), lawyers came more and more to fill the ranks of influential professionals. Despite a slight drop to 80 percent (eight people) in 1880, they still remained the primary component of the professional ranks. As attorneys increased in number among high powerholders, the number of physicians declined from three in 1850 to one in 1880. No physicians were large leaders in 1860; instead, two schoolteachers, J. D. Campbell and Richard Sterling, and teacher-minister-former attorney Calvin Wiley joined the ranks of professionals who were high powerholders. A minister, George W. Welker, and a teacher, F. S. Blair, were influential professionals in 1870 and 1880 respectively.

A nucleus of the same lawyers persisted among the large powerholders from one decade to the next. Their ranks expanded gradually in 1860 and sharply in 1870 as they were joined by a few Guilford natives who had not been high powerholders before and several newcomers to the community. Attorneys John Gilmer, Ralph Gorrell, and Cyrus P. Mendenhall were high powerholders in 1850 and in 1860. John M. Dick, a large powerholder in 1850, was not among the attorneys who wielded significant influence in 1860, but his son, Robert P. Dick, was there. Cyrus P. Mendenhall's uncle, George C. Mendenhall, was the fifth 1850 attorney. He was not included in the 1860 power group because he was killed in an accident in 1860. By the 1858–62 era, D. Frank Caldwell, who had intentionally retooled as a lawyer from a merchant, James R. McLean, and John M. Morehead joined Robert P. Dick, John A. Gilmer, Ralph Gorrell, and Cyrus P. Mendenhall as influential attorneys. In 1870, Caldwell, Dick, and Gorrell persisted, and John Gilmer, Jr., emerged in lieu of his dead father. Gilmer, Jr., was joined by John Morehead's nephew James T. Morehead, Jr., and Levi Scott as well as new arrivals in the community, Patrick F. Duffy, Thomas B. Keogh, Junius I. Scales, John N. Staples, and Albion W. Tourgée. In 1880, William S. Ball and George H. Gregory joined the existing nucleus of Caldwell, Dick, Gilmer, Morehead, and Staples, and C. P. Mendenhall, after a hiatus in 1870, returned to the fold. For a summary of attorneys by census year, see Appendix 6.

In contrast to attorneys, the rate of persistence for influential businessmen was high only between 1850 and 1860. Sixty-three percent (five of eight) of the businessmen who were influential in 1860 had been prominent in 1850, but between 1860 and 1870, not a single businessman continued in a position of substantial power, and between 1870 and 1880, only one, James W. Albright, did so. Among farmers who were leading powerholders, the continuation of the same people happened even less often than among businessmen. Only one farmer, Eli Smith, who was a high powerholder in 1850, remained one in 1860. None of the six farmers with substantial influence in 1870 had been in that position in 1860, and in 1880, again only one person, Joseph W. Gilmer, persisted from the 1870 high power group.

The failure of any businessman to continue after the war as a high powerholder may have been related to financial losses that some merchants incurred as suppliers of the Confederate army. James Sloan, for example, an influential powerholder-merchant in 1850 and 1860, who did not resurface after the war, informed Ralph Gorrell in 1861 that he could not superintend the acquisition of salt for county residents because he was engaged "in the important business of clothing the soldiers" and that he, at that time, had slightly less than $75,000 worth of clothing and goods in transit.[16] Additionally, two of the influential businessmen in 1860, Jonathan W. Fields, and Michael S. Sherwood, were dead by 1870, and, as the number of businessmen who were high powerholders dwindled, the death of even a few affected the small number available for exercising substantial influence. Farmers were unlikely to remain in positions of high power decade after decade because they derived much of their influence from having been in their respective neighborhoods a long time, and thus they were older than businessmen and professionals at the time they acquired significant influence. With the exception of 1880, when the average age of agrarians fell to a low of fifty, powerful farmers always averaged in the mid-fifties in age and were therefore considerably older than other leaders.

The decline of merchants and the rise of attorneys as important occupational groups between 1850 and 1880 resulted both from the growing wealth and specialization of the Guilford community in the 1850s as the railroad arrived and commercial agriculture accelerated and from the concerns and divisions generated by the war. That wealth in real property values was increasing for many in the county was demonstrated in Table 2 in Chapter 1. This table revealed that in 1850 71 percent of the households owned no property or property valued at less than $500, but by 1860, only

53 percent of the county's households were in these categories. Concomitantly, both absolute and relative expansion occurred for all real estate categories above $500, with the largest being in households with real property valued between $2,000 and $3,999. In the latter category, 110 households or 3 percent of the community in 1850 increased to 368 households or 13 percent of the community in 1860. These figures do not mean that every household in the community was prospering. The net decline in the free population between 1850 and 1860 indicated economic hardship for many, but wealth accrued to a number of households, particularly to those who already possessed sizable holdings and were near the railroad.

Powerholders, most of whom were already relatively affluent in 1850, were in an especially advantageous position to seize improved opportunities. As seen in Table 5, the average value of real property for all powerholders increased twofold between 1850 and 1860. The increasing affluence of attorneys such as Gilmer, Gorrell, and Mendenhall underscored this trend. Additionally, wealth was consolidated, along with power, by the middle of the nineteenth century through a series of marriages, which produced a coterie of "first families" in the Greensboro vicinity.[17]

As the wealth of Guilford citizens increased, so did opportunities for formal training. Ralph Gorrell, who in 1825 became the first Guilford native to receive a degree from the University of North Carolina, was one of the few leaders in 1850 to have a diploma, but by the 1850s, young men went to the state university as a matter of course. James Morehead, Jr., John Gilmer, Jr., Julius and Henry Gorrell, Samuel Adams, Samuel Weir, and William L. Scott, to mention a few, were all University of North Carolina alumni. Levi Scott, who never attended college, wrote his younger brother, William, in 1856 that he felt intimidated by his "indifferent education, lack of family prestige, [and] money."[18] His lack of education, Scott further explained, kept him from seeking opportunities outside of Guilford.

For young men with a university education in a predominantly agricultural society, the legal profession offered one of the few alternatives in the choice of a career. The limited options available were demonstrated by Nereus Mendenhall as he contemplated a career at midcentury: "Sometimes a little anxiety crosses my mind in respect of my prospects for an occupation—whether it would be best to remain on this road [as a railroad surveyor], to practice medicine, teach school, publish a paper, or what?" Similarly, Charles Shober, who admitted to his friend Bryan Grimes that he did not particularly like the legal profession, lamented that he did not know what other business to follow.[19]

Sometimes the occupation of lawyer seemed attractive to men in and of itself because it brought prestige and money. D. F. Caldwell determined in his forties to become an attorney, although he was already a successful merchant, railroad entrepreneur, and public official. Thus the upswing in Guilford's economic fortunes meant better educational opportunities for a number of young men, and the legal profession was one of the few attractive alternatives to them. The result, not unexpectedly, was a sizable number of attorneys in a relatively sparsely populated area.

The war and its aftermath brought additional lawyers into the area by encouraging geographic mobility, and it also accelerated the participation of lawyers in public affairs by making more frequent precisely the activities in which attorneys prevailed, even in 1850—partisan affairs and decision making. Influential farmers usually scored most of their points in public officeholding. The year 1870 proved an exception to this rule because party organizing was so intense at this time that even agrarians became involved in a significant way. In addition to officeholding, a sizable minority of farmers were decision makers, especially in 1850 and 1880, when railroad promotion was a top priority. Like farmers with substantial influence, businessmen tended to earn points via officeholding before the war. More than agrarians, businessmen were involved in decision making before as well as after the conflict, with the exception of 1860, when they, like farmers, were much less active. In contrast, professionals were always likely to be decision makers, especially in 1860, when issues like secession and the war effort prompted their involvement.[20] It probably seemed natural to lawyers and the general populace alike that attorneys, as legal advisers, should participate in activities surrounding the consideration of a legal question—secession. Additionally, "poor lawyers," who were "totally out of employment" during the war, no doubt found ample time to engage in war-related activities.

Attorneys also participated in partisan affairs at a higher rate than other important leaders, and their involvement in this area particularly accelerated in 1870, when participation for all groups was up. Furthermore, unlike farmers and businessmen, the participation of attorneys in party activities did not lessen dramatically in 1880. Thus the law of supply and demand was operative in explaining the burgeoning role of lawyers in public affairs. Enhanced opportunities for higher education for a number of young people before the war and geographic mobility resulting from the conflict ensured an abundance of legal minds in the community. At the same time, issues related to the coming of the war, the conduct of the fight, and the two-party system that grew from it provided exactly the questions with which these minds liked to grapple. The result was an expanded role for attorneys in public affairs at the expense of businessmen.

As attorneys replaced businessmen as the preponderant occupational group among high powerholders, occupation was becoming increasingly important in explaining variation in power scores, or the amount of power that one might achieve. Concomitantly, real property was declining as a relative contributor to power score variation. As seen in Table 9, although real property accounted for 31 percent of the variation in power scores in 1850, it explained only 4 percent in 1870.[21] Occupation, however, contributed 3 percent to the total variation in power scores or the R Square in 1850 but 9 percent in 1870.

Like occupation, place of birth also contributed an increasing proportion of the change in R Square between 1850 and 1870, but age contributed its largest portion in 1860. Unfortunately, although occupation and place of birth explained more and more of the variation in power, they did not contribute to R Square as much as real property had done, with the result that this particular combination of independent variables—real property, age, occupation, and place of birth—explained less and less of the total variation in power scores. Thus although occupation contributed more to the change in R Square in 1870 than any other variable, its contribution was not as important as real property was in 1850 or even 1860.

Although the changes in R Square produced by the addition of each independent variable were useful in comparing the relative contribution of each variable to variation in power scores between 1850 and 1880, unstandardized regression coefficients provide a clearer picture of the actual contribution of each independent variable to power. Table 10 shows that for every dollar increase in real property in 1850, power scores went up .001 of a point, or, to put it another way, for every thousand-dollar increase in real property in 1850, power scores rose 1 point.[22] In 1860, an increase of one thousand dollars in real property yielded only .3 of a point increase in power; the figure for 1870 was little different. Similarly, a year added to

TABLE 9.

Proportion of Variance in Power Scores Attributed to Selected Variables

| Year | R Square Change | | | | |
	Real Property	Age	Occupation	Place of Birth	Total
1850	31	0.9	3	.01	34
1860	12	3	6	0.1	21
1870[a]	04	.09	9	2	14

Source: Guilford County data base.

[a]Rounding of R Square change produced a total of 15 in 1870 rather than the actual 14 shown in the last column of this line.

TABLE 10.
Power Scores Regressed on Selected Variables

	Unstandardized Regression Coefficients			
Year	*Real Property*	*Age*	*Occupation*	*Place of Birth*
1850	.001	.12	4.34	−.86
1860	.0003	.17	4.24	−2.02
1870	.0002	.04	6.70	6.70

Source: Guilford County data base.

one's age produced an increase in power scores of .12 of a point in 1850, .17 in 1860, and .04 in 1870. Age was less important in the latter year because more young people gained high power in this year than in the others, so adding a year to one's age did not result in as dramatic an increase to one's power score as in the other years.

Unlike real property and age, occupation and place of birth are nominal variables. In the regression analysis, occupation was divided into two categories, farm and nonfarm, with farm being assigned a value of zero and nonfarm a value of one. Table 10 indicates that being a nonfarmer increased one's power score by 4.34 points in 1850 and 6.70 points in 1870. Hence being a nonfarmer in 1870 was more important in the attainment of power than it was in 1850. This measure, it should be underscored, indicated nothing about the type of nonfarmers who prevailed in 1870, only that being one was more important in the amount of power one achieved than it was in 1850.

Like occupation, place of birth was divided into two categories, South and non-South, with South being assigned a value of zero and non-South a value of one. Table 10 reveals that, like occupation, place of birth was becoming more important as a measure of power, but the negative and positive signs in front of these figures indicate something more. The negative .86 and negative 2.02 indicate that being born in the South (an assigned value of zero) enhanced one's power score .86 in 1850 and 2.02 in 1860, but in 1870, being born out of the South increased one's power score by 6.70 points.

The importance of the regression analysis lies in its verification of previously detected changes over time. First, it underscores temporary changes following the war. As young newcomers acquired significant influence, age mattered very little in the amount of power one acquired; further, being a nonsoutherner actually enhanced one's chances for additional influence. Though transient in nature, these alterations no doubt contributed to a general air of instability that intensified the seriousness with which the postwar partisan struggles were waged, and, also, they probably help explain the apparent challenges to the existing social order that many historians have perceived.

Additionally, the regression analysis reflects the growing specialization of Guilford society as real property became less significant in the acquisition of power and occupation became more important. The lessening in importance of real property as a factor in the attainment of influence did not mean that wealth was no longer an attribute of powerholders. Indeed, the average powerholder remained considerably more affluent than most Guilford citizens throughout the entire study. Instead, the relative decline in the importance of real property as an indicator of power suggested that most powerholders were increasing their property in the 1850s to the point that sharp differences no longer distinguished them from one another. Similarly, in the following decade many powerholders suffered financial losses from the war, and, since most were relatively depressed economically, that is, in comparison to one another, real property was not much more important in 1870 than it had been in 1860 in explaining the influence one might acquire. (See Table 6 for the growing similarity of medium and high powerholders in real property values.)

When wealth no longer dramatically differentiated powerholders in the amount of influence that they might secure, another attribute, occupation, became more important. Occupation, as measured by farm and nonfarm, suggested that being a nonfarmer was particularly important in the acquisition of significant influence. According to the earlier discussion of the socioeconomic attributes of powerholders, attorneys replaced businessmen as the most important nonfarm group on the eve of the war. Thus the occupation that became significant in the procurement of high power was one that usually required considerable resources and formal training—one that suggested a more affluent society that could afford to rely on trained legal specialists to direct its public affairs.

To recapitulate briefly, power arrangements following the war remained stable in most respects. Approximately the same proportion of the population garnered about the same amount of influence in the same ways as before the conflict. The most dramatic shift was in the number of people participating in partisan affairs. High powerholders in particular accelerated their involvement in party politics, while, in turn, lessening their participation as public officeholders.

Among all leaders, about the same percentage reappeared from one decade to another with the war years proving no exception, although a sizable number of large powerholders failed to survive the war. Many expired for reasons unrelated to the conflict, however.

The vacuum left by oldsters was filled by a number of young men who were either not from Guilford or who were born in the county but had been away for a while. Still, as wealthy professionals and businessmen who resided in Greensboro, the young leaders resembled those they replaced in most respects. Furthermore, once they became influential leaders, they tended to stay in the ranks. Thus the emergence of young men into positions of significant power after the war was only partially related to the conflict, and it was an ephemeral condition. No such phenomenon happened a decade later.

The most enduring change to occur between the mid-nineteenth century and the early 1880s was the rise of attorneys as the most influential figures in the community. Initiated on the eve of the war as the county grew more wealthy and specialized, this trend accelerated as the conflict encouraged geographic mobility among a number of young lawyers and produced affairs in which members of the legal fraternity engaged—decision making and party politics. The largest land- and slaveowners in the community, these attorneys saw their wealth increase almost exponentially before the conflict and decline just about as rapidly afterward, although they never became as poor as the vast majority of Guilford residents.

Businessmen, as well as land- and slaveholders, Guilford lawyers forged a consensus on economic issues in the antebellum years that persisted through the war, but, like the electorate, they too were affected by the bitter divisions that accompanied the conflict. Uncertain of the political future in 1865, members of the bar hesitated and eventually divided, with the majority going into Democratic ranks but with several very capable ones becoming Republicans. More accustomed than anyone else in the community to party politics, lawyers then fueled the flames of partisan warfare. Yet despite appearances of internecine wars, legal specialists cooperated far more frequently than they would have admitted. Drawn together by similar educational experiences, occupation of the same socioeconomic stratum, professional ties, and common economic assumptions and goals, the legal fraternity contributed a basic cohesiveness and stability to postwar society that its partisanship belied. It is to the attorneys' story of consensus, cleavage, and cohesion that we now turn to explore more fully the roots of "New" South leadership.

PART II

The Bar as a Strategic Elite

5. Lawyers and the Economy

The attorneys who rose to positions of significant influence on the eve of the war played a crucial role in the Guilford economy by bridging agricultural and business interests. Among the largest land- and slaveholders in the community, lawyers maintained numerous ties with rural elements, but as town dwellers who engaged in a variety of economic pursuits, they worked closely with local businessmen. Indeed, both the public and private activities of these planters-businessmen-attorneys suggested that their focus was more often the courthouse and countinghouse than the smokehouse. They were able, however, to ease potential tensions between agrarians who derived their living solely from the soil and businessmen whose well-being emanated largely from the town. The living arrangements of these multifaceted attorneys symbolized the pivotal role they played in the county's economic affairs. For these professionals, there were no planters to overcome or industrialists to thwart; all were one and the same and all were concerned with the same goal—making money.

Following the war, the economic consensus forged in the antebellum years persisted. Large landholding attorneys, regardless of partisan stripe, continued to dwell in town and to develop mines, railroads, and mills. Additionally, they worked in concert to repay the county debt and to encourage European immigration into the Old North State. In short, they reflected much more an extension of prewar sentiments and predilections than an aberration, and they agreed on economic matters far more than party politics suggested. Their capitalist consensus, in turn, coupled with their continued interaction in the face of bitter partisan warfare, discussed in Chapter 7, resulted in the accomplishment of at least a portion of their economic goals, an achievement that only this strategic social group could effect.

As discussed in the preceding chapter, attorneys such as John Gilmer, Ralph Gorrell, and Cyrus P. Mendenhall experienced an almost meteoric rise in wealth in the 1850s as their real and slave property expanded dramatically. By 1860, when lawyers had risen to the ranks of the most influential powerholders in the community, they were some of the largest propertyowners. Indeed, at a time when 42 percent of the county's households owned no property, 50 percent possessed real estate valued at less than $4,000, and the average powerholder held just over $4,200 in landed wealth (see Table 2, Chapter 1, and Table 5, Chapter 4), the seven attorneys who were high powerholders averaged real property worth $25,888. All held land valued at $10,000 or more except James R. McLean, who owned $4,700, but McLean had considerable personal property, including twenty-one slaves.

Like McLean, the other members of the legal fraternity who had become substantial powerholders possessed many more slaves than was customary in antebellum Guilford.[1] Although 88 percent of the households owned no slaves in 1860 and powerholders generally averaged four, attorneys averaged twenty-seven. Indeed, members of the bar owned well above the average for high powerholders—twelve. Only two of the seven attorneys owned close to the average number of slaves for large powerholders. D. F. Caldwell held thirteen and R. P. Dick, twelve.

With far more real property and slaves than other county residents, lawyers no doubt seemed to represent the interests of local agrarians. Additionally, some such as John Gilmer and John M. Dick had grown up on farms, and others like John M. and James T. Morehead on plantations. Dick had purportedly been forced to choose between a college education and a good farm, and Gilmer allegedly wore homespun until he was twenty. Thus these antebellum attorneys could seemingly identify with all elements of the rural population, wealthy as well as nonaffluent.

Even Greensboro natives who had no boyhood recollections of life on the farm managed to acquire real estate and demonstrate their love of agriculture. Ralph Gorrell, who owned three tracts of land totaling almost four hundred acres and two or three other parcels of unspecified acreage at the time of his death in 1875 despite large losses during the war, was described in the press as a "lawyer from duty and a farmer from the love of it."[2] Gorrell served as one of four vice-presidents of the prewar agricultural society and addressed assemblages at the courthouse on agricultural topics. D. F. Caldwell also managed to ingratiate himself with the "country people" and was allegedly disliked by the "moneyed men" of Guilford, although he lived in Greensboro from the time he was one until he died.[3]

Thus, when judged on the basis of their real estate and slaveholdings as well as their heritage and purported interests, influential attorneys resembled planters in other parts of the antebellum South on the eve of the war. Most held more than twenty slaves and possessed considerably more property than their neighbors. Their rural ties appeared strong, and one would expect, on the basis of this evidence alone, that their allegiance to a "planter mentality" as described by such recent historians as Eugene Genovese would be unshakable. Yet with the exception of John M. Morehead, who lived at a "delightful suburban seat," all of the well-to-do lawyers lived in Greensboro in 1860 and all, including Morehead, engaged in a variety of economic pursuits.[4]

These included the promotion of internal improvements, mining, and, when possible, mill building. Often, members of the bar purchased land for speculative purposes, farming it during economic hard times. Politically conservative, these entrepreneurs were bold in their economic endeavors, and though some of their financial ventures, such as slaveholding, may have hindered others, like industrialization, there was no evidence that these individuals perceived such negative relationships. Guilford attorneys were neither economists nor philosophers; they were practical men concerned with making a living, and in that respect, they were far more similar to their legal brethren in other parts of the nation than has been perceived.

The economic activities in which Guilford lawyers engaged included virtually every option available to them, with internal improvements, especially railroad building, the most conspicuous. The acquisition of a railroad necessitated not only the procurement of a charter and financial assistance from the state legislature but also fundraising efforts by private citizens. In all of these activities Guilford attorneys played an important role. The extent of their involvement is well illustrated by the exertions of three members of the bar: John M. Morehead, John Gilmer, and D. Frank Caldwell.

Both Morehead and Gilmer had apprenticed in the law office of Archibald D. Murphy, one of the state's earliest advocates of improved transportation facilities, and both were intimately involved with the formation of the Whig party in Raleigh in the mid-1830s, a party whose major goal was to improve transportation in North Carolina. As governor of the state in the early 1840s, Morehead advocated a comprehensive internal improvements program that called for the completion of railroad lines already begun in the state, improvement of rivers and harbors, and construction of extensive lines of turnpikes to link all the facilities together in one general transportation system.[5] Morehead's proposal was rebuffed by a hostile Democratic legislature, so by the latter 1840s, the attention of Guilford railroad promoters focused primarily on a single cross-state line linking Greensboro to the Danville-Richmond Railroad to the north in Virginia and to a South Carolina line, via Charlotte, in the south. To secure this end, D. F. Caldwell chaired a convention that met in Salisbury, North Carolina, early in 1849.

Frightened by the specter of a north-south line that would bypass their own vicinity, enough eastern Democratic legislators endorsed a railroad bill to secure passage late in January 1849, although, even in the face of a potential trade loss, so many continued to resist the measure that it passed the senate by a majority of only one vote and the Speaker, whose vote ratified it, was never again elected to public office.[6] According to the bill, the state would subscribe $2 million (ultimately it paid $3 million), but first, private subscriptions totaling $1 million had to be procured. Faced with considerable resistance in eastern North Carolina and the virtual bankruptcy of two previous state-supported projects, the Wilmington-Weldon and the Raleigh-Gaston, railroad enthusiasts confronted no small task in the procurement of the necessary $1 million.

The first step in the drive for subscriptions was the reconvening of the Salisbury convention, again chaired by Caldwell, and the development of plans for a later one in the same town. Shortly after the second Salisbury assemblage, a meeting was held at the Guilford courthouse at which ten delegates, including Morehead, were named to the third Salisbury gathering. Both Gilmer and Caldwell spoke at the county meeting.

Throughout the summer of 1849, Guilford railroad enthusiasts, paced by Morehead, Caldwell, and Gilmer, strove for stock subscriptions. In June, twenty-three counties sent representatives to a meeting in Greensboro. Caldwell called the meeting to order, appointed the president pro tem, and served on a committee to prepare business. Gilmer served on the resolutions committee and addressed the committee to prepare business, while Morehead was chosen permanent president and also addressed the committee to prepare business. Additionally, Caldwell, Gilmer, and Morehead were named a three-person committee to appoint a subcommittee to sell stock subscriptions. A joint meeting between Guilford and Davidson counties also occurred in June, and this was followed by several local addresses and written appeals by Caldwell and Gilmer.

A county meeting in October 1849, at which the same duo spoke, was followed by one in November in preparation for a general meeting to be held in Greensboro on November 29. By the time of the November county meeting, promoters of the railroad had agreed to sell the unsold portion of the $1 million appropriation in the form of one hundred shares of stock, rather than continue to rely on small subscriptions. At the preliminary county meeting, four companies, including that of C. P. Mendenhall and

James R. McLean, and eight individuals, including John Gilmer and John M. Dick, agreed to take twelve and a half of the remaining hundred shares.

This plan was effected at the North Carolina Railroad Convention in Greensboro on November 29. At this meeting, held in the First Presbyterian Church and attended by delegates from about twenty-five counties, a total of fifty-one of the remaining hundred shares were subscribed. Guilford led the way with the twelve and a half shares; only Rowan County (Salisbury) was close with eleven shares. The additional twelve and a half shares increased Guilford's total subscription from $60,000 to $150,000, $10,000 of which Morehead alone had subscribed.[7]

Morehead, Gilmer, and Caldwell not only played active roles in the general meeting on the twenty-ninth, but also Morehead subsequently sought subscriptions at a January meeting of counties west of Guilford through which the railroad would pass. Additionally, as a member of a committee of three appointed at the November convention to solicit stock from these counties, he traveled widely on the railroad's behalf. Gilmer participated in a local meeting at the end of February while Caldwell, Morehead, and eight other delegates from Guilford attended an assemblage in Hillsborough.

At the Hillsborough meeting, it was announced that $1 million had been appropriated but not all of the subscriptions were taken in compliance with the legislative act of 1849, so Caldwell was placed on a committee to sell additional stock and Gilmer and Morehead were designated commissioners in charge of reopening subscription books in Greensboro. Finally, on June 5, 1850, the $1 million subscription was achieved, and at a July meeting of the stockholders in Salisbury, Morehead was chosen president of the company, a position he held until he declined to run again and Charles W. Fisher replaced him in 1855. Both Morehead and Gilmer were designated directors of the company.

To coincide with the second annual stockholders' meeting in Greensboro the following year, a public groundbreaking ceremony was planned. At the celebration, Gilmer introduced a resolution and Morehead, the speaker. Like all of the promotional activities, the groundbreaking ceremony was bipartisan. Fewer local Democrats participated than Whigs because their numbers were fewer, but they demonstrated just as much enthusiasm. John M. Dick, who had attended the second Salisbury meeting and the convention of 1849 and who had subscribed one of the remaining one hundred shares of stock, invited Democratic Governor David Reid to stay at his home during the celebration. We are all "alive" on the railroad subject, Dick proclaimed.[8]

Hostility by eastern North Carolinians toward railroad efforts continued to plague Guilford promoters. Caldwell was warned that he should never venture into Beaufort or Hyde counties on the coast "or in fact, anywhere to the Eastward of Raleigh," and Morehead, fearing further opposition, hastened in the spring of 1851 to issue contracts for the construction of the road.[9] By January 1856, his efforts came to fruition. On the twenty-ninth of that month, D. F. Caldwell drove the last spike, connecting Goldsboro in the east and Charlotte in the west, a distance of 223 miles.

The completion of the central portion of the North Carolina Railroad moved Guilford much closer to the implementation of a north-south line, but eastern fears, coupled with the hostility of Democrats to any plans of the newly formed American party (mainly Whigs), thwarted efforts to connect with Danville before the war. State representative Levi M. Scott noted that the enmity of Democrats toward Americans was so great that even if the Democratically controlled assembly chartered a Danville road, it would probably be run in a way to spite Greensboro. "For this reason," he continued, "we are almost afraid to mention the matter."[10]

Scott's fears materialized when Democrats amended a railroad bill introduced by representatives from Rockingham County, just north of Guilford. The act did not involve a Danville link per se but would have chartered a railroad from Greensboro to the Dan River coal fields in northern North Carolina. Senator William S. Ashe of the seaport town of Wilmington, "to show his power and his desire to annoy," Morehead claimed, moved that Danville be inserted in place of Greensboro, and the Democrats carried the bill as amended, with the result that the railroad was to run from Virginia, near Danville, to the coal fields without coming within twenty miles of the North Carolina Railroad (or Guilford). "Thus," Morehead continued, "a North Carolina legislature, Democratic, refuse to let North Carolinians bring their own coal to their own Road, but compel them to carry it to another state."[11] The "controling [sic] influence of Wilmington" in this legislature, Morehead surmised, was "a curse to the state."[12]

Well aware of the constituency from which support for the North Carolina Railroad would have to come, Caldwell and Gilmer appealed to agrarians throughout the subscription drive. The railroad would open the markets of the world to western North Carolina farmers, Caldwell argued, and Gilmer stressed that improved transportation would make agriculture "a money-making business" in North Carolina just as it was in states with rail networks.[13] To a large extent, these efforts paid off, for about half of the initial $60,000 pledged in Guilford came in the form of small subscriptions, but though lawyers emphasized the profits that improved marketing would bring to farmers, they themselves envisioned financial gain from different quarters.[14] Specifically, they saw mining ventures as profitable corollaries to railroad construction, and they speculated in land, expecting prices to rise once the "iron horse" made its appearance.

Like other Guilford attorneys, D. F. Caldwell and John A. Gilmer were deeply involved in mining activities by the early 1850s. Both were among fourteen owners of the Taylor Coal Field in Chatham County, and they met in Greensboro in 1853 with others, including four New Yorkers, to form the Hillsboro Coal Mining and Transportation Company. Although Gilmer's portion of the stock was not as large as that of the northerners, he served as one of the company's directors. Initially, the owners of the Taylor Coal Field were very optimistic that their property's value would rise because of its proximity to a proposed railroad (probably the Western, chartered in 1849), but the enthusiasm proved unwarranted as mineral stocks generally declined and the railroad failed to materialize.[15]

Although Caldwell "made a failure" in his coal venture, as his cousin phrased it, he and Gilmer continued not only in these efforts but in other mining schemes as well. In conjunction with Orange County resident Hugh Waddell, who was also involved in the Hillsboro Coal Mining Company, Caldwell owned the Header property, which was, according to Waddell, one of the best places yet discovered for copper. Caldwell and Gilmer also possessed stock in the North Carolina Mining Company, another copper enterprise. Like the Hillsboro Company, this organization, which was managed by a New York firm, was adversely affected by the depression in mineral stocks in 1853.[16]

Besides these ventures, Caldwell had an interest in the Deep River Copper Mining Company, and Gilmer was one of the largest stockholders in the McCulloch Copper and Gold Mining Company.[17] One of the few local operations in which neither Caldwell nor Gilmer was directly involved was the Hodgin Gold Mine. Owners of this company included Ralph Gorrell, along with four other local businessmen and High Point physician Shubal G. Coffin.

Like Caldwell and Gilmer, other Guilford attorneys engaged in manifold economic activities, and these included manufacturing. As noted earlier, C. P. Mendenhall, James R. McLean & Company bought considerable stock in the North Carolina Railroad, and Mendenhall also engaged in banking. During the war, the enterprising lawyer was involved in the operation of a gun factory near High Point and afterward in a spoke and handle factory.

A director of the Bank of North Carolina, John M. Morehead possessed commercial interests in the present-day North Carolina coastal town of

Morehead City, and he operated a boat line on the Dan River. An early proponent of manufacturing, Morehead also served as one of the directors of Humphrey Cotton Mills, the textile plant established in Guilford in the 1830s, but his major business operation centered in Rockingham County, north of Guilford, the community where Morehead had grown up. There he established the Leaksville Cotton Mill in 1837, and to it he added a modest facility for carding and spinning wool. In 1876, when an agreement was filed in probate court following the deaths of Morehead in 1866 and his wife in 1868, the Rockingham County operation included cotton milling, grist and saw milling, "merchandising," and the farming of a tract of about 1,100 acres, a portion of which Morehead had probably inherited from his father.[18]

All of the attorneys bought land and farmed portions of it, particularly when they experienced financial reversals in other endeavors, but primarily they hoped to profit from rising land values. George C. Mendenhall in particular demonstrated the speculative fever that gripped Guilford lawyers. Besides some 1,400 acres in Guilford, Mendenhall owned on the eve of the war 160 acres in Arkansas, 920 acres in Iowa, unspecified acreage in Minnesota, and town lots in Indianapolis and St. Louis. His North Carolina holdings outside of Guilford included 100 acres in far western Buncombe County, which had been a part of his second wife's plantation, more than 200 acres in Moore County, which he owned outright, as well as an interest in the "John McLeod lands" and more than 500 acres in Randolph County.[19]

By no means was Mendenhall's land used entirely for farming. Besides the town lots that he possessed outside of the state, he owned several in the North Carolina towns of Asheboro, Gladesboro, and Albemarle. His Guilford holdings included eleven acres in Greensboro, nine town lots and three houses in Jamestown, and a homesite of almost seven hundred acres, which contained "mills and other buildings."[20]

Not only the extent and nature of Mendenhall's holdings but also the possession of at least some of it in conjunction with nonrelatives and the varied uses made of the property suggest a vigorous entrepreneurial spirit that is in striking contrast to the "antibourgeois" orientation ascribed by several recent historians to southern planters. Since Mendenhall gradually freed some of his bondsmen, he might be regarded as different from other southern aristocrats, but the boldness with which he approached economic affairs was emulated by all of the local attorneys, despite their reluctance to endorse democratic political measures like free suffrage in state senate elections.[21]

As noted in Chapter 2, local entrepreneurs secured a unique charter from the state legislature for a life insurance company, which permitted them to invest premiums broadly and to generate capital on the basis of funds they held in trust. By 1854, the company had issued $22,000 in one- and two-dollar bills. Throughout the venture, Guilford lawyers played key roles. D. F. Caldwell guided the bill through the house and John Gilmer through the senate, and Ralph Gorrell's picture appeared on the front of the company's two-dollar bill. The Greensboro Mutual Life and Trust Company also counted Cyrus P. Mendenhall among its directors.

When Lask & Company, exchange brokers of Tennessee, failed to se- cure the approval of local druggist David P. Weir, the manager of Greens- boro Mutual, in their scheme to circulate notes from the Greensboro com- pany in Tennessee, Arkansas, Mississippi, and Alabama, they turned to Gilmer and Caldwell for endorsement. Although Weir, the son-in-law of John M. Dick and brother-in-law of Robert P. Dick, had "no fancy for the name of *Wild Cat Currency*," the directors of Lask apparently assumed that Caldwell and Gilmer had no such qualms.[22] Whether Greensboro Mutual became involved with Lask is unclear, but it is apparent that the economic contacts of the directors generally and the legislative and economic con- nections of Caldwell and Gilmer in particular paid off, for the company declared an annual dividend of 67 percent from 1858 through 1861.[23]

The pivotal position held by attorney-planter-businessmen in the Guilford economy was graphically demonstrated by their living arrange- ments, for the wealthy residents of early Greensboro were able to combine town and country life in a way that is impossible in twentieth-century U.S. cities. Designated as the county seat in 1808, Greensboro was laid out in a grid pattern with the courthouse and public square at the heart of the town at the intersection of Market Street (running east-west) and Elm Street (on a north-south axis). Prime property stood at the four corners of the public square and sold in 1808 at an average price of $144 per lot, although some of the least expensive acreage a quarter of a mile away was valued as low as $4.80.[24]

By 1860, between 150 and 200 residences were arranged in a loose con- figuration within a square mile of the courthouse. These residences in- cluded town lots and "cottages," but the dominant feature was large es- tates consisting of seven to ten acres located within easy walking distance of the central square and often connected in the rear to large tracts of undeveloped or agricultural land. These estates were especially prominent on the north side of Market Street, the main thoroughfare leading west to Salem in Forsyth County, but they radiated from every direction of the courthouse except toward the northeast, where the land became low and marshy.[25] There, a few free blacks rented from white businessmen.[26]

The rural quality of the town was enhanced by the small size of the population and its proximity to vast expanses of open land. Mary Smith, wife of the pastor of the First Presbyterian Church, recalled that on their arrival in 1859, a single cabin sat between their house and the woods. "No street lamps illumined the darkness," Smith noted, "and the silence of the night was unbroken save by the wail of the whipperwill and the musical note of the screech-owl."[27] The closeness to an agrarian lifestyle was also underscored for many townspeople by the practice of some form of agriculture on their property. This was particularly the case on the large estates where not only a large family but also a number of slaves usually lived. "In a very real sense," a recent analyst of residential development in Greensboro noted, "these estates brought the country into the town, and throughout the pre-war period, there was little differentiation between the two."[28]

Virtually all of the attorneys who rose to prominence on the eve of the war lived on the town's large estates. In 1820, the Reverend William Paisley had purchased a block on west Market Street from D. F. Caldwell's father, Thomas, and near the courthouse he built a home in the early 1830s for the next to the youngest of his six daughters, Juliana, and her husband, John Gilmer. D. Frank Caldwell continued to dwell in his father's home on Market Street, and James T. Morehead lived on an estate in south Greensboro, not too far from Blandwood, built by his brother John M. Morehead. Cyrus P. Mendenhall also lived in south Greensboro in a large home on Elm Street, as did Ralph Gorrell, who owned an estate along Asheboro Street. On the north side of the town at the corner of Church and Elm streets stood the home of John M. Dick, and Dunleath, the estate of his son Robert P. Dick, faced Church.[29]

On their town holdings, lawyers combined business and agriculture. Ralph Gorrell and James T. Morehead located their law offices on their estates, and Gorrell's home in particular was known as a center for business and political as well as religious meetings.[30] "This pattern of convergence of real estate, financial, commercial, and industrial interests," residential analyst Jonathan Baylin concluded, "provides a major theme throughout the nineteenth century development of Greensboro."[31] No one harmonized those interests better than Guilford's powerful attorneys, and nothing symbolizes the integrating role they played more vividly than a description of Cyrus P. Mendenhall's home provided by a postwar admirer of Greensboro's antebellum dwellings: "The house which stood back in [the] yard was colonial in type, with beautiful old columns and seats on either side of the porch. . . . In front of the house one always noticed two large iron balls about two feet in diameter brought from the mining plant where now is Hayworth's Springs. This was also the home of Greensboro's first greenhouse."[32]

Undoubtedly, antebellum attorneys sometimes worked at cross-purposes in their economic endeavors. As they successfully expanded and concentrated their slaveholdings in the 1850s they unwittingly limited the profits of farmers, who might have provided a market for industrial goods and siphoned capital away from other ventures. There was no indication, however, that these enterprising lawyers perceived the conflicts inherent in their varied activities. They focused more of their time and effort on business ventures than agrarian ones, but above all, they were interested in making money, and in that way they were more like their legal brethren in other parts of the country than has been acknowledged. In assessing the role of lawyers in the development of the U.S. economy between 1820 and 1860, historian Charles M. Haar drew conclusions that could readily apply to Guilford attorneys when he wrote:

This is not to suggest that the lawyer . . . singlehandedly, or even deliberately, paved the way for economic expansion, even though he helped to devise the fundamental working arrangements of the industrial society. When he participated with full engagement in the expansion it was because his only choice was to adjust himself to the new era. There was nothing very philosophical about such a decision. If he wanted to prosper, he had to come to terms with emergent capitalism. . . . In many ways he was unaware of the implications of his actions. He had not studied economic theory, and what he knew of the "dismal science" had probably been derived from his own experience in business. . . . He was not an Olympian observer, standing outside the business process, predicting its course and moralizing about its significance, nor was he an idealist, hampered by theories or lost in refinement and abstraction: he was a practical man concerned with making a living.[33]

As late as 1880, a sense of rural life still pervaded the town of Greensboro, and affluent attorneys dwelled within its boundaries. Large estates persisted west along Market Street, north on Church Street, and even in south Greensboro near Asheboro Street, although the North Carolina Railroad, the black neighborhood of Warnersville, and a white moderate-income neighborhood known as Shieldstown had been constructed in the Asheboro Street vicinity by this time.[34] A booster pamphlet published around 1885 mentioned several factories, primarily spoke and handle, situated within the town but pointed also to Greensboro's possession of "the South's largest *dairy*."[35] Lawyers lived on the same estates as before the war, and newcomer Thomas B. Keogh purchased the residence of merchant Calvin McAdoo just behind Ralph Gorrell on Asheboro Street and Albion Tourgée located near the Dicks.

Like their predecessors, postwar lawyers continued a close association with the land, and some could still identify with an impoverished, agrarian background. D. F. Caldwell farmed his portion of the Taylor and Carlos mineral properties that he purchased before the war, growing cotton, corn, wheat, and oats, and Albion Tourgée operated a nursery which he bought upon his arrival in Greensboro in 1865 from C. P. Mendenhall, a venture into which Mendenhall had recently invested $17,000.[36] Reared on a farm a least as poor as that of Gilmer, Levi Scott determined that he had "borne up under a load of cares that would have driven mad almost any other man," while his younger brother William was cautioned by his parents about the dangers of city living.[37] "Your mother is mighty uneasy about you," John Scott explained to his son when the younger Scott was in Georgia, "for fear you [will] get burned to Death or have to jump out of the window of that 3 story high house if you stay there." Besides, he added, "A lawyer can't do no good up in a three story where the people [can't] git at you."[38]

Yet despite rural associations, attorneys continued as before the war to engage in a variety of economic activities, including the promotion of railroads, mines, and mills. Democrats and Republicans worked in concert to link Greensboro by rail with Petersburg, Virginia, Salem, North Carolina, and Cheraw, South Carolina. Republican Thomas B. Keogh joined Democrats D. F. Caldwell, John Gilmer, Jr., Ralph Gorrell, and Levi Scott in the spring of 1871 in the promotion of the Greensboro-Petersburg Railroad, and he worked alongside Caldwell, John Morehead's son Eugene, and John Gilmer, Sr.'s, son-in-law Charles E. Shober to complete the Central Railroad to Cheraw. Caldwell raged against "Holden's crowd" for making "such havock with our credit, Roads and Railroad men, it will be an uphill business now to get subscriptions to build railroads anywhere," but he had nothing but praise for local Republican merchant, manufacturer, and participant in all of the postwar railroad efforts D. W. C. Benbow.[39]

Similarly, leaders in both postbellum parties enthusiastically supported immigration into North Carolina, and despite charges by local Democrats of Republican extravagance at the state level, they worked in harmony to ascertain the amount of county indebtedness and find a way to repay it.[40] Finally, they worked jointly to acquire an appropriation from the legislature to build a new courthouse with Democrats Ralph Gorrell, C. P. Mendenhall, John Gilmer, Jr., and D. F. Caldwell, joining with Republicans

Thomas B. Keogh, William S. Ball, and Robert P. Dick in this effort.[41] The only difference of opinion expressed among Guilford lawyers over economic matters involved a single complaint by Democrat D. F. Caldwell about John N. Staples, a young Democratic attorney who approached county commissioners about buying grain in other counties to resell locally during the depression of the late 1870s. Staples, Caldwell grumbled, wanted the town to undertake too many ventures when he himself paid little in property taxes.

As before the war, attorneys continued to view mining as an attractive corollary to railroad building. Despite bitter political relations, D. F. Caldwell and the Gilmers retained joint ownership of the Taylor and Carlos properties, and they obtained a charter for the Altamahaw Coal Company from the legislature in 1872, serving as draftors of the company's by-laws and directors. Other mining interests of Caldwell included lime quarries and salt, but his economic endeavors did not stop with these. Shortly after the fighting ceased, he inquired about purchasing a hotel, and he owned the *Greensboro Patriot* for about ten years.[42]

Caldwell was also very enthusiastic about the possibility of iron mining and manufacturing in Guilford, enterprises in which John Morehead had shown an interest during the conflict.[43] Similarly, Albion Tourgée and Cyrus Mendenhall were interested in industrial ventures, operating spoke and handle factories in the 1870s. John Morehead's sons, like their father before them, also continued to build mills.

In 1881, J. Turner Morehead, Morehead's son and the nephew and cousin of the Greensboro attorneys of the same name, transformed his father's woolen operation into a separate manufacturing establishment. Then, in the 1890s, the Morehead holdings in Rockingham County were reorganized through the efforts of the Spray Water Power and Land Company, headed by B. Frank Mebane, the son-in-law of J. Turner Morehead. In rapid succession, "almost keeping pace with a mill-a-year plan," the company built textile mills in 1898, 1899, 1900, 1902, 1903, and 1905.[44]

While Turner Morehead pursued the family's textile interests to the north of Guilford, his younger brother, Eugene Morehead, encouraged the development of the tobacco industry in Greensboro.[45] In conjunction with his cousin Sam Hobson, Morehead created a tobacco association designed to promote Greensboro as a tobacco market. He envisioned a tobacco factory but was unable to do more than build a large warehouse because of financial difficulties with mills he owned in other parts of the state.[46] Early in the 1870s, Morehead relocated in Durham, a growing center for tobacco manufacturing in North Carolina.

Short on capital as before the war, Greensboro attorneys persisted in innovative efforts to generate cash. With the death of David Weir and the onslaught of war, the Greensboro Mutual Life Insurance Company collapsed, so lawyers shifted their emphasis in the postbellum years to savings and loan associations.[47] Probably they were attracted to these organizations because they permitted local businessmen, who had been badly injured by the war, to tap a large pool of small investors, but whatever the reasons for their appeal, savings and loans were avidly promoted by lawyers. Indeed, all three postwar associations met in the same law office, that of Republican William S. Ball and Democrat George H. Gregory.

To speak of strong rural-urban tensions in nineteenth-century Guilford County is inaccurate. Continuous struggles between businessmen and planters were not the order of the day either before or after the war, and no subservience of business to agrarian interests was evident. Instead, the community's largest land-, and before the war, slaveholders dwelt within the county seat town of Greensboro, where they spent most of their days in litigation, politics, or, even more likely, the promotion of various business schemes. They did not make great progress toward industrialization for several reasons, including a constant shortage of capital, characteristic of underdeveloped economies and intensified before the conflict by the slave-plantation system in which local entrepreneurs themselves participated; the downturn of national business affairs as in the mid-1850s and the mid-1870s; and, most significantly, sectionalism intermeshed with state politics, which constantly slowed the development of internal improvements. Nevertheless, interest in multifarious business ventures abounded, and because of the strategic position held by lawyers in the nineteenth-century Guilford economy, they were able to effect some of their goals of economic diversity and industrialization.

Their rapidly expanding land- and slaveholdings might eventually have made antebellum planters-businessmen-attorneys as resistant to economic change as their counterparts in the tidewater area allegedly were if the war had not come, but this process, if indeed it was under way, was far from complete by 1861. Instead, Guilford powerholders were heavily engaged in economic diversification when the war arrived, and they and their progeny continued to build railroads and mills in its wake. The orientation of turn-of-the-century industrialists was a logical manifestation of prewar attitudes and perspectives, not a sharp break with the past.

6. A State of Flux

❧❧❧

Considerable stress and uncertainty marked Guilford's transition from one-party politics and elite dominance to two-party strife and the domination of lawyers within the elite. Among voters, the rancor and division that characterized the peace movement of 1863 and the election of 1864 surfaced in a series of "Union" meetings held in the spring of 1865. Conflict deepened in ensuing months as former Confederates and Unionists attacked one another physically. Ultimately, these cleavages proved so intense that Unionists found it difficult to become Democrats despite their racism, and former Confederates shunned the Republican party whether or not they felt favorably toward blacks.

For leaders, the bitterly divided electorate heightened the uncertainties that accompanied military defeat and occupation. Particularly attorneys—those who had the most to lose—vacillated in choosing political affiliation, and it was not until the formation of the North Carolina Republican party in 1867 that their alignments crystallized. A variety of factors influenced individual partisan choices with Governor Jonathan Worth playing a crucial role.

When they finally became clear, alignments conformed closely to antebellum patterns, with lawyers, like other leaders, clustered in the same party. GOP legalists included only one former Whig, a perennial prewar Democrat, and three carpetbaggers. In the long run, the preponderance of Democratic attorneys encouraged conservative solutions to social and political issues, but during the tumultuous Reconstruction days, the presence of a few prominent lawyers in Republican ranks and the ties these legalists shared with their Democratic brethren proved crucial in promoting economic development and legitimizing partisan debate. Despite social conditions so chaotic that they degenerated into organized violence in the eastern section of the county, and politics so rancorous that compromise appeared out of the question, revolutionary change remained unlikely be-

cause the attorneys who managed the community's affairs continued to
relate to one another privately. Even as they engaged publicly in bitter
personal attacks, using every weapon in the awesome arsenal of nineteenth-century politics, they socialized, carried on their financial affairs,
and above all, fulfilled their professional commitments—together.

This chapter discusses the divisions among voters following the war,
the vacillation of lawyers, and the factors that influenced individual partisan decisions. A brief recount of the debate over revision of the constitution of 1868 illustrates the conservative solution of Democratic attorneys to
political challenges and the importance of having most of them arrayed on
the same side. Chapter 7 delves into the bitterness of partisan warfare and
the way that lawyers averted a revolutionary situation as they became professional politicians who treated contests for office as a business that could
be pursued and abandoned as election cycles demanded.

Despite, or perhaps because of, the extraordinary suffering of the local
populace caused by the unyielding demands of troop procurement, heavy
combat losses, and severe economic dislocation, Union meetings held in
the spring of 1865 were well attended, with more than seven hundred
Guilford residents at a meeting at Bloomington alone. Held ostensibly to
reunite North Carolina with the North, these meetings clearly demonstrated the divisions created in the polity by the war and the various positions wartime factions held in regard to the restoration of state government.

At the first of the springtime meetings, held at Greensboro on May 16,
the views of those who remained Vance supporters throughout the war
and who eventually constituted the heart of the Democratic party were
expressed. Written by former attorney and state school superintendent
Calvin Wiley, the original resolutions for this meeting were replaced by a
brief statement of loyalty at the insistence of U.S. Major General Jacob D.
Cox, but they are indicative of Conservative sentiment, for Wiley's views
were so close to those of John Gilmer that he had been asked on numerous
important occasions to ghostwrite for the former Whig and strong Vance
ally. Additionally, D. F. Caldwell implored Wiley to compose editorials
after Caldwell became a Conservative, and Wiley ghostwrote most, if not
all, of the important speeches and political statements, as well as a variety
of other communications, for his former University of North Carolina
classmate and ardent postwar Democrat, John C. Cunningham of Person
County.[1]

The first of Wiley's resolutions expressed a view that Gilmer stated
openly and that most former Whigs undoubtedly felt—that they had not
initiated the war, that they fought only because circumstances compelled

them to do so, and thus, by implication, that they were blameless for the negative consequences of the hostilities. Wiley followed this statement with a request that all counties in North Carolina join with Guilford in placing themselves under the authority of the United States and that they acknowledge that further resistance in the form of guerrilla warfare was useless. Then Wiley got to the heart of the matter. In an unyielding, almost arrogant tone characteristic of private statements by the school superintendent before the war, Wiley maintained that North Carolina expected confidence in return for her honesty and that, although the military government had given no cause for complaint, civil authority should be restored as soon as possible. Wiley was convinced that those in authority in the North would not wish "to destroy the fairest portion of what they call their own country" and to destroy the existing leadership was to do just that.[2]

Lincoln's assassination was regarded with "profound regret," Wiley continued, for all North Carolinians had "an extreme aversion to murder," even though, he insisted, they were "brave in war." In closing, Wiley offered "obedience" to President Andrew Johnson. His remarks included no mention of the abolition of slavery.

Despite the scuttling of Wiley's resolutions by General Cox, the import of the Greensboro meeting was readily discernible, for it prompted several other assemblages around the county. Many insisted that the Greensboro meeting did not represent the "true Unionists" of the community. Closest on the spectrum to the Greensboro affair was the well-attended meeting at Bloomington, near High Point. There, a close friend of William L. Scott, Clarkson Tomlinson, raised the American flag, and participants accepted the federal Constitution and the abolition of slavery. They expressed sorrow over Lincoln's assassination, as well as confidence in President Johnson. Their resolutions differed from those drawn by Wiley in two respects. Whereas the Wiley statements made no mention of slavery, the Bloomington resolutions did not deal with the restoration of state government.

In comparison to the Bloomington meeting, individuals who gathered in nearby High Point were very explicit about both a method for restoring civil authority and who they believed should assume command of the state. Following the usual expressions of regret at Lincoln's death but confidence in Johnson, these delegates advocated a state convention as the best way to reestablish state government. They endorsed Jonathan Worth as their choice for governor, although they would support others, including R. P. Dick and W. W. Holden. The High Point statements accepted emancipation as fact and urged the exclusion of Negro suffrage until the freedmen were qualified to enjoy the privilege. A subtle difference between the

High Point and Greensboro resolutions involved an explanation as to why North Carolina left the Union. According to Wiley's statements, circumstances compelled the state "to look for equality in a new national organization," and North Carolinians fought, not because they hated their enemies, but because they feared subjugation and its results. The High Point declarations, however, admitted a mistake on the part of the South, and, though they paid tribute to the fallen, they viewed them as having died out of a "false sense of duty against a government we should have loved and cherished."[3]

Unlike the affairs at Greensboro, Bloomington, and High Point, a meeting conducted at Pleasant Union Church in southeastern Guilford expressed hostility toward former Confederates and urged their exclusion from government affairs. Assemblages at Jamestown and Friendship were probably in the same vein as the Pleasant Union affair, although details of those meetings were sketchy. Led by a number of Unionists who had found it necessary to flee the community or remain "in the bushes" when conscription efforts intensified, Pleasant Union delegates heard Reverend George W. Bowman describe the horrors of a war brought on by "the secessionists and war men" and the necessity of electing to office men who had remained loyal to the United States during the "rebellion."[4] The resolutions adopted subsequent to Bowman's speech included a preamble that attacked the conductors of the Greensboro meeting as supporters of the war in every way except with their lives and property, and it further noted that those involved in the Greensboro assembly had condemned Union men as traitors. The statements that followed gave "cheerful support" to the U.S. government, which had come to rescue them from a government that had denied them civil rights and practiced "fraud and violence."[5]

Like the High Point resolutions, those adopted at Pleasant Union asked Washington officials to invoke a state convention, but they went further by urging that the leaders of the rebellion be excluded from office and treated as traitors. They would support no one for an official position, the delegates indicated, who had favored secession or conscription, repealed the bill of rights, used public office to "insult, harrass, oppress and murder loyal men," or upheld the rebellion and urged its prosecution to the point of extermination and starvation.[6] The Pleasant Union resolutions "rejoiced" at the elimination of abolition as the cause of sectional strife, and, in apparent anticipation of an upcoming fight at the polls with Conservatives, they urged the establishment of a "true union" newspaper in Greensboro.[7]

Ranging in opinion, then, from a ringing endorsement of the Vance government to the hope that all in it would be condemned as traitors, the resolutions offered at the Guilford Union meetings demonstrated the chasms the war had opened in the electorate. Although the original resolutions at Greensboro ignored abolition and those at Pleasant Union "rejoiced" at its occurrence, the major concern of all of the statements was who, among contending white forces, would control the postwar government.

The cleavages among voters expressed at the Union meetings deepened in the next few months as Unionists and former rebels attacked one another physically. Initially, there was no indication that former Confederates had the upper hand, but the position of Unionists deteriorated considerably by 1866. As Alexander McPherson described the situation to his friend Newton D. Woody, when the war ended, "all thing ar quiate in this country everybody hard at work. . . . Nead not antisipate any danger in coming home know not in that least for every man is a free man now here, White & black full privelidge to go Where tha pleas you cold of come home the first of may & not of bin in any danger you need not hisetate one moment for your have just as good & warm friend her know as you ever had." Mattie Corsbie wrote simply, "You can come home without being molested as there is no Sesesh these days they keep very small."[8]

Within a month after the communications of McPherson and Corsbie, however, strife between Unionists and Confederates was occurring. Still, according to Unionist D. M. Corsbie, "big times" were over for the "Secessionists," and occasionally one came "to the ground from the effects of a small stick handled by a bush fellow." A few weeks following Corsbie's comments, McPherson mentioned to his friend Woody that some of the "old secessionists talk big," but they had not murdered anyone. A threat had been issued against John Corsbie, but when confronted, the antagonist denied the charge.[9]

Yet conditions for Unionists worsened so much by the spring of 1866 that large numbers of Friends were reported fleeing the state. Nereus Mendenhall and Michael S. Sherwood denied charges of Unionist persecution at this time, but Mendenhall grew so concerned about the problem over the course of the next few months that he and Unionist Jonathan Harris, a friend of Delphinia and the late George Mendenhall, participated in the first of two meetings held in the fall to protest existing conditions and request stronger protective measures by the federal government.[10] The resolutions at this meeting were moderate in tone in comparison to those at the second assemblage, with Governor Worth describing them in retrospect as "cautiously drawn," but the gathering drew considerable attention and criticism by sending newcomer Albion Tourgée to a Unionist convention in Philadelphia. There, the young attorney claimed that Union men

were ostracized and proscribed socially in all parts of the state and that the
Unionist had only "a life of continual persecution for himself and poverty
and serfdom for his children" ahead of him, but it was Tourgée's alleged
comment that a number of Negroes had been murdered and thrown in a
mill pond in South Carolina that elicited the most comment.[11] The second assemblage, chaired by Abraham Clapp, a prewar Whig who served in
the state legislature from 1858 to 1860, criticized President Johnson and
complained of persecution of Unionists as well as oppressive taxation and
poor economic conditions generally.[12]

Despite strong indications of hard times for Unionists, Governor
Jonathan Worth refused to acknowledge the difficulties and to take action
to alleviate them. Instead, he chastised Mendenhall and Harris for participating in the fall meeting, urged John Gilmer to "see and post" Mendenhall about "passing events," and denied in a *Patriot* editorial that he
had forwarded complaints from seven hundred Unionists to local authorities in their respective home towns.[13] He hoped, Worth wrote to
Mendenhall and Harris, that their taking part in a political meeting did not
prove "prejudicial to their society," but in fact, Worth's concern stemmed
from two sources unrelated to the well-being of the Society of Friends.
First, he was afraid the Deep River meeting would be construed as suppor-
tive of the Fourteenth Amendment, under which, Worth reminded Mendenhall, neither D. Frank Caldwell, John Gilmer, nor Worth himself would
be allowed to hold office. Second, and even more important, Worth feared
that the Unionist meetings would be viewed as grounds for maintaining
federal troops in the state, a position Worth adamantly opposed, even in
the face of a combined request for such action a year later from Conservatives Gilmer and C. P. Mendenhall and Republicans R. P. Dick and
Thomas Settle.[14]

As Unionists and former rebels confronted one another, wartime cleavages deepened and the possibility that these antagonists would find their
way into the same political party lessened, regardless of their views toward
blacks. A number of Unionists had been slaveholders before the war, and
they continued to harbor racist sentiments after the conflict. As Albion
Tourgée explained in his novel, *A Fool's Errand*, many Unionists continued
to believe that abolition should have been punishment for those who
fought against the North and that, as Unionists, they should either have
been exempt from emancipation or compensated for the slave property
they lost. John Corsbie had owned six slaves at midcentury, John Boon's
family had the same number, and Charles Causey's father had one in 1850,
though none in 1860. Both Corsbie and Boon served for a time in the
Confederate army before leaving service and the county. Causey held a

variety of jobs that made him eligible for a deferment, one of which was in New Bern, where he smuggled letters in and out of the Confederacy for fugitives and their families.[15]

Following the war, Corsbie explained in a letter to fellow Unionist Newton D. Woody that Woody's financial woes stemmed "from the negroes being placed upon an equality with the white people," and young John Boon eventually participated in Ku Klux Klan raids in eastern Guilford.[16] But despite the racism of many Unionists, the continued clashes between them and former Confederates prevented partisan alignments solely on the basis of race. For some, such as Boon, racial attitudes would prove the overriding concern, and these individuals would emerge as Democrats despite their Unionist heritage, but for whites such as Corsbie, Causey, and Woody, the war proved too divisive to permit their joining in a white man's party.

The whites who met in Union meetings around the county to express their views on Reconstruction were not leaderless. Indeed, outspoken public officials ran every assemblage and some, like Mendenhall, Harris, and Tourgée, openly sought improved conditions for Unionists. Nevertheless, many leaders displayed considerable uncertainty about how to align themselves in the wake of war. Although powerholders could not determine with any precision the number of Unionists and Confederates, they could not miss realizing that whites had divided so badly in 1864 that they had endorsed rival candidates for the governorship and the legislature and that, if anything, the divisions appeared to be worsening. Confronted with a sharply divided electorate and an unknown federal policy, many leaders vacillated.

Eventually, far more powerholders made their way into Democratic ranks than Republican with 41 percent (211 individuals) of the 1870 power group and 35 percent (190 persons) of the 1880 power group emerging as Democrats. In comparison, only 13 percent of the 1870 and 1880 power groups (66 and 67 individuals respectively) became Republicans. Among high powerholders, the disparity was even greater with 78 percent (21) of the substantial leaders Democrats in 1870 and 70 percent (18) in 1880. In contrast, the proportion of Republicans who were high powerholders declined from 22 percent (6) in 1870 to 12 percent (3) in 1880. But despite the eventual preponderance of Democrats among leaders, considerable fluidity characterized local politics following the war. Unionists Nereus Mendenhall and Jonathan Harris ultimately split, with Mendenhall emerging after 1867 as a Democrat and Harris as a Republican. Even more revealingly, Calvin Wiley, who had remained in close contact with Vance supporters such as Gilmer throughout the war and who had constructed the original resolutions for the Greensboro Union meeting, felt so insecure immediately after the conflict that he composed a tortured, twelve-page epistle to Jonathan Worth asking him to assure Provisional Governor Holden that the former school superintendent was not his enemy.[17]

The choices were especially difficult for attorneys, and they exhibited considerable uncertainty of themselves and of one another for a lengthy period after the war. William L. Scott, who was allegedly involved in the peace meeting in Greensboro in 1864, supported Vance in the following campaign.[18] "Permit me to assure you," John Gilmer wrote the governor, "that few men in the State have labored more for your success in the late election, both in his conversation & with the pen, than Genl Scott."[19] Within six months, however, Scott was participating, along with his former military commander, attorney James M. Leach, in moderate Union meetings outside the county, and Provisional Governor Holden appointed the former captain of the Dixie Boys temporary mayor of Greensboro. Despite Holden's appointment of Scott to political office, the Guilford lawyer did not commit himself to the Republican party until the summer of 1868, almost a year and a half after the formation of the organization in Raleigh.[20] In contrast to Scott, Leach, a North Carolina native who moved to Guilford following the war, eventually made his way into the Democratic party and opposed his former ally in the fifth district congressional race in 1870.

Like Scott, Robert P. Dick kept members of the bar guessing about his partisan proclivities. Shortly after the election of 1864, Treasurer Worth recommended that the newly elected peace senator serve on what Worth regarded as one of the two most important committees of the legislative session, the Finance Committee. After his own election as governor in the fall of 1865, Worth continued to think highly of Dick and considered nominating him one of three members of the state Literary Board. Upon inquiring about his choice, the new governor learned that it was feared that Dick had "radical tendencies." "When the Confederacy failed," Calvin Wiley explained, "Mr. Dick took high and honorable ground, and won golden opinions on all sides," but in Wiley's view, Dick returned from a trip to Washington an "altered man" who lost much ground by the time the convention election of 1865 occurred. Wiley hoped Dick had "seen enough" and was "working back again," but he reminded Worth that nothing was to be gained by appointing a Radical to office. Wiley then vacillated, obviously uncertain about the partisan inclination of Dick, saying on the one hand that he had heard Dick was disgusted with Holden but on the other that he would recommend Dick only if Worth wished to appoint a "full Holdenite."[21]

In response to an inquiry from Worth similar to that received by Wiley, John Gilmer, after thinking the matter over carefully, concluded that the appointment of Dick would do Worth no harm. Within a few weeks after Gilmer's response, however, rumors were circulating that Dick was a member of a "Red String" association, an organization whose object was the election of Union men to office. Still, D. F. Caldwell pointed out, Dick had not worked against Worth in the election in 1865 but, instead, "did indirectly give you aid & comfort."[22] With the enactment of the radical Reconstruction Acts in March 1867, Dick's position finally became crystal clear. That month in a meeting in Raleigh attended by whites and blacks from some fifty-six counties, Dick proposed the formation of the Republican party.[23]

Among Guilford attorneys, no one found it more difficult to align himself after the war than D. F. Caldwell. A hard-core Unionist who was "mobbed" while speaking against the war shortly after Fort Sumter and who stood alone among the congregation of the First Presbyterian Church in Greensboro in opposition to a proposal to send the church bell to Richmond to be molded into cannon, Caldwell, according to his account, was shot and wounded while participating in the peace meeting in Greensboro in February 1864. A few months later, he was sent to a camp of instruction as a conscript, although he claimed he was within two months of being too old to serve. Fed only "1/4 lb of bacon bone . . . and 1 1/4 lbs of molded flower [sic] per day" and forced to stand guard duty two nights in succession, Caldwell, who suffered from "dropsey," managed to avoid further service by waging a successful campaign for the state legislature as a peace candidate.[24]

Following the war, harassment of Caldwell continued. John Gilmer, Jr., and his cronies "blated" at the middle-aged attorney in the streets as if he "were a sheep" and threw other insults at him. Caldwell believed, too, that John Gilmer, Sr., plotted to have his son serve as county solicitor in lieu of his longtime mining partner. Although no evidence was found that Gilmer intentionally tried to use this office in retaliation against Caldwell for his Unionist ways, Caldwell felt sufficiently alienated from those who continued to support Vance throughout the war that he warned Worth that "there is a class of old line Whigs of the Vance stripe that are more malignant and vicious than the worst secessionists." Clearly, at this point, Caldwell was estranged from the Gilmer faction, and John Gilmer, Jr., expressed "secret apprehensions," according to one of Worth's correspondents, that Caldwell was "going over to the Radicals."[25]

Yet instead of aligning himself with Republicans as Dick and Scott did, Caldwell eventually served as one of the county's most effective Democrats. When it appeared in 1868 that Caldwell would seek the Fifth District congressional seat, Republican Thomas Settle described the Guilford attorney as the most dangerous man who could have been put forward as an opponent, "an honorable man, a scholar and a gentleman,—an undoubted union man and an 'iron-clad.' "[26] Caldwell thus appealed to Unionists and Conservatives alike, and his support continued so strong that he outdistanced Democratic incumbents Junius I. Scales and T. M. Holt by more than two hundred votes in a bid for the state senate a decade later, although he was at odds with the local Democratic organization at the time.

To understand the decisions of lawyers like Scott, Leach, Dick, and Caldwell, one must consider a variety of factors. Racial attitudes certainly played a role, for Scott and Dick were able to work with blacks, urging their support in political campaigns and celebrating with them important events such as Emancipation Day, whereas Caldwell railed against those "who would place negroes above ex-slaveholders" and "fanatics" who talked about blacks being murdered and thrown into mill ponds (an obvious reference to Tourgée).[27] But racial attitudes did not tell the entire story, for Conservatives too sometimes demonstrated positive attitudes toward Afro-Americans, just as Republican and former Unionists revealed negative ones.[28]

Conservative John Gilmer, for example, freed his slaves so soon after the conflict that a Unionist friend of Newton Woody could only conclude, "Old John A. Gilmore [sic] must be turning abolitionist pretty fast." Northern Quaker Yardley Warner included Gilmer, along with Robert P. Dick, among the well-to-do in Guilford who demonstrated a "favorable animus" toward Negroes. Additionally, John Morehead's daughter, Lettia Walker, was commended by black delegates from Guilford at a convention of freedmen in Raleigh in 1865 for starting a school for former bondsmen, and Charles E. Shober spearheaded a drive to stop the execution of Afro-American Alfred Gilmer. Finally, Ralph Gorrell proved willing to take cases as he did in 1870 in support of Henderson Headen, a former slave who had saved for five years after he obtained freedom to purchase a mule, only to have the animal taken from him.[29]

Besides racial attitudes, several other factors figured in the partisan decisions of Guilford lawyers, with prewar alignments, federal policies, state leadership, and unique personal traits and life histories among the most important. Objective measures such as age, wealth, and occupation provided little assistance, for, as discussed in the following chapter, Democratic and Republican powerholders proved far more alike than different. All of the factors important in partisan choices surfaced in the decisions of lawyers Dick, Caldwell, and Scott.

For Robert P. Dick, whose family had long led the opposition party in the community and had suffered few ill consequences from it, the decision to challenge the Vance faction in 1864 and to move subsequently into Republican ranks was probably not overly difficult. As a Unionist Democrat who had remained at the Democratic convention in Baltimore in 1860, along with Holden and one other North Carolinian, and who served that year as an at-large elector for Stephen A. Douglas, Dick did not have the same perspective as prewar fellow Democrat James R. McLean, who led secession forces in the county. A victorious peace candidate for the state legislature in 1864, Dick established "kindly relations" with northern General Cox, who stayed at Dick's home while Union forces were in the vicinity at the close of the war, and he appealed to the general to aid in his enfranchisement shortly after the Reconstruction Acts of 1867.[30] Thus, despite the uncertainty surrounding Dick's partisan position in the months following the conflict, his involvement in the formation of the Republican party was not unpredictable.

In comparison to a Unionist Democrat like Dick, the decision to join Republican ranks was much more traumatic for former Whigs, for Vance himself was an old-line Whig, and his triumph over Democrats in 1862 marked the first time the Whig organization had controlled the state government in more than a decade. Therefore, to oppose the war governor in 1864 required most Guilford powerholders to break with the organization that had dominated the county for more than thirty years, and as powerholders who had benefited from existing arrangements, few found the incentive to do so. For many followers, the war proved a sufficient catalyst for severing their Whig ties, but for leaders, who possessed considerably more resources than the general populace, the ravages of war did not penetrate as soon or as extensively.

Once the bonds were broken, however, as in the case of Caldwell, realignment could be equally difficult. Federal policies, most notably the Fourteenth Amendment, and racism helped explain Caldwell's recommitment to Conservative ranks, but his ties to Governor Worth and the unwillingness of the governor to break with the Vance contingent figured most importantly in Caldwell's decision. As the independent attorney commented to Worth, some of the "best candidates" in Guilford were disqualified from seeking office before passage of the Fourteenth Amendment, and under this proposed legislation, even individuals like himself could not serve. "Old Frank is dead down against it and gives us all fits," Unionist David Hodgin explained to fellow Republican Tourgée. Caldwell in turn commented that the "National Union Republican party" considered anyone disloyal who did not support the amendment.[31]

Along with Caldwell's objections to the Fourteenth Amendment, his racism was unquestionable. When Sheriff R. M. Stafford worked to obtain a lighter sentence for Afro-American Robert Davis, who was sentenced to hang on a burglary conviction, Caldwell beseeched Worth not to pardon him, and he harangued endlessly about the Superior Court over which Tourgée presided, charging that blacks who were arrested for thievery were released on bail on bonds that were "notoriously insolvent" and that nothing was done when the "scoundrels" failed to appear in court. Privately, the cantankerous attorney rejoiced that many Afro-Americans appeared to be moving south to Florida following the war, and he suggested to William A. Graham that it would be politically advantageous for Democrats to spread the word that Loyal Leagues were "bands of thieves & murderers." Following this suggestion, the *Patriot and Times,* which Caldwell owned, began publishing a steady stream of articles about numerous crimes allegedly perpetrated by blacks.[32] (See the following chapter for more details.)

All of these comments and charges came after Caldwell rejoined Conservative ranks, however, and even his comment about blacks being placed above former slaveholders was made when he recommitted himself to Worth in the fall of 1866. In those crucial months between the close of the war and September 1866, it was Caldwell's ties to Worth and Worth's alignment with the Vance faction rather than his racism that figured prominently in his partisan decision.

A Guilford native and the son of a Quaker mother, Worth had been an active Whig attorney-legislator-planter in nearby Randolph County before the war, and as a participant in a variety of internal improvements projects, he had worked closely with leaders such as John Gilmer and John Morehead. Unlike these Unionists-turned-war-supporters, however, the Asheboro attorney refused to endorse secession after Fort Sumter. He not only voted against the majority at the May convention but also declined further service in the assemblage. In an about-face in 1862, however, he returned to the state legislature and was subsequently appointed treasurer of the state by Vance. Following the war, Worth also served as provisional treasurer under Holden.

Because of Worth's ties to Guilford and his involvement in Holden's provisional government, the moderate Union faction that met at High Point following the war named him as their choice for governor, although they also indicated they would accept others, including Holden or Dick. Worth was then put forward as an alternative to Holden by Conservatives after the provisional governor refused to endorse the pardon of the most likely candidate, former governor and Whig William A. Graham of Or-

ange County.[33] Thus Worth represented both Unionists and Conservatives after the conflict, and the way he aligned himself would be critical
in giving one wartime faction the edge over the other.

Despite private assurances to Dr. William Pugh that he was adamantly
"anti-secessionist" and would not be "the secessionists' candidate for governor," Worth never considered excluding such former Whigs as Gilmer and
Morehead from an important role in his government. When he solicited
advice from Wiley, Gilmer, and Morehead, he wrote Caldwell: "Surely, you
do not belong to that proscription class who would exclude from confidence all who aided the South after rebellion commenced." Then, in a move
that antagonized Caldwell even further, Worth appointed John Gilmer, Jr.,
and James Morehead, Jr., to the Board of Directors of the North Carolina
Railroad.

Caldwell was infuriated at this turn of events, and he explained to the
governor in no uncertain terms that he had expected him to turn to "old
union men" like himself, Dick, and Jonathan Harris for advice. He was
positive, Caldwell continued, that Dick owned more railroad stock than
John Gilmer, Jr., who, if he had any at all, had only recently acquired a
small amount. Caldwell then pointed out that he had defended Worth
during the hostilities, when he was denounced as a "d—— Nantucket
Quaker," and had worked for him in the county in 1865 although he did
not think he should have run against Holden. Similarly, Harris and other
former Holden supporters had worked "in concert and to same purposes,"
and in response, Worth had not only turned aside Union men but had
replaced them with "a class of old line former whigs who seek the political
death of all of our way of thinking."[34]

Caldwell's reprimand had little impact, however, for Worth continued
to align himself with Vance supporters and attempted to win Caldwell
over to their side. The governor saw that Caldwell received a pardon, and
he urged Gilmer to stop his son and his cronies from harassing this "ardent, honest, eccentric man," who had the ability to exert "much influence
among those of radical proclivities." Additionally, Worth continued to
write to Caldwell as a confidant, expressing dismay that the Guilford lawyer would wish him to ignore all those who aided the South after the war
commenced and assuring him that he did not intentionally overlook Dick
in his railroad appointments. By the fall of 1866, Worth's cajoling paid off,
and Caldwell wrote to the governor to explain how he might counteract
the "Radical spirit" that he saw on the rise in his area. Sensing the pulse of
the times, however, Caldwell called for aid for Unionists who had suffered
during the war; education, especially for the children of "conscripts" killed
in battle; and a township system of government, not too dissimilar from

the one Republicans would institute a few years later. "We must begin at the foundation and educate the people by letting the boys have a chance to act as constables, coroners, commissioners, magistrates, etc., etc.," he explained, as he described the popular system of government he envisioned.[35]

Undoubtedly, Caldwell's racism and his objections to the Fourteenth Amendment figured prominently in his realignment with Democrats, but a different posture by Worth might well have counteracted these influences. If Worth had truly represented those that Caldwell initially assumed he did, the governor himself, along with far more leaders in the Guilford vicinity, might have found their way into the Republican party, and election outcomes might have been very different than they were. Instead, Worth's reliance on longtime Vance supporters assured the continuation of the old prewar partisan organization among powerholders and prevented the development of a closely divided leadership reflective of the evenly divided electorate.

In view of these circumstances, the movement of William L. Scott into Republican ranks requires some explanation, for Scott was the only prewar Whig attorney to make such a move. Not only his cousin, prewar Democrat James R. McLean, but also his older brother, Levi, became Conservatives. Both Scott's personal makeup and his life history shed light on his decision to realign, although all the factors will probably never be known. His motives are important to consider, however, because they demonstrate the subtleness and elusiveness that characterized individual party decisions and the difficulty of explaining human motivation through objective measures. The course Scott followed also reveals how the Conservative press effectively maligned Republicans on the basis of actions taken during the war that were little different from those of Democrats.

Until the spring of 1862, Scott's life and career were not very dissimilar from those of other southern young men who managed to achieve a college education, although his family was not as affluent as some. Born in 1828, Scott entered the University of North Carolina in 1850 and supported himself in part by translating Greek manuscripts. A sharp debater, who completed his studies with first distinction in 1854, Scott taught for two years at Edgeworth Female Seminary and then read law in Georgia. Following a sojourn in the lower South and a trip northward with Samuel Weir, the son of druggist D. P. and Susan Dick Weir, Scott returned to Guilford to establish a law practice with his older brother. Early in the summer of 1861, the young attorney marched away enthusiastically as captain of the Guilford Dixie Boys, and within six months he was elected lieutenant colonel. Shortly afterward, during the military reorganization that resulted from the enactment of Confederate conscription, Scott was chosen colonel, but he abruptly resigned, going first to Richmond for a few days to await further orders and then home.[36]

Upon his arrival in Greensboro, Scott tried to get a position as a volunteer aide-de-camp and as the commander of a new regiment that was forming.[37] When these efforts proved futile, he obtained an appointment as brigadier general of a militia unit composed of troops from Guilford, Forsyth, and Rockingham counties. He was also appointed attorney for the town of Greensboro. Touched deeply by the deaths of numerous friends, including Lieutenant C. C. Cole and Samuel Weir, Scott memorialized several of them in biographical sketches, and he commenced an account of the Dixie Boys as well. The former Confederate captain also defended a number of conscripts trying to avoid military service.

Although Scott was not alone in his efforts to secure exemptions, his frequent involvement in these affairs possibly attuned him to the problems of conscripts and may have led him to support the peace movement of 1863 in some capacity, although his exact role in it, if indeed he played one, is unclear.[38] Additionally, after supporting Vance in 1864 and then failing to procure an appointment to a government post, Scott may have become disenchanted with the war governor. A sensitive man who worried at length about the well-being of his troops while captain of the Dixie Boys, the repercussions of a fray with local physician A. P. McDaniel while dealing with a typhoid outbreak in his company, the opinions of those left behind when he resigned from the army, and the loss of his friends in battle, Scott may also have been affected by the plight of Unionists following the war. Certainly he sympathized with Republicans who suffered at the hands of white terrorists once he became enmeshed in partisan politics. Aware that his narrow loss to Leach in the congressional election of 1870 resulted from Holden's sending the militia into his district to quell organized violence, Scott explained to his wife, Ella, that he preferred defeat "than the Ku Klux should not be put down—exterminated." "Defeat," he continued, "will not hurt me, and the stopping of violence and lawlessness would bless hundreds and thousands of good and unoffending people."[39]

Finally, Scott was not averse to working with blacks in political affairs. Whether he did so because of his sensitivity to human suffering or simple political expediency is unclear. His biracial activities may also have stemmed from his view of the war as a watershed from which there was no return. As he phrased it, the only "two immutable facts" to emerge from the hostilities were the abolition of slavery and the perpetuation of the Union, and on this basis he was willing "to forget, bury the past, and go forward."[40] Whatever his reasons, Scott addressed both mixed and all-black audiences, and he described slavery in retrospect as a "suicidal course." He was praised by Afro-Americans for speeches he made to them in his campaign for Congress in 1870, and, when too ill to attend the emancipation celebration in 1872, the forty-four-year-old lawyer composed a congratulatory letter to be read at the festivities. Within the year, Scott died from a steadily worsening paralysis.[41]

Scott's break with the Conservatives could not be explained on the basis of prewar alignments, federal policies, or state officials. Instead, it seemed to derive from his own personal inclinations and experiences. To him, as to most leaders in the spring of 1865, the political future appeared incalculable. Voters were badly divided, and state and federal officials sent mixed messages. Amid the uncertainty and confusion, the vast majority of those in power elected to stay with the party organization they had known before the war. Twice as many attorneys held firm as realigned. Those who made the commitment to a new organization differed in some noticeable way from their Conservative brethren. They included a respected member of the community's traditional minority, northerners such as Tourgée and New Yorker Thomas Keogh, and a former Confederate army captain whose wartime course and personal sentiments led him to the ultimate break with his former allies.

The preponderance of attorneys within Democratic ranks affected both the solutions proposed in the face of fierce partisan campaigns and the chances for success. Although D. F. Caldwell sensed the need for a more open system of government, he worked ardently alongside his Conservative allies for revision of the democratic constitution of 1868. During the campaign for a constitutional convention in 1871, Conservatives, including Caldwell, harped specifically on a heavy tax burden reputedly caused by an excessive number of local offices and generally on "every thing connected with the Politics of the state," according to one Republican observer.[42] In fact, they envisioned centralization of power at the state level and the abolition of local autonomy as a way to achieve political victory.

During the 1871 campaign, when William L. Scott and Robert P. Dick ran as anticonvention candidates against former Unionists Nereus Mendenhall and D. F. Caldwell, the more numerous Democratic lawyers managed to "double-team" on Dick, as Republican John Payne explained it.[43] Because Scott's worsening illness forced him to seek treatment outside the county and miss the entire campaign, one debate featured Mendenhall, followed by Dick, and then Caldwell and Gilmer. In retrospect, Payne noted that Caldwell campaigned for six weeks before the election, Mendenhall gave the county "a good canvassing," and attorneys John H. Dillard, Gilmer, Scales, and the Moreheads spoke. Then, "to wind things up," former Governor William A. Graham and Honorable Augustus S. Merrimon were brought in from the outside, and attorney Leach, who had spoken earlier at a barbecue with John Staples, made two additional speeches. In comparison, Dick returned home from his duties as an associate justice on the state Supreme Court in time to make "about 10 speeches."[44] In view of the barrage of Democratic legal luminaries who stumped the county, the loss of the election by anticonvention candidates by a mere four votes (1,745 to 1,741) underscored the depth of division within the electorate and the opportunity missed by most leaders for the creation of a new politics based on the war experience.[45]

Despite the eventual alignment of most Guilford attorneys with the Democratic party, conditions were fluid enough in the wake of the war to suggest that choices and outcomes could have been different. The course followed during this stage of the community's development was no more inevitable than that at any other time in its history, and one cannot explain partisan predilections in simple, unidimensional terms such as "rigidity" on the part of Conservatives or "racism" by whites. Instead, a myriad of factors combined to influence decisions, with Guilford native son Jonathan Worth playing a crucial role by bestowing legitimacy and positions on the allies of wartime Governor Vance.

The combined effect of all of these factors diminished the size of Republican leadership ranks, and the disparity between Democratic and GOP notables had important effects. But the Guilford Republican party included some very capable legalists whose ties to their Conservative brethren continued during the darkest days of Reconstruction. These ties encouraged the view of politics as a business to be pursued vigorously during election campaigns but laid aside as the important work of economic development persisted.

7. The Business of Politics

⌒⌒⌒

Once partisan alignments crystallized in Guilford, all the elements of the Reconstruction drama unfolded. Scurrilous personal attacks appeared in the press and on the stump, verbal abuse degenerated into physical confrontations, and social ostracism became the order of the day. Even more threatening to political order, organized violence erupted in the eastern section of the county, where White Brotherhood and Ku Klux Klan associations flourished.

Partisan efforts proved rancorous for several reasons, including the bitter divisions generated among white voters by the war and the important issues of local autonomy and black participation in politics raised by a new state constitution and black enfranchisement in 1868. The temporary disruption of some of the traditional patterns of leadership as a number of young newcomers assumed more prominent positions in the community further contributed to a sense of confusion in the political arena, but especially the permanent change in the occupation of large powerholders that came with the war intensified party politics.

Yet despite the bitterness and hostility that characterized postwar partisan clashes in Guilford, the central figures in the battles, the attorneys, continued to relate privately. As occupants of the same socioeconomic stratum and members of the same profession, lawyers had so much in common that even in the worst of times, they were rarely out of touch with one another. For them, politics was rapidly becoming a business, and as such, partisan fights could be waged and laid aside as the need arose.

The continued interaction and, on many nonpartisan matters, cooperation, among lawyers added an element of stability to southern society during Reconstruction that historians who emphasized the differences between Republicans and Democrats failed to discern. The triumph of Republicans over Democrats undoubtedly would have resulted in more humane treatment for blacks and greater local autonomy for all southerners, but this study has produced little evidence that it would have resulted in the massive upheaval that earlier historians feared and recent ones desired. Most important, the professionalization of politics allowed attorneys to continue working in concert toward common economic goals and to achieve a measure of success even in the darkest days of partisan warfare.

Partisan Tactics

Disagreements among Guilford lawyers, even among those in the same political party, were not new. On occasion before the war, they had confronted one another openly as in the controversy involving the expulsion of Wesleyan Methodist ministers from the community. In these instances, they usually assumed the expected Whig and Democrat stances, but more often they argued privately and without regard to party affiliation. Whigs Ralph Gorrell and D. F. Caldwell opposed Whigs John Gilmer and former Governor John Morehead in a congregational dispute involving the ouster of Reverend J. J. Smith as pastor of the First Presbyterian Church two years before the war, and Levi Scott and Julius Gorrell, both of whom were Whigs, squared off at the recruitment meeting of the North Militia in February 1862, when Scott contemplated challenging Gorrell for the position of commander of the regiment.[1] Although Scott eventually declined to run, he encouraged someone else to seek the position solely to keep Gorrell from getting it.[2]

Hostility between Scott and D. Frank Caldwell grew even more intense than the Scott-Gorrell dispute when Caldwell challenged Scott for the position of county solicitor in 1861. During the court session to fill this position, Caldwell asserted that Scott had charged the county excessively during his tenure in office and that he had occupied more than his share of appointed positions. The altercation became so fierce that James T. Morehead placed his chair between Scott and Caldwell, urging Scott in particular to hold his temper. Had he not been afraid it would prejudice the vote against him, Scott commented later, he would have "flogged" Caldwell. In the end, Scott prevailed, but the vote of 35 to 24 was much closer than he had anticipated three weeks earlier when he believed not a single justice, with perhaps one exception, would vote for Caldwell.[3]

Acrimony between Scott and Caldwell extended beyond the courtroom. Scott's wife, Mary Eliza Weatherly, refused to speak to Caldwell when she passed him in the street, and her father, Greensboro merchant Andrew Weatherly, who was at the courthouse the day Caldwell's charges were made, "came near to beating Frank." Caldwell himself publicized the controversy by charging in a thinly disguised newspaper article that the justices were incompetent for not choosing him as county solicitor. At that point, several magistrates, including attorneys James R. McLean, Scott's cousin, and Charles E. Shober accompanied Scott to the *Patriot* office, where they gave editor Michael S. Sherwood "some pretty plain talk" for permitting the article to appear in print. Scott's inclination when he saw the piece was to give Caldwell "a thrashing," he noted later, but he contented himself with having his father transfer some land to his brother William so that the younger Scott would be in a position to challenge Caldwell for a legislative seat if the latter decided to run.[4]

Antagonisms among prewar attorneys thus became so raucous on occasion that they verged on physical confrontations, but despite their severity, they remained largely private affairs which were seldom conducted along party lines. Even in the case of Caldwell and Scott, nothing appeared in the press except Caldwell's letter charging local justices with incompetency, and this public pronouncement elicited a strong response from those involved. With the exception of McLean, all of the disputes involved Whig attorneys. The Democratic lawyer invariably chose sides on the basis of kinship ties, aligning himself with his cousins Levi and William Scott in every fray.

Following the war, animosities among lawyers, again including those in the same political party, continued. Democrat Cyrus Mendenhall experienced difficulties with both James T. Morehead and D. F. Caldwell over matters related to litigation, and Caldwell and his brother, Robert N. Caldwell, belittled John Gilmer, Jr. "From what I learn," Mendenhall commented to Ralph Gorrell regarding a case Mendenhall had instituted, "Hon. J. T. Morehead is allowing himself to be a little too much exercised about me." Similarly, in regard to a case Caldwell had brought against Mendenhall, a friend and business associate of Caldwell's noted encouragingly, "I hope you may fling him and recover heavy damages." In 1875, when Gilmer and D. F. Caldwell competed for their party's endorsement for public office, Robert Caldwell described Gilmer as a "very nice clever little man But in comparison to you [D. F.] is a mere *Stripes* in politicks [who] . . . hasant the 'stabality,' or the 'abbality' to carry the flag through Guilford."[5]

Harmony proved equally elusive among Republican attorneys. Albion Tourgée initially did not trust William L. Scott or R. P. Dick, and native New Yorker and Republican Thomas B. Keogh hoped to prevent Tourgée from obtaining a seat in the constitutional convention in 1868 as well as the

Fifth District nomination for Congress the same year.[6] Another New York–born Republican attorney, William S. Ball, and Tourgée related poorly.[7] Yet, like the Democrats, Republicans tried to keep their differences private. The creation of a viable two-party system added a new element to the dissension among leaders, however, as Democrats and Republicans began to attack one another openly and personally along strict party lines. Before the war, local Whigs had reserved attacks of this nature largely for nonlocal opponents in statewide races.

Democrats seized the initiative in launching a stream of printed abuse because they managed to convert the established Whig newspaper into a Conservative mouthpiece. Local press coverage therefore initially emphasized the intraparty fighting of Republicans and viciously attacked Republican leaders through distortion and innuendo. Once a Republican newspaper was on surer footing in the 1870s, its editors engaged in the rabid journalism characteristic of the day, attacking especially a courthouse ring that allegedly emerged in the wake of constitutional revision.

About 150 freedmen and "quite a number of the 'Conservative' white trash" attended a Radical meeting, the Democratic *Times* reported in April 1868, but it was determined to postpone a nomination until Governor Holden could be present. At a follow-up assemblage a week later, a Colonel Morehead allegedly arose and nominated himself after the slate of officers had been presented. At this point, Albion Tourgée supposedly got up and misrepresented Morehead, and "a general row" almost ensued.[8]

In a similar vein, the *Patriot and Times* described efforts by Republicans to nominate a candidate for the Fifth District congressional seat in the fall. These efforts especially provided the Democratic press with ammunition because Republicans split when William F. Henderson was nominated by a small majority, and several delegations, including those of Guilford, Forsyth, Person, and Randolph counties, walked out of the convention and subsequently nominated Tourgée as a means of securing Henderson's withdrawal from the race. "Windy Billy" Henderson procured the nomination, according to the *Patriot and Times,* through "irregularities" at some county meetings, and because he was of "such questionable character" that "honest men" could not vote for him, "respectable" delegates walked out. They preferred, the editors explained, "a high-toned honest man."[9]

Both the Reverend George W. Welker and Robert P. Dick had been ardent secessionists before the war, the *Patriot* maintained in 1869. Welker had allegedly made speeches encouraging volunteers, and Dick had "'longed to trample the accursed banner (the stars and stripes) under his feet, as a hated emblem of tyranny.'" Personally, the editors conceded, they had high regard for Dick, but "'as a politician,'" he was "'as deep in the dregs and as low in the mire as any of them.'"[10]

William L. Scott "came home when the battle waxed hot, in order that a 'historian' might be spared to write of their gallant deeds," the *Patriot* continued in its caricatures of Republican leaders. A "peace man" who resigned from the army because of his views, Scott managed to secure a militia appointment just in time to avoid conscription. Interestingly, the local press intimated, a health problem improved considerably after his militia appointment. Scott then spent his time advising conscripts on how to avoid the army, a service for which they "had to pay dearly," according to the editors.[11] But the worst was reserved for newcomer Albion Tourgée, who was forced to deny publicly that he was "a cannibal (a gorilla, the wandering Jew, a Ku Klux or Anti-Christ)!"[12] Nor had he served time in a penitentiary, Tourgée insisted on numerous occasions.

In the late 1870s, after the appointment of most local officials had been centralized at the state level, the Republican *North State* launched an aggressive attack on a "court house ring" that allegedly consisted of Democrats united only by their "thirst for gold" and their "useless regret for losses sustained in the late war." The alleged ring was also charged with extravagance and the maintenance of too many public officials, the same charges made by Democrats against Republicans at the state level when the GOP was in office. Someone had offered to feed county prisoners for 25 percent less than the current cost, the paper charged, but the county commissioners turned the offer down because they wished to aid their cronies. Likewise, a county treasurer was unnecessary but was retained by the party in power at a cost to taxpayers of $800 per year.[13]

The editors of the *North State* also chided the county commissioners for doing everything the ring asked of them, including the payment of money into an account in the name of a young lady called "'Miss Cellaneous.'" In selecting candidates for office, the press charged, "The most unsuspecting must see at a glance that the 'Court House Ring' is pulling the wires and these puppets are only dancing to music which the 'bosses' make," and in a strike for morality, the paper noted that jurors were boarded during court at a licentious haven for immoral females [the county poorhouse]. When Democrats asked for evidence to support these claims, Republicans termed the request an "artful dodge."[14]

According to the *North State,* John N. Staples, the "Bismarck of Guilford," withdrew his nomination for the state legislature solely as an expression of "unwavering loyalty" to a county boss, while R. M. Stafford, the "Chief Engineer" of the courthouse ring, prepared for the election campaign, and Julius Mendenhall, though the " 'boss' " of the county commissioners, did whatever the ring asked. Emsley Armfield reputedly had the job of "gobbling up fat contracts" to provide for the county jail and poorhouse, a task he apparently did well because the overseer of the poorhouse lived in "a fine house" while the poor dwelled in the " 'nigger' cabins" in the rear. Cyrus Wheeler, "the Ring's candidate" for the senate in lieu of Staples in 1878, reputedly was so "contemptuous of Quakers" during the war that he threatened to hang Elihu Mendenhall, and when captured during Stoneman's raid, he had the audacity to claim that he was a Friend. This same person also allegedly maintained that any white man who received a vote from a " 'nigger' " was "beneath the notice of a dog."[15]

The rabid journalistic style of the Guilford press was only part of a more general climate of aggressive personal interaction among politicians characterized by rowdy attempts by the opposition to break up political meetings, verbal abuse of one another, physical confrontations, and social ostracism. According to Tourgée, about two hundred "Rebs," representative of the "whole secesh elite of the county with Reverend Smith at the head," attended a Republican county convention in 1868, and, after the session "Young Jim" [Morehead?] charged to the front of the room and announced his candidacy for the state senate. R. P. Dick expelled "a few pungent remarks," and Tourgée attacked Jim verbally, telling him to sit down and keep quiet—which he did, apologizing for his rudeness. Similarly, Republican speeches were halted in an 1872 convention by tactics by the opposition such as yelling, hissing, and beating on boxes.[16]

Rude interruptions of public gatherings were usually attributed to young people, but older leaders were not above verbal assaults on one another, and they avidly repeated alleged scandals. In Tourgée's words, Zebulon Vance was a "Conscript hunter and woman torturer," and Vance repeated the charge that Tourgée had spent time in prison.[17] In an address called "In Contempt of the People," Tourgée launched a blistering attack on Nereus Mendenhall in which he asked rhetorically, "Is Nereus Mendenhall honest? I never asked it. I *know* he is honest for I have heard him say so often. But people who do not know him so well as he does himself may be pardoned for making the inquiry."[18] Republican DeWitt C. Benbow was reportedly in Raleigh in 1879 "lobbying and talking scandal," Tourgée readily admitted, and the northern-born attorney was delighted to learn in the midst of his 1878 bid for Congress that Alfred M. Scales, his opponent, had been accused of seducing a woman while he was in Mississippi.[19]

For their part, Democrats charged at the 1875 constitutional convention that T. M. Shoffner, "late Republican senator from Alamance," was involved in taking the corpse of a colored man from a grave in 1858, boiling the body, and selling the skeleton to Dr. Abner S. Holton, also a Republican, of Greensboro. It was rumored during the gubernatorial race of 1876 that Thomas Settle appeared drunk at Jonesboro, and he said he was disgusted with the entire campaign.[20]

On occasion, verbal abuse degenerated into physical threats or attacks, as leaders openly brawled with one another. Attacks on newspaper editors were not infrequent, and Tourgée launched a scathing verbal attack on one Gus Atkinson, who alleged that he kicked the judge in the derriere as he walked down the street. Tourgée also dropped a platter on the plate of an opponent at a public dinner because the opponent had called him a rascal, and he described a tense moment after dinner one evening during the constitutional convention of 1875 when he confronted convention president Edward Ransom who, it was rumored, was going to shoot Tourgée for claiming that his photograph belonged in the Rogue's Gallery. Someone placed a revolver in Tourgée's hand as he faced Ransom for two minutes or so, but nothing happened.[21]

Like verbal abuse and physical threats and assaults, social ostracism occurred in state races both before and after the war. John Gilmer recalled that because of his continued Unionist stance before Fort Sumter, he was "not only denounced and persecuted with unusual bitterness, but in social intercourse was slighted and regarded as a sympathizer with abolitionists and a traitor to the South."[22] Similarly, Calvin Wiley indicated that he found it difficult during the war to adhere to his principles and maintain his social relationships.

With the development of two-party politics locally and the participation of a relatively large number of nonnative southerners in the high power ranks as Republicans, social ostracism became a favorite Democratic weapon. Although a resident of the community for twenty-seven years at the time of his candidacy for office in 1868, Reverend Welker was labeled by the Democratic press "an exotic from the state of Pennsylvania"; those who had only recently arrived made even better targets. In reference to Thomas B. Keogh's wife, Eugene Morehead commented, "She is a beautiful, fat, catholic, irish, yankee, one of our *carpet baggers*," whose "soiree" was attended by all the young people, "—*which was condemned by no few*."[23] The Tourgées especially were slighted by their neighbors. When Albion was away at the constitutional convention of 1875 and Emma ran low on horse feed, she noted, "I was determined I would ask no one to trust me if they [the horses] had to eat each other," and, again, when her cows failed to give their usual supply of milk: "I could not see what I was going to do, for I had steadfastly determined not to run the risk of insult by asking any one 'to trust' for necessaries." For his part, Albion warned a northern relative that if her daughter came for a visit, company would be scarce: "We don't grow popular in the social acceptance of the town a bit but rather the reverse." Six years later, conditions appeared little improved as Tourgée explained to his doctor, "Times are better here, for such men as I am only in the sense that Hell is better than Purgatory."[24]

Finally, alongside all the other attributes of Radical Reconstruction politics, organized violence beset the community. Tourgée and his wife received notes threatening the attorney's life as early as 1866, when he traveled to Philadelphia to participate in the fall Unionist convention, although violence was still sporadic and unorganized at this time.[25] The judge grew increasingly concerned in the spring of 1870, when white Republican leader John W. Stephens was killed in nearby Caswell County, and he mentioned a plot on his life in the midst of the Ku Klux Klan trials in 1872 as a result of the Stephens murder.[26] According to Tourgée's account, a member of a Klan camp was supposed to start a row in the courtroom, and when Tourgée sentenced him to jail, he would shoot the judge. The court was insulted and the man sentenced but nothing further happened, although Tourgée recalled later that, at the moment of sentencing, "Gen. Scales became as pale as a ghost."[27]

In the campaign of 1870, the tables were turned briefly when Governor Holden sent the militia into neighboring Caswell and Alamance counties. "A bloody scene" seemed about to occur, according to William Scott, when soldiers surrounded the Caswell County Courthouse and someone struck a member of the militia. In fact, nothing of consequence happened, although Democratic leaders, including Scott's opponent for Congress, James M. Leach, were badly frightened.[28] This tense situation was unplanned, however, and no Democratic powerholders ever faced the danger that their Republican counterparts experienced.

For Republican followers, especially blacks, times were even more precarious than for leaders, and though the worst of the troubles occurred in Alamance and Caswell counties, Guilford was not exempt. Indeed, it was Guilford powerholder Obediah McMichael who spearheaded the creation of a White Brotherhood chapter in Alamance County in 1868, and both White Brotherhood and Ku Klux Klan chapters flourished in the eastern segment of Guilford by 1869.[29]

In June of 1869, the *Patriot and Times* admitted that a *Standard* article describing the beating of a black man by individuals in disguise was accurate, but the editors tried to minimize the incident by arguing that no alarm was manifested by the citizens because the sheriff had not been contacted. The writer then attempted to deflect blame from Democrats through the use of D. F. Caldwell's favorite argument, claiming that "even Radicals" tired of seeing Negroes arrested and either fed by "rebel taxpayers" or, as happened too often, pardoned by the governor.[30] In the fall of 1869, the Republican press appealed to Guilford citizens to check the lawlessness with "public opinion & demonstration" and urged the establishment of a vigilance committee.[31] By this time, even the *Patriot* was forced to acknowledge that atrocities were occurring in Guilford as elsewhere, and the editors agreed that Holden acted correctly in calling out the militia in Lenoir, Orange, Chatham, and Jones counties, although they continued to decry the alleged use of Afro-Americans among the armed forces.[32]

Greensboro Conservatives reacted to the murder of John W. Stephens in much the same way as their counterparts in other communities, determining that Stephens's "bad character" justified retribution against him, but privately they began to express concern about violent excesses.[33] Frank Caldwell was warned that the "infernal agitation" in the South was perpetuating "Holdenism," and another correspondent worriedly reported to him that "a great many" say they will not vote for "a Ku Klux."[34] The murder of Stephens, however, finally prompted Holden to send the militia into Caswell and Alamance counties, an action that ironically proved costly to Republicans in the Guilford vicinity.

In the wake of criminal charges that followed the military campaign, Obediah McMichael appeared in court, "looking about as sorry as you could imagine," Tourgée commented to Thomas Settle. Two more Ku Klux raids were reported in the county early in 1871, but by this time, their fury had lessened considerably in comparison to the peak years of 1869 and 1870. Stronger federal measures and Tourgée's success in extracting a number of confessions from Klan members late in 1871 helped considerably to curb the attacks.[35]

Thus despite the reported "high-toned" quality of Republican leaders in Guilford County and the favorable feeling on the part of many Conservatives toward blacks, the community did not escape the excesses of Radical Reconstruction that were experienced in other parts of the South. These excesses included threats against some Republican leaders and violent attacks on a number of Afro-Americans. It is therefore important to consider whether organized violence kept legitimate leaders from positions of influence, for if the arrangements described in Chapter 4 resulted from force, the image of the community is very different from that which emerges if powerholders served with the consent of the polity.

Implications of Organized Violence

There is little question that virtually all of the organized violence was directed toward Republicans or potential Republicans. Even in 1870, when the GOP in Caswell County, backed by the militia, temporarily gained the upper hand, the threats against Democratic powerholders had no lasting effects. In comparison, William L. Scott commented on the "heretofore intimidated colored and white Republicans," and Tourgée claimed that "of the scores and hundreds who had suffered outrages at the hand of these organizations—every one had been a Republican."[36] The judge also maintained that victims were informed that their membership in the Republican party prompted the assaults, but blacks in Guilford may not have been as intimidated and reluctant to participate in the political process as it initially appeared.[37] J. Morgan Kousser argued in his work on southern politics that the effectiveness of violence and intimidation in keeping black and white dissenters out of power has been overrated. Voter turnout in gubernatorial races in Guilford, including that of Republicans, consistently increased between 1868 and 1880, growing in the case of the GOP from 1,739 in the former year to 2,248 in the latter.[38] (see Table 3, Chapter 2). By 1888, Republicans overpowered Democrats 2,680 to 2,470.[39]

Additionally, because individuals identified as leaders in this study included those who garnered influence outside of elected positions, as well as those in elected office, it was possible to be a powerholder without winning an election. Therefore, even if some voters were so intimidated that they stayed away from the polls, individuals they might have endorsed could have surfaced in other leadership capacities. Many candidates labored in party organizations and were thereby included in the analysis in this manner.

Finally, and most important, in the opinion of both Republicans and Democrats who participated in the critical election of 1870, when organized violence was at its peak in the Fifth District, the subsequent Republican loss resulted from the dissatisfaction of voters with Holden's sending the militia into the vicinity and not from violence and intimidation per se. His prospects for election to Congress were bright before the militia was called out, William Scott explained to his wife just after the courthouse confrontation, but this action may have cost him enough votes to defeat him.[40] Tourgée was even more critical of Holden's handling of the affair, claiming not only that the use of the militia but the way it was done proved costly to Republicans. "A magnificent fizzle," he described the military campaign, because the governor did not send competent detectives into Caswell and Alamance to gather evidence before the arrival of the troops. Therefore, they were forced to strike "entirely in the dark" and in a way that resulted in freedom for the perpetrators of violence and, the judge intimated, the probable continuation of their activities. "A first class bungler," Tourgée privately called the governor.[41]

R. W. Glenn, a Democrat and brother-in-law of John Gilmer, Sr., expressed views similar to those of Scott and Tourgée, although he was delighted rather than chagrined at the outcome of the militia's foray into Caswell and Alamance. "I think Kirk & his militia did us good services," he commented to Calvin Wiley. "It is true it was hard to put up with but we determined to bear it. Thank God for the results," he concluded.[42] Thus there is no indication, based on the assessments of Republicans and Democrats who were intimately involved with the 1870 election, that intimidation and assaults explained the outcome at the polls. Instead, ironically, it was the efforts to quell the violence, not the violence itself, that produced a negative response on the part of voters toward Republicans.

The significance of the violent excesses in Guilford was not, then, that it explained the stability that prevailed in power arrangements throughout the war era. Instead, its import lay in what it suggested about the nature of Guilford society generally, for it implied a community in considerable disarray. When this condition is added to the bitter political divisions that beset the county in the postwar years, it becomes obvious that, as in the controversy over abolition, Guilford once again followed the path of other southern communities, a fact that is very significant in light of the continued association and even cooperation among Guilford attorneys discussed later in this chapter.

Reasons for Rancorous Politics

Partisan politics in Guilford proved bitter and intense for several reasons. First, the war divided white voters in a way that no previous crisis had done, and continued confrontations between Unionists and former rebels in the wake of the conflict hardened the cleavages. The congressional Reconstruction Acts of 1867, which resulted in a new state constitution in North Carolina and the enfranchisement of black men, intensified these differences in two ways. First, the enfranchisement of black males and the new constitution with its guarantee of local autonomy brought issues to the public forum that were very important to all participants. Second, the movement of most black voters into the Republican party and the clustering of many whites in the Democratic party made the race issue more volatile than it had previously been, although race was certainly not a new subject in southern politics.

Among leaders, the emergence of several young newcomers as high powerholders disrupted traditional powerholding patterns and thereby contributed to a sense of confusion and desperation. More important, the prevalence of attorneys among the community's most influential citizens intensified the partisan battles, for once the electorate divided, lawyers, who had traditionally devoted considerable time and energy to party affairs, brought home all of the trappings of two-party politics that they were accustomed to using in their fights against Democrats in other parts of the state.

The ravages of war on the personal fortunes of members of the legal community intensified their intra- as well as interparty struggles. Even in the best of times, young lawyers had often found it difficult to maintain their practices and devote time to campaigning for office, and balancing the two became more difficult than ever after the war, when both winning office and attending to their personal finances required more time. To make matters more galling, their desperate financial situations followed on the heels of the most prosperous decade that most of these attorneys had ever experienced.

In their desperate attempts to achieve public office, lawyers, like other leaders, focused on the issues of black involvement in politics and local autonomy in part because the solutions to these questions would go a long way toward determining who among them would achieve office. They also seized on these topics because few other issues of substance separated them. Especially Guilford attorneys agreed on economic matters.

To a large extent, the intense partisan struggles following the war stemmed from the importance of the issues to the voters. To black citizens, political participation represented one of the few tangible results of emancipation as well as hope for better times, and they began mobilizing even before the adoption of a new state constitution and the Fifteenth Amendment. To whites, constitutional issues had long been important in and of themselves, sometimes overshadowing the race question, although the significance of the latter issue cannot be ignored.

Early in 1868, the Democratic *Times* reported a Republican meeting "at the negro village of Warnersville," a residential area established by Yardley Warner, a Pennsylvania Quaker, at the close of the war, and similar reports were issued the following year by the *Patriot*.[43] Additionally, Harmon Unthank, a forty-five-year-old carpenter and former slave, who purchased a lot in Warnersville in 1871 and subsequently built a house on it, began lining up support for Tourgée's bid for the Fifth District congressional nomination while the Greensboro attorney attended the constitutional convention in Raleigh. At Tourgée's behest, Unthank intimated to white Republican John A. Pritchett that he could become a state legislator if he would work for Tourgée's nomination as a congressional representative, and the Warnersville resident approached the white sheriff Stafford about working for Tourgée as well.[44] Also, when the Republican party in Greensboro endorsed Tourgée's candidacy for the Fifth District congressional seat in mid-February, Unthank, among others, circulated petitions in the attorney's behalf.[45]

Like Unthank, a number of other blacks assumed leadership roles in organizing efforts. Frank Jordan, a fifty-five-year-old carpenter with $300 in real property, served as a delegate to the Republican state convention in 1872, as did Unthank, and Zephiniah Mitchell, a sixty-three-year-old brickmason, who was never enslaved and who accumulated real property valued at $1,600 and personal property worth $300 by 1870, served as a delegate to a Republican state convention in 1868.

Even more involved in Republican organizations than Unthank, Jordan, or Mitchell was George M. Arnold. Arnold, who was probably not a Guilford native, reported to the *New York Times* in 1872 on the proceedings of the Democratic convention that was meeting in Greensboro.[46] Besides giving a lecture at the courthouse in 1871 titled "The American Negro in National Politics," Arnold served as secretary of the Republican county convention, speaker at a county rally, and secretary and a member of the resolutions committee of the district congressional convention in 1872. That same year, he was chosen as canvasser for the state at large by the Republican state convention, and he addressed an all-black convention in Greensboro.[47] In March 1873, Arnold invited black Republicans of Guilford and surrounding counties to a meeting in Greensboro at which Thomas Settle would speak, but he did not reappear in the political arena after that date.

In contrast, Unthank continued to toil in Republican ranks a decade later, serving as an alternate delegate to the district convention in 1878 and as vice-president of the county committee on permanent organization in 1880. Besides Unthank, other black leaders active in partisan affairs in the 1878–82 era included Charles Lambeth, a delegate from Friendship Township to the Republican county convention in 1880; John Dyson, a Jamestown delegate to the same meeting attended by Lambeth; John McAdoo, a member of the resolutions committee of a county meeting in 1878 and an alternate delegate to a judicial district convention in 1880; and A. C. Davis, who was chosen a delegate to a congressional convention in 1880 by the county executive committee of the Republican party and who served as secretary of the central executive committee for three years.

Of the Republican activists in 1878–82, all except Dyson, a thirty-one-year-old laborer from Jamestown, were artisans. Lambeth and McAdoo were blacksmiths, and the twenty-six-year-old Davis, a native of Virginia and the only nonnative North Carolinian of the group, was a shoemaker. Generally, like white leaders, most black powerholders owned property, although they were by no means as affluent as their white counterparts. (Mitchell, with $1,600 in real property, was the wealthiest.) Most Afro-American leaders also had a trade, although the number of artisans declined slightly between 1868–72 and 1878–82.[48]

Zephiniah Mitchell, the antebellum free black who had accumulated property "despite his condition," as the *Greensboro Register* phrased it, was elected to the highest office of any black Republican, a county commissioner's seat in 1868. He also served as county ranger in 1869 but failed the following year in his bid for reelection as county commissioner, trailing behind the next lowest Republican, the *Patriot* was quick to point out, by one hundred votes.[49] Though respected in the community, a political organizer, and a director of a building and loan association, Unthank served only as a member of the school committee in Morehead Township. Afro-American Frank Jordan was appointed town commissioner by Governor Holden but failed to recapture the seat in the subsequent election.[50]

In spite of slights by white Republicans when it came to nomination for important public offices and overtures from Democrats that ranged from simple declarations of friendship to published economic threats, the overwhelming majority of Afro-American powerholders joined the GOP.[51] Of nine black leaders in the 1868–72 era, seven were Republicans. Similarly, seven of eleven Afro-American powerholders affiliated with the Republican party in the years 1878–82.[52] The remainder avoided partisan ties; no black powerholder emerged as a Democrat.

To some extent, pressure from other blacks encouraged Afro-Americans to affiliate with the Republican party. Stanhope Young and Clay Albright were allegedly mobbed for associating with Democrats. The Republican press derisively mentioned that "a nigger," Sam Wiley, signed a certificate supporting Junius I. Scales in his bid for the state senate in 1878.[53] But the historical positions of the two major parties; Republican support for the Thirteenth, Fourteenth, and Fifteenth amendments; and the working relationship between local white and black Republicans were most important in attracting blacks to the GOP.

To many white voters, the involvement of blacks in politics represented more of a threat than an achievement, and the race issue was consciously manipulated by local Democrats as a way of attracting white support for their own party. The use of the race issue in politics was not new. Fifteen years before the war D. F. Caldwell inquired about the authenticity of a rumor that Jonathan Worth ate with Negroes at his table as his own family, only to learn that it was "a campaign smear tactic." Charges that John Gilmer was a "black republican" and the linking of Guilford Whigs to abolitionism by the Democratic press were obvious attempts to gain political mileage out of racial fears among whites.[54] But conscious exploitation by local leaders was a new phenomenon triggered by the elimination of slavery and the participation of the overwhelming majority of Afro-Americans in the Republican party.

D. F. Caldwell especially illustrated the consciousness with which Conservatives linked black crime and Republican organizational activities. In August 1868, in a letter to William A. Graham, Caldwell referred to an editorial in the *Standard* which the Guilford attorney interpreted as encouraging blacks to steal livestock. In the same edition of the paper, another article reported that the combined membership of the Loyal Leagues, ad hoc associations of the Republican party, had reached seventy-two thousand. Caldwell then got the notion that the Loyal Leagues were arming, and he suggested to Graham that it would raise "a storm of indignation" and result in "great capital" for the Democratic party if the press and public speeches suggested that there was a link between the arming of the Loyal Leagues and the alleged call for Negroes to steal. In short, Caldwell suggested that it would be politically advantageous for Democrats to spread the word that the Loyal Leagues were "bands of thieves & murderers" united under the direction of "one of the worst Carpetbaggers in the state."[55]

At this point, the *Patriot and Times,* which was owned by Caldwell, commenced a steady stream of articles about crimes allegedly perpetrated by blacks. Stealing was growing more common and appeared to have increased with the "new government," the paper cried the same month as Caldwell's letter to Graham. Moreover, there was no punishment for Negroes, and now Judge Tourgée wanted to provide the jails with stoves, an action that would result in many more prisoners, the *Patriot* lamented. A neighbor of D. F. Caldwell had had his entire wardrobe stolen, editor Albright interjected, and in the eastern part of the county, a black man fired through a window in an attempt to murder a Mrs. Clapp. And the reports continued. A year later, the *Patriot* concluded that burglaries occurred with such frequency that most people carried firearms.[56]

Guilford whites did not always respond hysterically to rumors of black crime and racial unrest. In 1871, an extra edition of the Democratic *Sentinel* reported that five thousand Negroes who had arrived in Goldsboro from New Bern on a train chartered by the Republican State Executive Committee had become intoxicated, and a riot had ensued. In Greensboro, it was rumored that there would be "h——— . . . to pay between the races." In fact, the alleged riot turned out to be "a small matter," and John Payne indicated to William Scott, "The people here are disgusted with the account which is so different from the reports yesterday and the inconsistencies therein."[57]

The concern of many whites over the involvement of blacks in politics was tempered by their worry over the fate of local autonomy. Since the state constitutional convention of 1835, white voters had been discussing constitutional issues and political procedures, and they were not easily persuaded to relinquish their newly acquired opportunities in 1868, even if it meant the appointment of most local officeholders by state officials and the consequent elimination of blacks from public office. Many of these citizens had gone to war because they believed a tyrannical government threatened their individual liberties, and a good number broke with Governor Vance during the conflict because they thought the Confederacy represented a similar threat. To these persons, constitutional issues and political forms mattered.[58]

Thus to both blacks and whites, the issues of black involvement in politics and local autonomy had considerable import. Politicians attempted to manipulate these matters to their own advantage, but their attention to them did not give the issues their significance. Leaders were inclined to exploit black participation in politics and local autonomy, however, because of the similarity of their stances in regard to most other matters, especially those related to economic development, and because of the desperate financial circumstances in which they found themselves at the close of the war.

For attorneys whose financial situations had deteriorated during the war, economic problems were compounded by the considerable time they had to spend away from their practices organizing political parties and campaigning for public office. The allocation of time between private practice and politics had always been a problem for lawyers. That was why *Patriot* editors counseled John Gilmer not to seek political office at midcentury. Gilmer, they pointed out, was a man of "moderate means" with a growing family to support. But the problem of dividing time between business and politics worsened for members of the legal community as politics required more time and fewer of them had wealthy families to aid them. In 1860, Charles E. Shober explained that he planned to practice law, not because he was dependent on the profession but because he did not wish to spend his time in idleness.[59] Few young men were in a position to make such a statement after the war. Indeed, James Leach warned William Scott in 1870 that his business might suffer if he entered politics, and Thomas B. Keogh concluded late in the decade that he had suffered precisely that fate. Hence in the wake of financial disaster resulting from the war, lawyers naturally sought public office, and because they spent considerable amounts of time attaining this goal, they grew increasingly dependent on political success.

Democratic lawyers demonstrated their need for political jobs through explicit appeals to one another to stay out of certain races and keen competition for nomination for office. Three years before William Scott's conversion to Republicanism, his old friend and commander, James M. Leach, pleaded with him not to run for the legislature, for "the loss of my cotton crops, bank stock, and over $18,000 in Alabama leaves me not worth a *pocket knife*, & besides have 5 children to support & try to educate." Similarly, a gentleman from Mt. Airy urged D. F. Caldwell not to seek the Fifth District congressional seat in 1870 because he himself was in economic straits and sorely needed the nomination. Caldwell's opponents for this particular spot were numerous, "too many to give your party even the shade of a shadow of success," a friend of Caldwell's feared.[60]

When James Leach secured the Fifth District nomination in 1870 over Caldwell, considerable disappointment was expressed by Caldwell's supporters, one of whom raised the charge that Leach ran for office constantly, even without his party's official endorsement—a charge that seemed valid in light of Leach's earlier plea to Scott. Leach continued so desperate for the congressional seat that he again appealed to Scott not to run, although Scott was in the opposition party by this time. Leach pointed out that he and Scott had many friends in common and then argued that Scott would undoubtedly lose and would be in "a predicament" with a loss in politics and a neglected law practice.[61] Like Leach, John N. Staples was also accused of running for office without his party's endorsement. Interestingly, his accuser, D. F. Caldwell, indicated a few years later that he intended to do precisely the same thing.

Competition increased among Democratic aspirants as the nation's economy worsened in the 1870s. "Greenbackism" was reputedly appealing more to Democrats than Republicans in the election of 1878, and Junius I. Scales in particular was rumored to be a Greenbacker.[62] Zebulon Vance expressed concern to Julius A. Gray that Scales might challenge him in the race for the U.S. Senate, although Gray assured him that Scales's name was put forward by the "numerous aspirants" who wanted his current position.[63] Ultimately, the Senate race was a hot one in Guilford, not because Scales challenged Vance, but because Vance's main opponent, A. S. Merrimon, was supported by D. F. Caldwell.[64]

Like Democrats, Republican attorneys competed for political jobs out of financial need. When William Scott's rheumatism and partial paralysis worsened in the summer and fall of 1871 and he could no longer practice law, he appealed to Senator John Pool for Frank Wheeler's assessorship with the Internal Revenue Service for the Fifth District. A number of local Republicans were dissatisfied with Wheeler's performance, and thirty-nine party members signed a petition favoring Scott's appointment, but Pool could not replace Wheeler without near unanimous support. If a vacancy existed, he indicated to Scott, and Scott and Wheeler were vying for the spot, the senator would be free to choose the ailing lawyer, but he could not simply remove Wheeler from office, especially when he had the support of Robert M. Douglas, Thomas Settle's brother-in-law, who claimed Scott's district as his home while serving as private secretary to the president of the United States. Too many requests like Scott's came to Pool, the senator explained.[65]

Albion Tourgée also had his economic ups and downs, and he sought public office in part to alleviate his financial problems. As a newly appointed code commissioner with a salary of $200 per month for three years, Tourgée felt "tolerably well provided for" in 1868. The following year, his business prospects were described as "extremely good," and in the 1870 census, he owned real estate valued at $15,000. Unfortunately, Tourgée was adversely affected by the panic of 1873. With "rapidly maturing liabilities of $30,000 and nothing but bad debts and a lot of unsalable stock," he considered giving up but hoped he could recover before people learned of his desperate condition. Then, in 1874, Tourgée's spoke and handle factory collapsed, and the following year, he expressed regret to his wife, Emma, concerning "the necessity of constant care and economy to make both ends meet." The following year, the Tourgées moved to Raleigh, where Albion secured a post as a federal pension agent and Emma was designated as a clerk to administer oaths in the pension office. A few months later, the Tourgées sold their home in Greensboro, although they did not dispose of all their property there until they left the state in 1879.[66]

Like Albion Tourgée, Thomas B. Keogh experienced financial difficulties after his arrival in Greensboro and, like Scott, Keogh appealed for a local political position in his time of economic need. As a law partner of Democrat John A. Barringer and editor of the *North State,* whose circulation trebled in the late 1870s, Keogh was doing well in 1878 and con-

templating a trip to Europe. By the following year, however, his fortunes
had taken a downturn, and he, like Scott before him, sought Frank Wheeler's assessorship. Failing in his efforts to secure this position, Keogh appealed the following year for a solicitorship. He did not wish to oust in-
cumbent solicitor Rayner until he had a new job, Keogh explained to
Settle, but "the time has come when I must have something for the reason
that I need it—and not for the fun of the thing."[67]

Thus as the economic fortunes of attorneys experienced a dramatic
downturn and two-party politics blossomed, lawyers increasingly became
professional politicians whose livelihoods depended on the procurement
of public office. These circumstances combined to produce cutthroat competition within the same party, an intensive struggle for votes, and
mudslinging campaigns which implied that postwar partisan leaders held
markedly different views from one another. In fact, leaders assumed many
similar postures, especially on economic development, and this similarity
in outlook helped account for their hysterical rhetoric and slanderous personal attacks. Aside from local autonomy and the role of blacks in politics,
few substantive issues separated the two parties. Indeed, a generation gap
was more important than partisan differences in explaining different perspectives on the role local government should play in economic matters.

In summary, partisan politics intensified in Guilford following the war
because of the importance of the issues and the changes in the nature of
leadership that accompanied the conflict. Especially, the increasing involvement in public affairs of attorneys who were already skilled in campaign
techniques and whose personal fortunes experienced dramatic fluctuations
in the 1850s and 1860s intensified the competitiveness and bitterness in the
political arena. On many economic matters, these lawyers agreed, but their
very consensus sparked vituperative personal attacks. Yet despite the inten-
sity of their confrontations, these same attorneys continued to interact with
one another socially, economically, and, most of all, professionally.

Persistent Relations of Attorneys

The continued interaction of lawyers derived both from their occupation
of the same socioeconomic stratum and from their shared profession.
Most were much more affluent than the general population, and as demonstrated in Table 11, Democrats and Republicans were even more similar
in wealth than antebellum Democrats and Whigs.[68]

Republicans and postwar Democrats were also similar in occupation,

TABLE II.

Mean Age and Wealth of Powerholders by Political Party

Year/Party	Age	Real Property ($)	Personal Property ($)	Slaves
1850				
Whig	46	5,684	NA	10
Democrat	43	1,972	NA	7
1860				
Whig	47	13,075	30,455	13
Democrat	47	4,147	8,804	4
1870				
Democrat	46	3,856	1,863	—
Republican	44	2,505	1,776	—

Source: Guilford County data base.

residence within the county, and place of birth. The majority in both parties engaged in agriculture (62 percent for Democrats and 53 percent for Republicans), but a plurality resided in Greensboro (37 percent of the Democrats and 39 percent of the Republicans).[69] The leadership of both organizations derived overwhelmingly from the South with 98 percent of the Democrats and 92 percent of the Republicans born in the Confederacy, although a slightly higher percentage of the Republicans than the Democrats were born in southern states outside of North Carolina (a difference of 4 percentage points).

Among high powerholders, 85 percent of whom were attorneys by the years 1868–72, Democrats and Republicans were also far more alike than different. When the very wealthy Republican DeWitt C. Benbow was excluded from the calculations, Democrats still averaged only slightly more real property than Republicans ($6,460 to $5,000), and they possessed less personal property than their GOP counterparts ($4,100 to $3,329). Additionally, both resided in Greensboro at the overwhelming rates of 76 percent for Democrats and 67 percent for Republicans.

The birthplace of influential Republicans was the primary characteristic distinguishing them from their Democratic counterparts, although they also differed slightly in age. Among high powerholding Republicans, only 50 percent were born in the South, while the comparable figure for Democrats was 95 percent. Republicans were also slightly younger than Democrats in the high power ranks with an average age of thirty-nine in comparison to the Democrat's forty-six. Thus the young, nonsouthern newcomers who arrived in the community after the war and emerged as large powerholders became Republicans, not Democrats, and this tendency lent credence to the Democratic charge that Republicans did not represent the "natural" leadership of the region, even though Republican leaders generally were natives of the South and, indeed, of the Old North State.

As in other nineteenth-century American towns, members of the Greensboro elite often interacted socially, and these frequent exchanges were reinforced for lawyers by their shared profession.[70] Certainly the practice of law did not have all of the accoutrements that it came to possess in the twentieth century, but lawyers constituted a distinct group in nineteenth-century America. Legal historian James Willard Hurst argued that attorneys were distinctive not only because of their high position in the social structure but also because they shared a special body of knowledge, practiced their craft only after satisfying some standard set by the state, and affiliated with one another through an internal organization. Judith Shklar maintained that attorneys shared the same ideology—legalism— whereas Charles M. Haar noted that even though the public was often critical of lawyers during the antebellum years, members of the bar had a positive image of themselves and that they "did in fact constitute a profession *ipso facto*."[71]

To prepare for a career in law throughout the period encompassed by this study, one usually apprenticed in a law office or simply read law, although at least two of the Guilford attorneys had more formal training. John Gilmer and John Morehead both apprenticed with Archibald D. Murphy, and several younger attorneys prepared for their law careers locally. James R. McLean and Charles E. Shober read law with Gilmer, as did John Gilmer, Jr., although the latter also completed a law course at the University of Virginia before returning to Greensboro in 1860 to enter practice with his father. Similarly, Robert P. Dick prepared by reading with his father and George C. Mendenhall. Following a slightly different path to the bar, James T. Morehead, Jr., became a student of Judge Richmond M. Pearson in a well-known "law school" run by the judge at Richmond Hill, North Carolina.[72] By the eve of the war, most of the young men entering the legal profession in Guilford also had common undergraduate educational experiences at the University of North Carolina, an institution, as noted in Chapter 4, attended by Gilmer, Morehead, Julius Gorrell, and William Scott.

Regardless of where they trained, most of the Guilford attorneys probably read treatises common among legal practitioners throughout nineteenth-century America. These included an edition of Blackstone edited by St. George Tucker and published in 1803 and James Kent's *Commentaries*, a four-volume series published between 1826 and 1830. The *Commentaries* rapidly became the standard treatise on law in the United States, according to Hurst, because they dealt mainly with constitutional law and the law of real property. As a constitutional law treatise, the *Commentaries* were used widely for instructional purposes, while as a real property treatise, they constituted, in the words of Hurst, "the mainstay of law practice throughout the country throughout much of the nineteenth century."[73]

Besides the possession of a special, common body of information, attorneys had to be admitted to the practice of law, and though admission consisted of nothing more than an oral examination by an attorney or a judge and certification by the courts, law was the only profession besides medicine for which there were any admission standards in the antebellum United States.[74] Similarly, the legal profession usually maintained some type of internal organization. Even in the absence of formal associations, Hurst maintained, there developed "a substantial corporate sense" and "a close sense of what was done and what was not done" because lawyers rode rural circuits together.[75]

The "corporate sense" described by Hurst obviously developed among circuit-riding Guilford lawyers as is demonstrated later in this chapter in the case of William L. Scott. In addition, the more formal Guilford Bar Association was active throughout the period studied. Meeting on a regular basis to hear invited guests and attend to other business, the association also reinforced a sense of collegiality by paying tribute collectively to fallen members without regard to party affiliation. Whig James T. Morehead chaired a tribute by the bar to Democrat John M. Dick in 1861, and Republican William Scott spoke and served on the resolutions committee honoring Whig/Conservative John Gilmer, Sr., in 1868. In turn, four of the five individuals who were active in the commemoration for Scott four years later were Democrats, with Ralph Gorrell playing a particularly conspicuous role, introducing resolutions honoring Scott and presiding over meetings that eulogized the deceased Republican both before and after his funeral. In short, the constant exchanges among attorneys as they traveled the circuits together, interacted in court, and met regularly in professional assemblages encouraged cordiality and respect even as they hurled abusive epithets at one another in their bids for elective office. Indeed, nothing better demonstrates the stability in power arrangements described in Chapter 4 than the continued interaction, and even cooperation, of members of the legal fraternity in the face of partisan strains.

For the Dicks, longtime members of the community, politics rarely got in the way of social interaction. Before the war, when John M. Dick and his family constituted one of the few leading Democratic households in the vicinity, the young R. P. Dick frequently stopped by the Gilmers to see the family, and Mrs. Gilmer and Mrs. John Dick exhanged visits often. In June 1848, when R. P. Dick was married, Whigs John Gilmer and Charles Shober and Democrat James McLean attended the wedding, and all attended a party before the affair. Additionally, Robert P. Dick worked to secure the release of James T. Morehead, Jr., from prison in New York at the end of the war, assuring the young Morehead that he had not visited him only because he had been away from home longer than he had expected and was short on funds. Dick commented to Thomas Settle during the postwar partisan clashes, "I have always had as high a social position as I wanted and have nothing to gain in that direction."[76]

William L. Scott, a member of Greensboro's younger set before the war, continued to find a ready welcome when he returned home from an absence in the midst of the political turmoil of 1867. To his new bride, Ella, he wrote: "Though I have often been from home, and even longer than my last absence from here; yet, on my return, never before did I meet at the hands of my townsmen a more hearty and cordial greeting than at this time. Such have been the gratulations, that I feel that marrying has made me a more important character, and I know a better man."[77] A cousin of John Staples and a close friend of Charles Shober, Ella Scott helped her husband maintain those ties even during the heated congressional campaign of 1870.

Social interaction also occurred between Democrats and carpetbaggers on occasion. In regard to a party held by Thomas Keogh's wife, Eugene Morehead concluded, "Affiliation goes mightily against the grain in word, but it seems somewhat easy, when eating & drinking soirees are on hand." Tourgée joined in a deer hunt with Democrats, including, among others, Cyrus Mendenhall, John Staples, and John Gilmer, Jr., in 1873 and was a frequent participant in Confederate Memorial Day ceremonies, writing a poem which John Gilmer, Jr., read at the ceremony the year preceding the deer hunt. The northern-born judge also expressed distress over "poor Jno. Gilmer," whom he visited about the time the Tourgées were departing from the community permanently. As Tourgée's departure date approached, despite all the problems his family had experienced, he still hesitated in leaving. To his wife he wrote that the best course of action would be for her to return from Pennsylvania to Guilford so that they could work things out in Greensboro. "I may be wrong," he reflected, "but somehow I can see light in no other direction."[78]

Although Tourgée had limited social contact with Guilford Democrats, he had business relationships and, more important, professional ties with them.[79] Tourgée, as secretary of the Republican executive committee, and D. F. Caldwell, president of the Seymour-Blair Club, agreed to exchange dispatches they received concerning elections in the North in 1868, and Tourgée also served as a member of the lecture committee of the Guilford Bar Association. In that capacity, he extended invitations to Republican Thomas Settle and Democrat James M. Leach to deliver addresses. Additionally, Tourgée sought legal advice from Ralph Gorrell, and in keeping with the tradition among attorneys of honoring one another in time of death, regardless of partisan ties, the Ohio native gave what he described to his wife as "*the* speech of the occasion as is admitted by all" at the constitutional convention of 1875 honoring former Governor William A. Graham (labeled a Conservative white supremacist by Tourgée's biographer). In turn, in 1879, when Tourgée completed the analytical index to his *Digest of Cited Cases,* Democratic Judge John H. Dillard hailed it as "the very thing the profession has long needed."[80]

Even during one of the worst periods of Tourgée's sojourn in Guilford, professional ties were strained for a time, not broken. Shortly after the murder of white Republican and Tourgée's friend John W. Stephens, Tourgée wrote a letter to Senator Joseph C. Abbott detailing Klan outrages in his district. A copy of the letter was sent to Governor Holden and subsequently found its way, with several inaccuracies, into the *New York Tribune.* This exposure of southern atrocities, like his speeches in the fall of 1866, brought such wrath on Tourgée's head that he attempted to secure a foreign post, at least for a time.

In response to the turmoil, the Guilford Bar Association appointed a committee consisting of Ralph Gorrell, Cyrus Mendenhall, and Levi Scott to communicate with Tourgée to learn whether he really wrote the letter. They did not wish to do him an injustice, they explained, and, in fact, given the makeup of the committee with the highly respected Gorrell and William Scott's brother and continued law partner, Levi, on it, apparently they were attempting a fairly moderate response. After correcting the errors in the letter as it was printed, Tourgée stood behind everything he said, and, understandably, chastised the bar for condemning his outspokenness rather than the atrocities, but he qualified his statements by suggesting that perhaps the members of the bar were unaware of the situation: "I am aware, gentlemen, that many, perhaps all of you have frequently heretofore, and perhaps until the present, strenuously asserted that no such system of organized violence has existed in our midst—many of you have regarded the outrages of a trivial nature and hardly worthy of serious attention." At the same time, Tourgée admonished them for not knowing enough about the situation to gauge its severity: "I may be allowed to suggest, gentlemen, that the views and utterances of the Bar of Guilford have not been of a character to invite the confidence of the victims of these outrages, and enable them to obtain sufficient data to judge correctly of their number and character."[81] Tourgée closed his response with an impassioned description of the outrages and with expression of regret at both the problems that prompted his letter and the bar's response to it.

Despite the strained relations, as Tourgée held a special court during the two weeks following his letter, both he and the attorneys maintained their "respective dignities," and, though some members of the bar proposed for a time not to practice before him, they had "to come down a little" because they feared, according to Tourgée, that such an action would cost them money. Three weeks after his response, Tourgée still expected an answer from his legal brethren, but R. P. Dick and several others assured him no reaction from the association would be forthcoming. Two weeks later, the judge commented only that the "Bar is very quiet."[82]

Tourgée was most maligned in areas of the state where he was rarely seen. At the end of his first circuit as Superior Court judge of the Seventh District, he was encouraged sufficiently by the response of local attorneys to offer a "hearty thanks" publicly "'to the bar of the Seventh Judicial District (with one *exception*) for the uniform kindness and courteous deference with which they have aided me in the performance of new and onerous duties, the manly forbearance which they have exercised toward unavoidable defects, and the cheerful grace with which they have yielded in cases of difference.'"[83]

Besides Tourgée's interaction with Conservative lawyers, numerous other instances of professional contact and courtesy were evident. When Ralph Gorrell felt rushed in presenting his arguments before the state Supreme Court, even though Republican Judge Thomas Settle had extended the hours beyond the usual adjournment time, Gorrell appealed to Settle when they met in conference as "a respected colleague and friend" to read his brief to the court. In turn, when Settle attempted to secure a federal judgeship, Democratic Judges Dillard and Gilmer, along with other members of the Guilford bar, signed his petition, just as many of them did for Republican William Ball when he tried to secure political office. R. P. Dick continued to express warm regard for Zebulon Vance, despite their participation in opposite partisan camps: "I beg you to be assured that no political differences,—have ever changed my friendship for you.—I can never forget your many kindnesses, and you will ever have my best wishes and warmest regard."[84] John M. Dick remained on the "roll of honor" among the older generation commemorated at events such as Fourth of July celebrations, and, from a suggestion initially proposed by D. F. Caldwell, R. P. Dick and John Dillard established a law school together.[85]

Finally, at least three law partnerships consisted of Democratic and Republican attorneys. These included Gregory and Ball, Keogh and Barringer, and Scott and Scott.

No one better demonstrated the way in which professional ties between partisan opponents were formed and maintained than William L. Scott in his relations with other Guilford lawyers. A cousin of James R. McLean, the Whig Scott had close ties with one of the community's few leading Democrats before the war, and, though Scott chafed at the "mean fling" thrown at him by the *Patriot* when he came out in support of Grant and Colfax, his interaction with other professionals changed little as a result of the innuendo.[86]

Before the "mean fling," Scott described a train trip to High Point which he took with "Mr. Gilmer" and "Major McLean." The next day they met James M. Leach, "a very kind and especial friend" with whom they all rode on the stage to Salem. As Scott summarized the trip for his wife, "We had a merry and delightful journey. Such excursions of the legal fraternity are, likewise, highly improving." In Winston, the party had tea with a sister of Charles Shober's. Such social entertainments were not infrequent in the different towns at which the courts were held, William explained to Ella, and "we enjoy them exceedingly after the labors of the day and the toils of the night through which we legal men are obliged to pass." On his return trip, William rode with John N. Staples, "with whom I am well pleased . . . and much obliged to him for his good opinion of me." A month later, Scott described a trip with Judge Dick, "a boon traveling companion and real lover of the natural world."[87] In the midst of constant professional interaction, then, ties were formed that were not readily broken when partisan politics intensified.

Following the war, William continued in partnership with Levi, his brother and a very active Democrat, and he maintained his friendships with other Conservatives, including his opponent in the congressional campaign of 1870, James M. Leach, although their relationship was strained for a while. Scott was so close to Leach in 1865 that he determined not to oppose him at the latter's behest because, in Scott's words: "I cannot run, after your appeal, though I sacrifice a cherished hope, the first child of my ambition. For rather would I blight my own aspirations, than even mar the close friendship between us."[88]

In 1870, when Scott determined to challenge Leach, the Democratic lawyer rebuked him for his failure to schedule joint canvassing appointments as was the custom, and, even more indicative of the heated campaign, Leach noted that he had heard that Scott had attacked his "private character." He warned his old ally, "Now this must not only stop, but be satisfactorily explained or I tell you not threateningly but calmly and firmly, trouble will come of it." Scott assured Leach that he would be happy to canvass with him after he completed his rounds with Samuel F. Phillips; he also insisted that he had done nothing to slander Leach. The following week Scott indicated to his opponent that he regretted not seeing him in High Point so that they could arrange joint canvassing, but he suggested privately to his wife that Leach was responsible for their failure to campaign together. "James" has "dodged thus far," he explained.[89]

Scott and Leach finally met under very stressful conditions in mid-July at Yanceyville, where the soldiers under Colonel George W. Kirk's command had surrounded the courthouse as they made arrests for alleged complicity in the Stephens murder. Although Scott had little sympathy for the Ku Klux, who "have had their day," he interceded for "old Democrats" and conversed with the officer who had been struck, assuring him that all would submit peacefully. Besides alleviating the tension generally, Scott gave protection personally to Leach.[90]

Two months after the strident campaign and Scott's narrow loss to Leach, the Guilford Republican headed north for a vacation in New York City. There he shared a state room at the Grand Central Hotel with none other than John Gilmer, Jr. Their room, Scott laughingly told his wife, was described by Gilmer as "one half a *mile from the sky*." Ralph Gorrell was also along on the trip, and he and Scott enjoyed an outing to Central Park together to hear the famed Henry Ward Beecher.[91]

Thus the relationships that Scott formed with the Gilmers and other prominent Guilford families before the war persisted through the strident postwar partisan battles. The press might attack Scott's courage during the conflict and derisively question his activities once he returned home, but Scott maintained his professional friendships privately and continued to think with fondness of individuals who had become his political opponents. To Ella he wrote of John Gilmer, Sr., while he was visiting New York: "Last night, my sleep was delighted by a dream of the elder John A. Gilmer, my excellent and distinguished friend. He was with me at our home; and, after some talk, inquired for dear little Clarie. . . . After many fond attentions to the sweet child, the poor, good, old man walked off much as I have seen him in his days of affliction."[92]

The divergence in public pronouncements and private relationships suggested that politics had become a business to Guilford lawyers. Sharp, painful barbs were the order of the day, but they did not necessarily carry over into one's private affairs. Affluence, residence, and choice of career set these leaders apart from their followers, and their common experiences produced cohesion in society that their rancorous politics belied. This cohesion, in turn, facilitated the efforts of members of the bar in obtaining a diversified, industrialized economy.

If politics had become a business and partisan differences did not hinder capitalist ventures, one might ask why Democrats dismembered the Republican party through disfranchisement at the turn of the century. Although this study does not extend into the 1890s, the findings in this chapter suggest two possible scenarios. First, because of occurrences such as Scott's death in 1872 and Tourgée's departure from the community in 1876, the number of Republican lawyers may have dwindled to the point that GOP party leadership seemed alien to Democratic attorneys by the Populist decade. Additionally, hard economic times may have brought new faces into the upper echelons of power. Conservatives, then, could have ceased viewing partisan conflict as acceptable and determined once and for all to smash their opponents to ensure the survival of the economic system they cherished. More likely, disfranchisement simply represented another conservative solution to a severe political confrontation, just as the abandonment of local autonomy did in the 1870s. Indeed, it is not improbable that attorneys readily turned to constitutional remedies to political challenges because, as legalists, their chosen profession inclined them in this direction.

Because this investigation ceased in 1882, these suggestions are obviously speculative. This chapter does underscore, however, the non-revolutionary nature of partisan politics during the Reconstruction era and the similarities in the economic views of Democratic and Republican leaders. Both were ardent capitalists. Neither envisioned an economy markedly different from the one they had promoted in the past, and, working together, they achieved at least some of what they intended.

Conclusion

❧❧❧

As debate over the nature of the nineteenth-century South continues, this study supports aspects of both the elitist-precapitalist perspective and the democratic-capitalist view.[1] Large slaveholding planters were found to be preeminent before the war, as Eugene Genovese argued, and wealthy agrarians in power following the conflict, as described by Jonathan Wiener and Dwight Billings.[2] This study challenges the notion that these leaders were precapitalist patriarchs who promoted landed interests above all others. In fact, Guilford planters promoted every capitalist venture available to them, from land speculation and the development of mines and railroads to the construction of mills. Following the war, as before, they gave little indication that they preferred one method of making money over another. If anything, they spent most of their time on business affairs and concentrated on agriculture during economic hard times.

Although the war altered none of these economic tendencies, it shattered a prewar partisan consensus among the electorate and produced intense two-party politics until the end of the century.[3] Aware of the strong divisions among voters, Democratic and Republican leaders assumed divergent positions on political questions such as suffrage and local autonomy, but they never divided over economic matters. Republican notables were far fewer in number than their Democratic counterparts, but they were not their social inferiors, and political differences did not translate into economic discord.

Rural-urban conflict seldom surfaced before the war and continuity prevailed in the economic sphere following it because a strategic elite, composed of lawyers, assumed growing importance within the community. Attorneys with multifaceted concerns smoothed potential differences between agrarian and commerical interests and continued to cooperate with one another in the midst of political turmoil in a way that no other group in the county could have done. As they became professional politicians during the turbulent Reconstruction years, they viewed politics as a business that did not have to interfere with the management of other aspects of society. Conservative legalists supported structural changes in state government as a means of ensuring political success. They did not oppose local autonomy and black suffrage because they regarded two-party politics and their Republican foes as conditions they could not countenance.

The crucial role played by the bar in Guilford County naturally raises questions about its influence in other communities. Although studies of local power similar to this one are unavailable for comparative purposes, certain developments suggest that the course of affairs in Guilford was not unique to that community. Just as the county manifested its "southern-ness" during the abolitionist controversy, the war, and the darker days of Reconstruction, it also replicated the experiences of other southern communities, particularly in the upper South, in the increasingly important role that attorneys came to play in its public affairs.

J. Mills Thornton III indicated in his work on Alabama that lawyers increased as a proportion of the state legislature from 16 percent in 1828 to 26 percent in 1849 and that, outside of agriculture, law was "the only other vocation which consistently had substantial representation. He also indicated that though attorneys traditionally gravitated toward the Whig party, their power within the Democracy was growing in the 1850s so that by the end of the decade "lawyers at last began to be accorded some degree of leadership even in the hill counties." Still, attorneys in Alabama did not increase as a proportion of the legislature between 1849 and 1860, in contrast to the situation in the upper South.[4]

Like Thornton, Ralph Wooster found attorneys important among state legislators in Alabama as well as in other states of the lower South, but he discovered their numbers diminishing in the 1850s. In comparison, he found a growing number of lawyers in upper southern state legislatures during these years. The number of lawyer-legislators increased between 1850 and 1860 in every state of the upper South except Missouri, Wooster noted, and he could not assess the situation there because of incomplete occupational data. Taken as a whole, 26 percent of all legislators in the upper South were lawyers in 1860, compared to 20 percent in the lower South. In North Carolina, the proportion of lawyer-legislators in 1860 stood just slightly above average (26.7 percent), an increase of 2 percent since 1850.[5]

The Guilford analysis further suggested that the increasingly important role played by attorneys in antebellum public affairs accelerated after the war for two reasons. First, the conflict increased mobility among young professionals, both North and South, and heightened their influence temporarily because a number of older leaders, ravaged by wartime losses and age, succumbed. More significantly, the traditional involvement of attorneys in partisan affairs increased their participation in the public arena because party politics intensified in many southern communities in the wake of war and Reconstruction.

As in the Guilford study, Jack Maddex found young men schooled in war very prominent among postwar Virginia officials, and J. Morgan Kousser stressed the viability of the southern Republican party into the late nineteenth century.[6] Morgan noted that participation by white Republican voters proved especially high in the upper southern states of North Carolina and Tennessee as late as the presidential election in 1880, the year North Carolina elected a GOP governor.[7] Furthermore, the electorate in the Old North State consistently gave the Republican party between 40 and 49 percent of its ballots in every gubernatorial election between the war and the disfranchisement of blacks in 1900.

The argument that old-line Whigs prevailed in several southern states after the war also lends indirect support to the notion that lawyers continued to be important in southern public affairs because attorneys had a much higher propensity for the antebellum Whig party than for the Democracy.[8] Former Whigs especially dominated state affairs in postwar Virginia, Tennessee, and North Carolina—precisely the states where attorneys had come to the forefront on the eve of the conflict.[9] Additionally, although these old partisans lost considerable influence in the midst of agrarian insurgency in all three states during the latter part of the century, Dwight Billings recently concluded that, at least in the case of North Carolina, those who ousted the Populists were the same as those who had preceded them in power. "My research strongly suggests," Billings wrote, "that, contrary to popular opinion, these were not new men in state politics."[10]

Certainly, comparisons drawn over long periods of time must be viewed with a healthy skepticism, but it is also significant that V. O. Key's description of North Carolina leadership in the first half of the twentieth century exactly fits nineteenth-century Guilford powerholders writ large. "An aggressive aristocracy of manufacturing and banking, centered around Greensboro, Winston-Salem, Charlotte, and Durham, has had a tremendous stake in state policy and has not been remiss in protecting and advancing what it visualizes as its interests," Key explained in 1949. "The state," Key concluded, "has been run *largely by lawyers*."[11] William Chafe in his work on civil rights efforts in Greensboro in the 1960s echoed both Key's findings and those of the Guilford analysis in his description of modern Greensboro. "Greensboro was a microcosm of the state at large," Chafe explained in his description of the community at the outset of the 1960s. "Like the state," he observed, "the city was governed by sophisticated lawyers associated with large corporations."[12]

The data thus suggest that lawyers grew increasingly important among state legislators in the lower South in the years preceding 1850 and then declined or remained the same thereafter, while their numbers accelerated among upper southern legislators during the 1850s. By the end of the decade, lawyer-legislators were much more prevalent in the border states than in the Deep South. Additionally, there are indications that lawyers persisted in power in upper southern states following the conflict, dominating North Carolina in particular well into the twentieth century. Only in the tumultuous 1890s were legalists possibly ousted from power in this state.[13] In short, considerable evidence concerning states in the upper South corroborates the major change detected in the Guilford study—that attorneys played an increasingly important role in public affairs in the 1850s and that their opportunities for power improved in the fifteen years following the conflict.

Although differences appeared in the rate of involvement of attorneys in state legislatures in the upper and lower South in the 1850s, the rising significance of legalists in the antebellum South in general probably derived from similar sources—the same sources as those deemed significant in the Guilford study. First, the spread of the market economy prompted the involvement in public affairs of those who were, in the words of Thornton, "agents of the world of contract and commerce." Thornton commented specifically on the important role played by the bar in the Black Belt, which he described as "the area most involved with the market economy," and he also noted that lawyers tended to be more prominent within the Democratic party "*in the market regions.*"[14]

Second, the growing specialization of society that accompanied the market economy prompted management of affairs by "specialists," and in a world based on written constitutions where law played a central role, "specialists" were those associated with the law. As French traveler Alexis de Tocqueville noted on a visit to the United States in the 1830s, America was a law-dominated society, and "as the law grew," Charles Haar explained, "so too did the role of the lawyer." The revision of state constitutions and discussion of constitutional issues, including states rights and secession, in the three decades before the war stimulated the involvement of attorneys in southern public affairs. As nineteenth-century Justice Joseph Story suggested, "The discussion of constitutional questions throws a lustre round the bar, and gives a dignity to its functions which can rarely belong to the profession in any other country."[15]

The differences in the rate of involvement of attorneys in the antebellum state assemblies of the upper and lower South probably stemmed from the disparate fortunes of the political parties in each vicinity. Attorneys tended to be Whigs, and the fortunes of this party plummeted in the lower South in the 1850s. In contrast, after experimenting with the American party and obtaining few positive results, Whigs staged a comeback in the upper southern states beginning in 1858. Furthermore, Whig organizations, allied with a few old Union Democrats, grew stronger, not weaker, in the elections of 1862 and 1864 in the upper South as Democrats were blamed for secession and the hardships that accompanied the war.[16]

The lengthy persistence of attorneys in power in North Carolina was possibly related to the unusual sectional characteristics of the antebellum parties in this state, for unlike all other southern states, Whigs in North Carolina derived their strength from the piedmont while Democrats were centered in the coastal plain.[17] Therefore, following the war, as before, commercially oriented legalists, regardless of party, had the continued support of the state's most populous region.

The increased involvement of attorneys in public affairs in the upper South during the war era and the persistence in power of lawyers in North Carolina into the twentieth century suggests a divergence in leadership patterns not only between the upper and lower South but also between the upper South and the North. Morton Keller argued in his impressive work that attorneys in northern states withdrew from the public arena during the middle of the nineteenth century, "in part because of the growing importance of businessmen, in part because of the character of the national crisis during those years." "The ideologue, the publicist, the politician, and the soldier took center stage in the determination of public policy," Keller explained. Particularly, the rise of urban machine politicians pushed lawyers out of public activities. According to Keller, James Bryce, "the leading English observer of post–Civil War America," noted this development when he commented, "The function of a class of men who devote themselves to politics solely . . . has done a good deal to jostle the legitimate lawyers out of political life." "Men of the law assured one another," Keller also noted, "that they were well advised to avoid the seamy life of public office."[18]

Despite their withdrawal from public affairs, lawyers continued important in northern society through their service as advisers and counselors to large corporations.[19] This involvement in turn heightened their conservatism, according to Keller, as they came to regard themselves as "the chief engineers of the new business economy." Law school graduates were told, Keller noted, that "the Bar is the natural enemy of anarchy and despotism," lawyers were reminded that they "ought to constitute a conservative class," and one spokesperson referred to the legal system as "the conservative power which has . . . reconciled diverse and conflicting interests and held the safeguards of life and property secure amid this surging sea of popular suffrage."[20]

The leadership of attorneys in local and state affairs in the upper South at a time when they were withdrawing from public activities elsewhere had important implications. First, it prompted a more favorable response among upper South officials toward industrialization than was the case in the Deep South, and second, it resulted in a more conservative political environment in the border states than in the North. Leaders in Virginia, Tennessee, and North Carolina fit much better the image of C. Vann Woodward's Redeemers than did their counterparts further South. Recent state studies of South Carolina, Alabama, Texas, Louisiana, Mississippi, Georgia, and Florida, for example, emphasized the importance of agrarian elites in effecting legislation favorable to rural interests following the war, while analyses of Tennessee, Virginia, and North Carolina stressed the industrial bent of the leaders in these states.[21] Tennessee Redeemers were not simply Whig-industrialists, Roger Hart concluded, but they were "more favorable to capitalist enterprise than the Bourbon Democrats of the 1880's."[22] Similarly, Maddex determined in his study of Virginia leaders that "the principal conservative leaders . . . consciously strove to adapt their part of the world to the tendencies of the bourgeois revolution of their time and to confer on it the benefits of industrial capitalism," and Hugh Lefler described "the conservatively controlled Democratic party" of North Carolina as "the ally and guardian of the railroad and industrial interests."[23]

The significance of having attorneys in positions of influence in local and state affairs lay not simply in their having an industrial orientation, however, but in their ability to effect at least some of what they wanted. As shown in the Guilford study, lawyers were inclined by training and experience toward a world of "contract and commerce," and their involvement in public affairs, particularly the legislature, placed them in a position to learn of new, wider opportunities and to make things happen as they did in the case of railroad construction and the establishment of the Greensboro Life Insurance Company.

Following the war, members of the legal fraternity continued to interact, despite raucous, divisive partisan politics, and in concert they per-sistently pushed toward common economic goals. As professional politicians, attorneys also added a measure of stability to society when it appeared in considerable disarray, and although their ranks did not divide evenly along partisan lines, a number of very respectable members of the bar chose the GOP. Social revolution was therefore less a possibility in upper southern states during Reconstruction than in the Deep South, and two-party politics persisted longer and stronger in the former area than in the latter.[24] As large landholders, lawyers also managed, as before the war, to project their economic visions in ways that were nonthreatening to farmers and thereby they prevented potentially explosive confrontations between business and agrarian interests.

Thus the most significant fact about advocates of industrialization in the upper South was not that they were Whigs but that they were lawyers. The strategic position of members of the bar in their state and community allowed them to accomplish at least a portion of their goals, despite serious "impediments," as Maddex termed their economic challenges, and in the face of considerable social and political upheaval. James Roark noted that planters with diversified interests made the fastest recovery after the war, but it was North Carolina that served as a particularly instructive example of the achievement of attorney-leaders.[25] The poorest southern state in 1860, the Old North State became the region's acknowledged industrial leader by 1900. Manufacturing products outstripped agricultural goods by several million dollars by the turn of the century, and by 1940, a larger proportion of the state's labor force was in manufacturing and the total value added by manufacture exceeded that of all other southern states.[26]

In contrast to their economic boldness, attorneys were often arrayed against social and political change. Oriented toward the past and precedent by training, southern lawyers had their conservative tendencies reinforced by their Whig origins and by the growing conservatism within the legal profession that emerged late in the nineteenth century. Especially in North Carolina, where attorneys persisted in power well into the twentieth century, the dual tendencies toward economic progressivism and social conservatism are observable.

Dwight Billings detected the dual nature of North Carolina's leadership in his study of the political economy of the state in the late nineteenth century, although he mistakenly attributed the conservatism to the persistence of a prewar, anticapitalist bias among North Carolina planters.[27] Additionally, Key emphasized the progressive side of North Carolina officials as he described a "progressive plutocracy" consisting of "top politicians and policy makers," who acted in concert with industrial leaders. "It would be inaccurate to portray a direct line of authority, or even of communication, from the skyscraper offices of industrial magnates to the state capitol," he wrote. Instead, "The effectiveness of the oligarchy's control has been achieved through the elevation to office of persons fundamentally in harmony with its viewpoint." The economic elite's interests were served, Key concluded, "without prompting." Key also detected an uprightness among North Carolina's leadership reminiscent of Ralph Gorrell a century earlier. "While many of its governors may have been stodgy and conservative," the political analyst explained, "they have never been scoundrels or nincompoops."[28]

Like Key, Jack Bass and Walter DeVries discovered a close connection between business and government in their survey of post–World War II North Carolina, but they viewed this alliance with suspicion, emphasizing the conservative tendencies of government officials and terming the state a "progressive myth." North Carolina possessed not only a low industrial wage base but also the lowest rate of unionization in the nation, these political analysts pointed out in the mid-1970s. Additionally, they argued, the state's congressional delegation had been among the most conservative in the country in recent years. Pejoratively they commented, "The giant tobacco companies, the textile and furniture manufacturers . . . the insurance industry, and the electric power companies tend to be as satisfied as the bankers with state government."[29]

In conclusion, this study shows that although the U.S. Civil War did not dramatically alter power arrangements in the nineteenth-century South, it did produce subtle changes in the leadership which help explain the different responses of postwar leaders in the upper and lower South toward industrialization and the dual nature of officials in upper southern states, who proved at once economically progressive and socially conservative. The one permanent change detected in this work involved the rise of attorneys to positions of significant influence on the eve of the war and the subsequent improvement in opportunities for this group to exercise power during the 1860s and 1870s. The change did not result from the conflict alone. It derived from the spread of the market economy into the southern uplands and the rising fortunes of the Whig party in the upper South, as well as from issues related to secession, war, and rancorous two-party politics.

The increasingly important role played by attorneys in the southern piedmont and, in turn, in upper southern state legislatures was important because these individuals were at once legalists, businessmen, and planters, and the consolidation of all of these attributes within the same persons had important ramifications. As planters, attorneys were in a position to ameliorate the fears of landholders, large and small, who derived their living solely from the soil, while as businessmen, they carried on an aggressive program for economic expansion. Additionally, as lawyers who were constantly in touch with a wider, modernizing world, legalists had their capitalist tendencies reinforced, and equally important, because of their strategic position in society, they made progress toward their goals. At the same time, members of the legal fraternity tended to be cautious in regard to social and political change.

The timing of the war proved important because it occurred after the market economy had begun to spread into the interior of the South but before enterprising attorneys acquired land and slaves in the same large aggregates as planters further South. Eventually, planter-attorneys might have become as resistant to economic change as their Deep South counterparts, but in 1861, they were builders of railroads, mines, and mills, as well as land speculators, and the war served only to strengthen their commitment to economic diversification. At the same time, the conflict increased the participation of lawyers in public affairs, and it was their continued public service that made the upper South the home of a distinctive blend of capitalism and conservatism, a mixture that would lead political analysts of modern, lawyer-dominated North Carolina to conclude that it represented both a "progressive plutocracy" and a "progressive myth."

Appendixes

Agriculture
  Farmer
  Nurseman
  Overseer
Business-Commercial
  Printer-editor
  Tavernkeeper
  Merchant
  Innkeeper
  Stage contractor
  Merchant and farmer
  Store clerk
  Tobacco trader
  Manufacturer (tobacco–cigar,
    cotton, spoke)
  Horsedealer
  Colporteur
  Peddler
  Trader and farmer
  Cashier
  Teller
  Treasurer
  Banker
  Railroad agent
  Mail contractor

Business-Commercial (continued)
  Druggist
  Jeweler
  Building contractor
  Telegraph operator
  Book agent
  Auctioneer
  Insurance agent
  Land agent
  Sailor
  Bookkeeper
  Sawmill owner
  Express clerk
  Speculator
Professionals
  Lawyer
  Medical doctor
  Schoolteacher
  Dentist
  Minister
  College president
Government Officials
  Clerk of court and register of
    deeds
  Judge

Occupations were derived from the Seventh, Eighth, Ninth, and Tenth Censuses of the United States, 1850, 1860, 1870, and 1880: Guilford County, North Carolina, Population Schedules; originals in NCDAH.

Government Officials (continued)
Keeper of poor
Township justice
Constable or city marshal
Deputy sheriff
Sheriff and tax collector
Superintendent of common
schools
Federal employees (postmaster,
postal clerk, U.S. deputy
marshal)
Artisans
Wagonmaker
Carpenter
Blacksmith
Miller
Fanmaker
Tanner
Tailor
Hatter
Saddler and harness maker
Carriagemaker
Surveyor
Millwright
Carpenter and farmer
Saddler and farmer
Brick mason
Brickmaker

Artisans (continued)
Tinner
Cabinetmaker
Artist
Gunsmith
Wheelwright
Mechanic
Shoemaker
Machinist
Architect
Clock repairer
Marble cutter
Laborers
Domestic
Unskilled worker in grist mill
Miner
Miner and farmer
Factory work (handle foundry,
spoke, cotton)
Prison guard
Keeper of livery stable
Tree dealer
Laborer (day)
Plasterer
Not Employed
No job
Student
Housewife

APPENDIX 2
Relationship between Individuals Held in High Public Esteem and Participation in Honorific Affairs

Sociologist Floyd Hunter developed the reputational approach to power as he posed the question, "Who rules in Regional City?" to Atlanta, Georgia, residents in the early 1950s.[1] Specifically, he asked a panel of fourteen individuals who had lived in Atlanta for several years to pare lists of civic, business, government, and status leaders to ten notables in each category and then to choose a total of ten top leaders from the pared list of forty people. Interviews were thus crucial to Hunter's approach, and initially it appeared unsuitable for a study of a nineteenth-century county where potential interviewees were long dead.

It was hypothesized in the Guilford study, however, that Hunter's concept of "deference" could be equated with the term "public esteem" and that individuals who had a reputation for commanding respect would surface in affairs that were by nature honorific and prestigious. To test this hypothesis, I assessed the extent to which four individuals, who reputedly possessed special attributes that set them apart from others and engendered considerable respect, appeared frequently in commemorative and celebrative affairs. Once a link between the possession of public esteem and participation in prestigious affairs was confirmed, I then included honorific affairs and positions within them in the power scale described generally at the outset of Chapter 4 and in detail in Appendix 3.

Initially, it appeared that Calvin Wiley was an exception to the generalization that individuals who elicited respect within the community would surface in prestigious affairs, for Wiley, who was suggested as a minister for the First Presbyterian Church of Greensboro in 1859 and who ghostwrote for a number of prominent politicians, including John A. Gilmer, did not participate in commemorations and celebrations to any great extent. Wiley's lack of involvement in prestigious affairs stemmed, however, from his absences from the community. Because, in his own words, he had "to strain every nerve of body and mind to make money," Wiley was forced to be away from Guilford first as a young lawyer practicing in Oxford, North Carolina, and then as superintendent of the common school system. After the war, he worked as an agent for the American Bible Society in Tennessee before returning to North Carolina in 1874 to settle permanently in Forsyth County.[2]

Individuals who confirmed a link between a reputation for commanding respect and the occupation of posts within prestigious affairs included Whig/Conservatives Ralph Gorrell and D. Frank Caldwell and Democrat/Republican Robert P. Dick. Like a number of other powerholders, all three individuals had deep, illustrious roots in the community and considerable wealth. Additionally, they occupied important official positions and could influence people. Beyond these characteristics, however, these three individuals had special qualities that engendered respect from their fellow citizens, and all three were increasingly tapped for participation in commemorations and celebrations as they aged.

Born in 1803, Gorrell was the grandson of another Ralph Gorrell, who immigrated to Guilford via Boston in the company of Robert Lindsay, the grandfather of banker Jesse Lindsay, in 1750. During the American Revolution Grandfather Gorrell raised forces to keep Indians in check, and he subsequently served in the House of Commons and the North Carolina Constitutional Convention in Halifax. In 1808, he sold for $98 the twelve acres of land on which the town of Greensboro was built.

Reportedly the first Guilford native to graduate from the University of

North Carolina, Grandson Gorrell served as a member of the House of Commons in 1834 and 1835 and in the North Carolina Senate in 1845 and 1858. He was an attorney for the North Carolina Railroad Company, and he engaged in the postwar years in the collection of debts for out-of-state firms that had claims against Guilford estates. Besides financial remuneration from public positions and legal pursuits, Gorrell owned shares in the Bank of North Carolina, and he consistently bought land.[3]

Among the local citizenry, Gorrell was renowned not only as a public speaker but also for his knowledge of the law and his integrity. Among his better-known speeches was one delivered during the presidential campaign of 1840 and another welcoming Governor Morehead to Greensboro in 1842. A number of individuals, ranging from conservative Governor Jonathan Worth to carpetbagger Judge Albion Tourgée, sought legal advice from Gorrell. His reputation for integrity was so widespread that his picture was used on the two-dollar bill issued by the Greensboro Mutual Life and Trust Company.

As Gorrell grew older, he was increasingly asked to participate in commemorative events. In the 1848–52 years, he took no part in such activities, but in 1861 he played a conspicuous part in a commemoration for Judge John M. Dick, and by 1870, he chaired not only a commemorative affair for attorney William L. Scott but also the Guilford Bar Association meeting and a general meeting in Randolph County for Governor Worth as well as the resolutions committee for John A. Gilmer.

Like Gorrell's ancestors, Robert P. Dick's great-grandfather arrived in the county before the American Revolution, and his grandfather fought as a young man in the revolutionary Battle of Guilford Courthouse. Shortly after the battle, Grandfather Dick received a grant of land in Guilford's Rock Creek Township, and there a son, John McClintock Dick, was born in 1791.

John M. Dick, Robert P.'s father, attended the University of North Carolina and then read law. Elected a state senator in 1819 and again for three consecutive terms following reelection in 1829, John M. was named a Superior Court judge in 1835. Besides the salary from this position, which he held until his death in 1861, and income from his law practice, Dick also acquired considerable property, which included a large estate in Greensboro, a plantation of about a thousand acres, and stock in the North Carolina Railroad. To Robert, one of his eight children, John gave cash, slaves, and an education at the Caldwell Institute and the University of North Carolina.[4]

Following his years at the university, Robert P. Dick read law with his father and local attorney George C. Mendenhall. In the spring of 1853, when only twenty-nine years of age, he was appointed U.S. district attorney for the state of North Carolina, an office he held until he resigned in February 1861. A prewar Democrat like his father and a peace candidate for the legislature in 1864, Dick eventually became a Republican, serving as an associate justice of the state Supreme Court from 1868 until 1872. In conjunction with attorney John Dillard, he founded a law school in Greensboro in the late 1870s.[5]

Even more than Dick and Gorrell, D. Frank Caldwell had illustrious connections, for he was the grandson of the Reverend David Caldwell, who started Caldwell Institute, and Rachel Craighead Caldwell, the daughter of another well-known Presbyterian divine. Caldwell's uncle, Samuel Craighead Caldwell, married into the prominent Alexander family of Mecklenburg County and then, after his first wife's death, into the Lindsay family of Guilford.[6] D. Frank Caldwell served in the state House from 1848 through 1859, although he did not undertake a career in law until the late 1850s, and as a state senator in 1879. As discussed in greater detail in Chapter 5, he also engaged in a variety of economic activities, which included mining, railroad promotion, and farming.

Similar, then, to Gorrell in lineage, wealth, and official position in the community, Robert P. Dick and D. F. Caldwell also had personal qualities that distinguished them from others in comparable situations. Dick especially was lauded by Republicans and Democrats alike as a gifted orator, and he spoke not only at the Alamance celebration and an organizational meeting for the Centennial Association but also at the memorial to honor Whig Henry Clay, though Dick himself was a Democrat, and at the decoration of Confederate graves when a Republican. He also served in several other capacities in the Centennial Association and participated in commemorations for John A. Gilmer, William L. Scott, and President Garfield.

Caldwell, although described as a speaker of "eloquence," appealed especially to the "country people." His advice concerning railroads and banking was sometimes sought privately, although, admittedly, it was difficult to determine when his expertise was sought and when he simply gave it. Caldwell was involved along with Dick in the Clay commemoration at midcentury, and, like Gorrell, his rate of participation increased as he aged. He played conspicuous roles in honoring Gilmer and Worth in the immediate postbellum years and in the Centennial Association and memorial services for Joseph W. Glenn and President Garfield during the early 1880s.

Thus, Caldwell, Dick, and Gorrell exhibited special qualities that elicited respect, along with those common among many leaders. Because of these attributes, this trio would probably have been named as powerful by local citizens if one could have traveled to nineteenth-century Guilford and conducted interviews as Hunter did in Atlanta. Since Caldwell, Dick, and Gorrell also appeared frequently in honorific affairs, particularly as they grew older, a relationship between the possession of community respect and involvement in prestigious events was confirmed, and this indicator of influence was incorporated into the Guilford study, although, as indicated in Chapter 4, few persons garnered power in this manner.

APPENDIX 3

Ranking and Point Assignment Procedure

The ranking of institutional and extrainstitutional affairs involved the interplay of theory and empirical evidence concerning the nineteenth-century South, North Carolina, and especially Guilford County. The general definition of power, the capacity to affect the lives of others, served constantly as a guide in the categorization process.

The point scheme presented below reflects the rationale for all of the various categories. As seen in this scheme, the two major divisions, Institutions and Episodes, contained high and low components. Within Institutions, the political segment was classified as high, and the social and economic portions were rated low. Within Episodes, decisive affairs were ranked high and prestigious ones low. The political institution was ranked high because it could affect almost everyone in the community through its power to levy and collect taxes; the economic and social institutions influenced a much more limited segment of the population. Decisive episodes yielded considerable community interest and participation; prestigious ones engendered limited enthusiasm and involvement.

Within the high-ranked political institution, the category Officeholding was rated high and Partisan Activities low, because one could acquire legitimate authority to impose his will on others only through the occupation of an official position. Participants in party politics might select a candidate for office, but one had to attain a position for the maximization of influence.

Specific offices within the category Officeholding were ranked high or low on the basis of the opportunities for independent action afforded by an office and the duties associated with it. Popularly elected sheriffs, congressional representatives, county treasurers, Superior Court clerks, and state legislators were regarded as less likely than appointees to be influenced by a single individual or a small group of individuals, inside or outside the county. Additionally, although nominated by state legislators from their home counties rather than popularly elected, magistrates in the

Point Scheme

Institutions
  Political (High)
    Officeholding (High)

Office	Years Held	Points
High	4 or 5	8
High	3	7
High	2	6
High	1	5
Low	4 or 5	4
Low	3	3
Low	2	2
Low	1	1

    Partisan Activities (Low)

Position	Level	
High	High	4
High	Low	3
Low	High	2
Low	Low	1

  Social and Economic (Low)

Organization	Position	
High	High	4
High	Low	3
Low	High	2
Low	Low	1

Episodes
  Decisive (High)

Decision	Specific Activity	Role	
High	High	High	8
High	High	Low	7
High	Low	High	6
High	Low	Low	5
Low	High	High	4
Low	High	Low	3
Low	Low	High	2
Low	Low	Low	1

  Prestigious (Low)

Specific Affair	Role	
High	High	4
High	Low	3
Low	High	2
Low	Low	1

antebellum period served for life and were thus free to act independent of any other official body. In the mid-1870s, when justices were again appointed, they served six-year terms. Even though selected annually by their peers, members of the Finance Committee and the County Court were also substantially free of clandestine control because they were chosen by majority vote of a large number of magistrates. Some fifty magistrates chose the five members of the Special Court in 1849. These individuals were themselves magistrates for life and thereby possessed a certain degree of authority apart from their positions on the Finance Committee or County Court. In comparison, local appointees, such as school committeemen or patrols, not only had duties with very limited scope but very little opportunity for independent initiative in the exercise of these duties.

A high degree of autonomy did not automatically result in a position's receiving a high ranking. Register of deeds, surveyor, and coroner were popularly elected county officials after the war, but because the duties associated with them did not significantly alter the lives of county residents, they were rated low. Interestingly, the only time magistrates received a low ranking was during the period when they were chosen by popular vote. Their duties during those years were simply too petty to warrant a high classification. Similarly, town officials, though popularly elected throughout the years under surveillance, were categorized as low for two reasons. First, the mayor and town council had authority over a relatively small proportion of community residents. Also, lopsided elections and voter apathy suggested that Greensboro residents regarded municipal officials as unimportant.[1]

On the basis, then, of the powers and duties of an office, with some consideration for the autonomy of the position, magistrates were ranked high in 1850, 1860, and 1880 and low in 1870. Superior Court clerks were ranked low in 1850 and 1860 and high in 1870 and 1880. The prewar Special Court and Finance Committee, along with sheriffs, state legislators, congressional representatives, and Superior Court judges were ranked high in each five-year period; all other county officials were given low classifications.

In addition to being ranked high or low, official positions were related to length of service. It was assumed that an individual who occupied an office for a long period of time would influence more members of the community than one who held office briefly. Because information was collected within two years of each census year in this study, the maximum time one could serve in each of the four sample periods was five years. Thus one who officiated in a high capacity for four or five years was regarded as more powerful than one who occupied a high position for one, two, or three years.

Within the low category, Partisan Activities, attention was given to the level of activity at which organizational efforts occurred and to positions within meetings and organizations. As described in Chapter 2, party activities were carried on at five levels—township, county, district, state, and national—and political clubs appeared occasionally in the town of Greensboro. Of the various levels, county and district meetings were ranked high because it was at these levels that actions were effected which had communitywide impact and in which the largest proportion of the local populace participated. All of the partisan candidates for the popularly elected offices that were ranked high in the officeholding category were nominated at these gatherings, and executive committees that guided political affairs between conventions were selected there.[2] Frequently, at the county convention delegates were chosen to attend the state, as well as the district, meetings. If state delegates were not selected at county gatherings, they were appointed at district conventions. All eighteen townships were represented in the Republican county convention of 1880 and more than two hundred delegates attended the Democratic county convention of 1870. Moreover, the Seymour-Blair Club alone sent fifty delegates to a district convention in 1868.[3] In addition to county- and district-level activities, mass meetings and small organizational groups were also ranked high. This was done because mass meetings, unlike staged rallies, were voluntarily attended by sizable crowds of Guilford residents, and small organizational groups acted as catalysts for more formal political organizations.

Within the partisan affairs carried on at various geographic levels, positions that involved the organization of a group or the direction of it were rated high, whereas those that were merely vehicles for the implementation of orders were assigned a low rating. Positions ranked high because of their role in the creation of a political organization included committee to draft an organization's constitution, organizer, and permanent committee on organization. Among party officials who directed the course of action of a political association were president, chairman, executive committee, central executive committee, resolutions committee, nominating committee, elector, frequent speaker, or any other individual who occupied a pivotal role in a group's actions. A number of Guilford delegates, for example, bolted the Fifth District Republican convention in 1868, held another meeting in which a new congressional candidate was nominated, and ultimately forced the selection of a third individual as the Fifth District Republican congressional candidate.[4] Although instances such as this were exceedingly rare, they were important when they occurred.

Examples of party officers ranked low because they simply executed the orders of others included arrangements committee, secretary, invitation committee, vice-president, correspondence committee, and committee to

inform nominee of his nomination. Delegates were ranked low because
they were usually so numerous that no single individual could exert extensive influence. Candidate for office was not included among party positions,
high or low, because in too many instances a person simply nominated
himself a candidate without any party sanction, campaigned minimally, if at
all, and either withdrew from the race early or received few votes. Hence
being a candidate did not necessarily mean that an individual was persuading others to accept his views or even that he represented a particular
political philosophy. Furthermore, as indicated by election results, prewar
Democratic candidates invariably garnered such a small proportion of the
total vote that, even if they were official party candidates, there was no
reason to believe they influenced very many people. At the same time, Whig
candidates were included in the power scale by virtue of their ultimate
occupancy of various official positions. Although elections were closer after
the war than in the antebellum period, with minority party candidates
persuading quite a few voters to accept their opinions, self-nominations
continued, and on the whole, the position of candidate was too erratic to be
meaningful in the construction of the index scale.

Voluntary associations within the low-ranked social institution were
classified high or low on the basis of community involvement and interest
in them. Prewar fraternal orders and temperance and monument associations, along with the postwar Grange, were assigned a high rating,
whereas an organization such as the Guilford Agricultural Society, which
had a very difficult time attracting members and sustaining itself once it
got under way, was classified low. Protestant churches were also placed in
the low category, not because they were viewed as unimportant by county
residents but because each one involved only a small segment of the total
community and because available information concerning churches and
their officers was highly uneven. Thus, like militia officers, church officials
were assigned a low rating partly to avoid giving undue weight to those
few individuals whose names happened to have been preserved.

Positions within social organizations were rated high or low on the
same basis as that used for ranking partisan positions. Positions committed
to the creation or direction of an organization were rated high; those responsible for the execution of orders were rated low. Fortunately, information concerning the formation of organizations was available twice for the
years analyzed because a number of associations, like the agricultural society, were founded in the early 1850s and then had to be resuscitated after
the war. Occupations that might initially appear to be positions within the
social institution, such as minister, teacher, and editor, were excluded from
the index scale because they were correlated as occupational variables with

power scores. Thus, like every individual in this study, ministers, teachers, and editors had to take overt action such as occupying an official position within a community organization or speaking to one of those groups to be included as leaders. Their mere existence did not constitute the exercise of power. A concerted effort was made throughout the investigation to analyze the exertion of influence and not simply the socioeconomic structure upon which inferences about power were based.

Similar to voluntary associations, economic organizations within the low-ranked economic institution were categorized high or low on the basis of community involvement. Additionally, some consideration was given to the contribution of the organization to the county's economic development. Using these criteria, all of the railroad companies with the exception of the Western, each of the banks, the prewar insurance company, and the postbellum savings and loan associations were classified high, whereas the short-lived tobacco association and the brief effort to stimulate home-ownership were rated low. The Western Railroad Company was placed in the low category because the line did not reach Guilford during the course of the investigation nor were Guilford entrepreneurs actively involved in the company's operations until its absorption into the Cape Fear and Yadkin Valley Railroad.

Positions within economic associations were placed in a high or low category on the same basis as those in social organizations with creators and directors of affairs ranked high and followers of instructions rated low. Also, for the same reasons as with social organizations, occupations such as planter and manufacturer, like editor, minister, and teacher, were not included among positions in the economic institution; instead, participation in organized economic activities constituted a prerequisite for inclusion as a powerholder.

Decisive and prestigious episodes were ranked high and low respectively on the basis of community interest and participation. Within the high-ranked category Decisive Episodes, Decisions, Specific Activities within Decision, and roles were designated high or low. As indicated, major decisions included railroad promotion, abolitionism, secession, war, constitutional revision, and prohibition. The high ranking of all of these crises, with the exception of secession, derived from the large proportion of the community involved in them. Secession was rated high because of the sizable number of persons affected by its outcome. High-ranked Specific Activities included those such as a fundraising assemblage held in Greensboro in November 1849, which was attended by twenty-four Guilford promoters of the North Carolina Railroad. In contrast, a meeting of twenty-three counties west of Guilford attended by only one

Guilford resident received a low ranking. Roles were labeled high if they were instrumental in the development of a crisis or if they were central to the occurrence or direction of a specific activity within a decision. A role such as railroad stock seller in which an individual merely followed orders was ranked low.

Within the low-rated category, Prestigious Episodes, the only affairs to receive high classifications were the commemoration for Henry Clay and the two efforts to pay tribute to the Battle of Guilford Courthouse. Roles within commemorations and celebrations received a high or low ranking based on the extent to which they involved planning or executing the affair. Unlike the low classification assigned the position of speaker in social organizations, this role was rated high in prestigious events because it often constituted the raison d'être of the gathering. In comparison, voluntary associations rarely convened for the primary purpose of listening to an oration. For a complete list of the institutions, organizations, positions, prestigious affairs, crises, activities within crises, and roles, along with the categorization of each, see the Power Index Scale at the conclusion of this appendix.

After the categorization procedure was completed and the point scheme designed, points were assigned by computer to individuals on the basis of the institutional positions they held and/or the episodic roles they played. As seen in the Point Scheme, 8 was the maximum number of points one might acquire for any one activity. This number could be attained through the occupation of a high public office such as state legislator for four or five years or by playing an important role, such as fundraiser, in a high-ranked activity, like the North Carolina Railroad Convention, within a high decision such as railroad promotion. Through involvement in a low-ranked institution or episode, one might acquire a maximum of 4 points. The minimum a person could achieve was 1 point. The sum of the points acquired by an individual for each of his activities constituted his total power score. As indicated in the text, subtotals were derived in the following categories: public office, party work, political institution, social institution, economic institution, total institution, prestige, and decision making. The following discussion illustrates the application of the point scheme and concludes the comments concerning the point assignment procedure.

Ralph Gorrell earned 1 point in the public office category for his service on the Greensboro Board of Health in 1849 (a low public office for the minimum time). Very active in partisan affairs, Gorrell scored 4 points as chairman of a county Whig meeting to choose delegates to congressional and electoral district conventions in 1848 (high position in party work category plus high level). He also acquired 2 points as a delegate to a meeting to choose a presidential elector of the Seventh District (low position plus high level). In 1852, Gorrell earned 4 points again as chairman of a county Whig meeting (high position plus high level) and 4 additional points as a county elector (high position plus high level) and 4 points as a Fourth District elector (high position plus high level). He scored an additional point as a delegate to the Whig National Convention (low position plus low level) and a point for a speech he made before the local Scott and Graham Club (low position plus low level). Finally, Gorrell picked up 3 points in the party work category for serving on a committee to draft a consitution for the Scott and Graham Club (high position plus low level), 1 point for serving on the committee to nominate officers for this organization (low position plus low level), and a point for serving on the club's committee of correspondence (low position plus low level). Gorrell's total score for partisan affairs, then, was 25. Added to his point for serving on the Board of Health, Gorrell's score in the political institution was 26.

This Greensboro attorney also scored 2 points in the social institution category for serving as a Greensboro High School trustee in 1849 (low organization plus high position), 2 points in this category for being a member of the committee to draft a constitution for the local agricultural society (low organization plus high position), 1 point for making the arrangements for a meeting of the agricultural society (low organization plus low position), 2 points for speaking at two separate meetings of the agricultural society (in each case, low organization and low position), and 1 point for serving as one of four vice-presidents of the organization (low organization plus low position). Gorrell's total score in the category social institution was 8, and because he did not score any points in the economic institution, his total institution score was 34 (1 for public office plus 25 for partisan activities or a total political score of 26 plus 8 for involvement in social organizations). Finally, through his work in railroad promotion, Gorrell scored 14 points in the decision-making category, 7 as a delegate to the North Carolina Central Railroad Convention in Greensboro (high decision plus high specific activity plus low position) and 7 as a delegate to the Hillsboro Railroad Convention (high decision plus high specific activity plus low position). Because he had no involvement at this time in prestigious affairs, Gorrell's total power score was 48 points (34 institution plus 14 for decision making).

In comparison to Gorrell, Robert F. Armfield earned 1 point in the public office category for serving on patrol to check free persons of color for their appropriate papers in 1850 (low position for minimum time). Since this constituted Armfield's only involvement in public affairs, his score in all of the other subcategories was 0 and his total power score was 1.

Gorrell and Armfield received points in the preceding example only for the years 1848 through 1852 because points were assigned to Guilford residents for their participation in public affairs within two years of and including each of four census years, 1850, 1860, 1870, and 1880. Point assignment was limited to the five-year spans 1848–52, 1858–62, 1868–72, and 1878–82 because census manuscripts constituted the only source of socioeconomic information about individuals active in public affairs, and, for purposes of this study, it was important that participation rates and socioeconomic factors exist in proximity to one another.

Power Index Scale

I. Institutions
  A. Political
    1. *Officeholding*
      High
        State representative
        Special Court
        State senator
        Chairman, County Court
        Sheriff
        County commissioner
        Chairman, county commissioners
        Superior Court judge
        Congressional representative
        Finance Committee, County Court
        Confederate congressional representative
        County treasurer
        Magistrate (High—1850, 1860, 1880)
        Clerk, Superior Court (High—1870, 1880)
      Low
        Assessor
        Register in bankruptcy
        Member, 1868 constitutional convention

Low (continued)
    Township clerk
    Associate justice, Supreme Court
    U.S. district judge
    University of North Carolina trustee
    City attorney
    Committee to build new courthouse
    General superintendent of public roads (county)
    Examiner of applicants to teach in public schools
    Code commissioner
    Superintendent of county poor
    County committee to lobby 1868 constitutional convention for railroads
    County auctioneer
    Assistant U.S. district attorney
    Chairman, justices of the peace (1870)
    Superintendent of health (county)

Power Index Scale (*Continued*)

Low (*continued*)
County revenue deputy
Aide to governor
Director, North Carolina
   Penitentiary
Electionholder
Town commissioner
Orphan's Court
Poor warden
Patrol
Patrol checker
Superintendent of com-
   mon schools
Deputy sheriff
Constable
Member, committee to
   examine teachers
County ranger
County surveyor
Militia captain
Militia colonel
Militia brigadier-general
Chairman, town commis-
   sioners
Postmaster
Coroner
Counselor of state
Chairman, poorhouse
   buildings
Militia lieutenant colonel
Chairman, Board of
   School Superinten-
   dents
Greensboro Board of
   Health member
County Court clerk
Greensboro Board of
   Health chairman
Checkmaster in equity
Solicitor
County trustee
State commissioner for
   hospital for insane

Low (*continued*)
Chairman, state railroad
   commissioners
Road overseer
Standard keeper of
   County Court
Treasurer, public build-
   ings
Assistant marshal (census
   taker)
Officer, local military unit
School committee
Relief commissioner
Captain, state military
   unit
Major, state military unit
Town mayor
Member, Board of
   Superintendents,
   Common Schools
Jailer
State superintendent of
   common schools
Public register
Registrar
Magistrate (Low—1870)
Clerk of Superior Court
   (Low—1850, 1860)
U.S. marshal
U.S. deputy—internal
   revenue collector
*Number of Years Office Could Be
Held*
4–5 years
3 years
2 years
1 year
2. *Partisan Activities*
Position: High
   Chairman, convention or
      meeting
   Resolutions committee
      (*continued*)

Power Index Scale (*Continued*)

High (*continued*)
Chairman, resolutions
committee
Elector
Nominating committee
Committee to draft orga-
nization's constitution
President
Introducer of resolutions
Organizer of organization
Executive committee
Frequent speaker
Permanent committee of
organization
Chairman, nominating
committee
Instrumental in group's
course of action
Chairman, executive com-
mittee President's
committee on perma-
nent organization
Central executive com-
mittee
Position: Low
Delegate
Arrangements committee
Secretary
Speaker
Invitation committee
Vice-president
Correspondence committee
Alternate delegate
Treasurer
Committee to select busi-
ness
Committee to inform
nominee of his nomi-
nation
Campaign committee
Committee to choose
elector

Low (*continued*)
Director
Explainer of object of
meeting
Platform committee, per-
manent organization
Committee to appoint
campaigners in every
tax district
Marshal
Credentials committee
Subelector
Vice-president of rump
meeting; conference
committee to address
voters, rump meeting
Canvasser
Level of Activity: High
Mass meeting or small or-
ganizational group
County
District; congressional
Level of Activity: Low
Unknown
Township or city
State
National
Gubernatorial
Political club
Rally
B. Social
Organizations
High
North Carolina Sons of
Temperance and other
local chapters
Guilford Masonic chap-
ters
Odd Fellows, local chap-
ters
Greensboro Monument
Association

Power Index Scale (*Continued*)

High (continued)
Mount Vernon Association
Local Grange organizations
Low
Greensboro Fire Company
Alamance Classical School
Select Primary English School
Guilford County Agricultural Society
Church—Protestant Sects except Quakers
Greensboro Female College
Greensboro High School
Grand Section of the Cadets of Temperance (district meetings)
Guilford Bible Society
District temperance meeting
Springfield Academy
Guilford Medical Society
Guilford Teachers and Friends of Education/ Guilford Education Society
Edgeworth Female Seminary
Philomathian Society
Fourth of July celebration
Greensborough Guards
State Education Association
YMCA
High Point Female Normal School
State Bible convention

Low (continued)
Eclectic Literary Club
Border Agricultural Society (Va.-N.C.)
State Masonic/Odd Fellows organizations
Society of Friends
Local agricultural society (township)
County Society for Sabbath School Workers
Benevolent club
Raleigh State Fair
Atlanta Sunday School convention
Lenoir College Institute
Friends Normal School
Brotherhood of Locomotive Engineers— Greensboro Division
Oak Ridge Institute
American Bible Society
Positions within Organizations
High
Trustee
Subscription committee (fundraisers)
President
Organizer
President, Board of Trustees
Executive committee
Committee to draft constitution
Nominating committee
Chairman
Influential member (reputedly)
Director
Low
Correspondence committee
(*continued*)

Power Index Scale (Continued)

Low (continued)
Delegate
Speaker
Principal
Witness
Vice-president
Secretary
Arrangements committee
Fourth speaker (repre-
  senting organization)
Introducer of speaker
Finance committee
Proprietor
Deputy grant master
Lobbyist for particular
  legislation from the
  state legislature
Committee on ques-
  tion(s)
Furnishing committee
Manager
Chairman, relief committee
Advisory committee
Treasurer
Chairman, literary exer-
  cises committee, reli-
  gious exercises com-
  mittee, and removal of
  Confederate dead com-
  mittee
Lecture committee
Librarian
Vice-regent or vice-
  director
Various and sundry un-
  known officers, such
  as N.G., P.S., E.S.
Seed distributing com-
  mittee
Committee to address
  farmers on tobacco
  culture

Low (continued)
Chairman, elders and dea-
  cons
Committee to solicit
  members
Depository (Bible Soci-
  ety officer)
Secretary pro tempore or
  assistant secretary
Elder; deacon
Solicitor of stock sub-
  scriptions
Gatekeeper; overseer
  (local Grange)
Foreman
Assistant manager
Chaplain
Master
Agent
C. Economic
  Organizations
  High
    Greensboro Mutual Fire/
      Life Insurance Com-
      pany
    North Carolina Railroad
      Company
    Guilford Building and
      Loan Association
    Northwestern North Car-
      olina Railroad
    Central North Carolina
      Railroad
    Mechanics Building and
      Loan Association
    Greensboro Bank
    Cape Fear and Yadkin
      Valley Railroad
  Low
    Tobacco Association
    Guilford Co-op Business
      Company

Power Index Scale (*Continued*)

Low (*continued*)
Western North Carolina
Railroad (did not go
through Guilford)
Oakdale Manufacturing
Company
Positions within Organizations
High
Director
Executive committee
Attorney
President
Trustee
Organizer
Trustee, sinking fund
(North Carolina Rail-
road Company)
Low
Secretary-treasurer
Vice-president
Treasurer
Secretary
Finance committee
Committee
Secretary, organization
meeting or general
meeting
State proxy
Director—representing
state
Cashier
II. Episodes
A. Decisive
Decisions
High
Railroads
Efforts to rid county of
abolitionists
Secession issue
War effort
Post-1868 constitutional
convention

High (*continued*)
Prohibition
Low
Public display of union
sentiment
Efforts to control small-
pox
Yadkin River improve-
ments
Bill to extend legislative
term
Attempts to discredit op-
ponents (political)
Disabilities
Passage of bill in House
to appropriate money
for a public building
Organization of postwar
military company
Specific Activity within Decision
High
Hillsboro convention
Guilford County meeting
North Carolina Railroad
convention at Greens-
boro
North Carolina Railroad
convention (23
counties)
County meeting to rid
county of abolitionist
preachers
Tri-County meeting
North Carolina Railroad
convention
Meeting called by Jeffer-
son Davis to consider
Greensboro-Danville
Railroad
Vigilance committee
Indignation meeting
(*continued*)

Power Index Scale (Continued)

High (continued)
County meeting to pro-
mote Petersburg-
Greensboro Railroad
County meeting to select
constitutional conven-
tion delegate (Con-
servative)
General meeting
County association (sup-
porting)
Low
No specific activity
North Carolina Railroad
meeting
Salisbury railroad con-
vention
Local meeting
Crooks-McBryde case
Railroad convention
(counties west of Guil-
ford)
Groundbreaking celebra-
tion/preparation meet-
ing
Doweltown meeting
Meeting to complete or-
ganization of Central
North Carolina Rail-
road
Proposed convention
Meeting offering Greens-
boro as a drill center
Local committee or
group
May convention
Local meeting to form
Home Guard
Peace conference in Balti-
more
Raleigh textbook meeting
Local group promoting

Low (continued)
Western legislative group
promoting
Local group in opposition
Northwestern North Car-
olina Railroad
North Carolina delega-
tion to Baltimore
Meeting with Virginia
delegates leasing
North Carolina Rail-
road
District group meeting
Township meeting
Fourth of July celebration
Ladies society (promot-
ing)
State convention (pro-
moting)
Antiprohibition Liberal
party
Cape Fear and Yadkin
Valley Railroad town-
ship meeting
District group opposing
Role in Specific Activity
High
Speaker
Chairman
Resolution committee
Fundraiser
Introducer of resolutions
Permanent president
Explainer of purpose of
meeting
Organizer
Initiator of meeting
County canvasser
County canvasser in favor
of proposed constitu-
tional convention,
1870

Power Index Scale (*Continued*)

High (continued)
Chairman, resolution
committee
Committee to solicit
members
Committee to suggest re-
moval of disabilities to
Congress
Executive committee
Central campaign
Committee on permanent
organization

Low
Delegate
Secretary
Contractor for section
Purchaser of 100 shares
of stock
President pro tempore
Committee to prepare
business
Committee to appoint
stocksellers
Stockseller
Committee to notify abo-
litionists to leave
Arrangements committee
Defending attorney
Vice-president
Contractor for largest sec-
tion
Distributor of Bibles to
troops
Salt procurer
Committee to prepare by-
laws
Member textbook com-
mittee
Commissary
Lobbyist to convention of
1868

Low (continued)
Signer of western legisla-
tive address
Conference committee
Candidate for delegate to
convention (opposi-
tion), 1870s
Secretary-treasurer
Introduced speaker
Candidate for delegate to
convention (in favor
of), 1870s
Anticonvention speaker
Campaign committee

B. Prestigious
Prestigious Affairs
High
Commemoration for
Henry Clay
Alamance celebration
Centennial Association,
Battle of Guilford
County Courthouse

Low
Commemoration for John
M. Dick
Washington Birthday
celebration
Commemoration for J.
W. Field
Rowan Rifleman anniver-
sary celebration
Odd Fellows fortieth an-
niversary celebration
Commemoration for J. A.
Gilmer
Commemoration for
Governor Worth
Decoration of graves of
Confederate dead
(*continued*)

Power Index Scale (*Continued*)

Low (*continued*)
Commemoration for W.
L. Scott
Emancipation celebration
Local meeting
Commemoration for J.
Scales
Confederate Memorial
Day celebration
Commemoration for
Joseph W. Glenn
Commemoration for
President Garfield
Commemoration for
Joseph W. Gilmer
Role in Prestigious Affairs
High
Speaker at commemora-
tion/celebration
Chairman
Introducer of resolutions
Popular lecturer
Organizer: executive com-
mittee; committee
chairman; presenter of
preliminary resolutions
Organizer: program com-

High (*continued*)
mittee, city meeting;
speaker at organiza-
tional meeting (Cen-
tennial Association)
Chief marshal
Committee on permanent
organization
Central executive commit-
tee
Resolutions committee
Low
Arrangements committee,
local meeting
Invitation committee,
local meeting
Secretary, local meeting
Secretary, commemora-
tion/celebration
Assistant marshal
Marshal
Sender of letter which
was read
Committee on reception
of orator
First vice-president
Treasurer

APPENDIX 4
Location of Powerholders in the Censuses

Because census records were the major source of information for the socioeconomic attributes of the powerholders, it was crucial that as many
members of the power groups be located in the population schedules as
possible. Fortunately, the proportion found in all four periods was consistently high, and no bias was discovered in the distribution of power
scores between those located and those not located in the census schedules. Of the 427 individuals who scored one or more points in 1850, 321 or
75 percent were found in the census. They constituted the 1850 power
group. The figures for 1860, 1870, and 1880, respectively, were 433 of 539 or

80 percent, 518 of 668 or 78 percent, and 538 of 771 or 70 percent. The term "power group" thus refers throughout this analysis to powerholders located in the census in contrast to those who earned points for participation in public affairs but could not be found in the population schedules.

Several explanations accounted for the powerholders not found in the censuses. A few individuals died or moved away from the community before they were taken. Census takers probably overlooked some people and failed to make follow-up visits to others who were not at home at the time of the first visit. Some of the omissions were undoubtedly attributable to researcher error. The Guilford census data are not computerized, so original handwritten, unalphabetized population schedules had to be compared with lengthy lists of powerholders. Also, some individuals assigned points for participation in public affairs may not have been Guilford residents, although so many of the organized activities included in the power scale were limited to the county that this situation did not occur often.

The important issue was whether the sizable proportions of powerholders located in the census manuscripts were representative of all of the powerholders in each of the five-year periods. To examine this matter, powerholders were grouped into small and large categories on the basis of their power scores. To attain a large score, a person had to hold at least one major position in a major institution, play a major role in an important

TABLE 12.

Percentage of All Low and High
Powerholders Compared to Percentage
of Low and High Powerholders
Located in Census Schedules

Year	Small	Large
	All	
1850	62	38
1860	68	32
1870	63	37
1880	60	40
	Located in census schedules	
1850	57	43
1860	65	35
1870	58	42
1880	56	44

episodic affair, or occupy numerous minor positions or play numerous minor roles in institutions and affairs. One or just a few minor positions resulted in a small score. On the basis of the point scheme, 5 or more points yielded a large score, while 4 or fewer points produced a small score. See Appendix 3. (These point categories were consistent with the "natural" clustering of power scores observed in scattergrams.) Table 12 indicated that power scores were distributed similarly among all power-holders and powerholders located in the census records. Indeed, no difference greater than 5 percent existed between all small scorers and those found in the population schedules in 1850, 1860, 1870, and 1880. Likewise, the same situation existed for the two sets of large scorers. Although large power scorers constituted a slightly higher proportion of those located in the census schedules than for all powerholders, again, the differences were very small.

Because socioeconomic variables and involvement in public affairs were computerized only for those powerholders located in the census records, all of the comparisons made in Chapter 4 that involved the use of the computer were limited to the 75 percent found in 1850, the 80 percent located in 1860, the 78 percent in 1870, and the 70 percent in 1880. Of the five major categories of comparisons, actual to potential powerholders, clustering of power scores, repeaters in successive groups, achievement of power scores, and relationships between power and socioeconomic variables, all but the first necessitated computer technology. Therefore, only in the case of actual to potential powerholders were all of the powerholders used; all other comparisons involved the portion located in the census records.

APPENDIX 5
High Powerholders

| Powerholders | Total Points by Census Years[a] | | | |
	1850	1860	1870	1880
Adams, Peter	52	39	47	
Albright, James W.	(3)	(9)	43	52
Apple, Abner	(17)	30	(10)	
Apple, Bingham	24			
Armfield, Emsley	(2)	(10)	28	

[a]Points in parentheses indicate the scores of powerholders when they did not exceed 20, the criterion for high power.

APPENDIX 5 (*Continued*)

Powerholders	Total Points by Census Years[a]			
	1850	*1860*	*1870*	*1880*
Ball, William S.				46
Benbow, DeWitt Clinton			39	36
Benbow, Jesse	(18)	22	(2)	(15)
Blair, F. S.				23
Caldwell, D. Frank	66	25	67	32
Campbell, J. D.		21		
Coffin, Dr. Shubal G.	40	(9)	(2)	
Davis, Joseph A.			22	(16)
Deans, James			(3)	21
Denny, Dr. Rufus K.	(12)		21	(15)
Dick, Hiram C.		(9)	27	(4)
Dick, John M.	22	(3)		(1)
Dick, Robert P.	(12)	50	29	30
Duffy, Patrick F.			37	(11)
Eckel, Alexander P.		(2)	36	(19)
Fentress, Frederick	34	23	(5)	
Fields, Jonathan	49	31		
Foust, D. P.		(3)	(8)	27
Fulghum, R. T.				29
Gardner, Abel R., Jr.	23			
Gibson, Joseph	48			
Gilmer, John A.	113	36		
Gilmer, John, Jr.			68	23
Gilmer, Joseph	(10)	(5)	26	28
Gorrell, Ralph	48	22	69	
Gott, William	21			
Gray, Julius A.			25	39
Gregory, George H.				32
Gretter, John B.			36	(17)
Hardin, William D.			(5)	21
Hiatt, Joab	26	21	(1)	
Hill, William H.			(7)	29
Hill, Wilson	28	(5)		
Hodgin, David			26	
Hoskins, Joseph	(15)	20	(18)	
Hunt, Nathan	21	22		
Keogh, Thomas B.			45	(17)
Lindsay, Jed. H.		45	27	

(*continued*)

APPENDIX 5 (*Continued*)

Powerholders	Total Points by Census Years[a]			
	1850	1860	1870	1880
Lindsay, Jesse H.	(16)	(19)	(17)	48
Long, James A.		20		
Mebane, Dr. James A.	38	(18)		
Mendenhall, Cyrus P.	26	34		34
Mendenhall, George C.	23			
Morehead, James T.	(13)	(9)	46	
Morehead, James T., Jr.				39
Morehead, John M.	109	35		
McLean, Dr. James A.			(12)	24
McLean, James R.		38		
McLean, Joel	29	(9)		
Ogburn, Edmund W., Jr.	30			
Ogburn, J. Lee				20
Ragsdale, James S.				33
Rankin, William S.	23	(1)		
Reece, William H.	(16)	28		
Reid, Anselm		39		
Scales, Junius I.			25	
Scott, Levi M.	(1)	(12)	50	(16)
Shelly, Jesse	26	(1)		
Sherwood, Michael S.	(16)	48		
Shober, Charles E.			51	
Simpson, Frances L.	31			
Sloan, James	67	33	(16)	
Smith, Eli	39	24		
Staples, John N.			30	26
Sterling, Richard		27		
Summers, Ludwick	26	(15)	(3)	
Swaim, Lyndon	44	22	(11)	(7)
Tatum, Allen E. D.	(17)	22		
Thomas, Robert			27	
Tourgée, Albion W.			35	
Unthank, Harmon				21
Weir, Dr. David P.	28	(12)		
Welker, George W.			48	
Westbrook, Samuel W.	(8)	23		
Wheeler, Cyrus J.				20
Wheeler, Jesse	31	(11)		
Wiley, Calvin H.		27		

APPENDIX 5 (*Continued*)

	Total Points by Census Years[a]			
Powerholders	*1850*	*1860*	*1870*	*1880*
Wilson, Archibald	38	(18)	(9)	(4)
Winchester, Dr. J. W.				20
Yates, C. G.				29
Frequency of High Powerholders	31	28	27	26

APPENDIX 6
High Powerholding Attorneys by Census Year

1850
John M. Dick
John A. Gilmer
Ralph Gorrell
Cyrus P. Mendenhall
George C. Mendenhall

1860
D. Frank Caldwell
Robert P. Dick*
John A. Gilmer
Ralph Gorrell
James R. McLean*
Cyrus P. Mendenhall
John M. Morehead

1870
D. Frank Caldwell
Robert P. Dick**
Patrick F. Duffy

1870 (*continued*)
John Gilmer, Jr.
Ralph Gorrell
Thomas B. Keogh**
James T. Morehead, Jr.
Junius I. Scales
Levi Scott
William L. Scott** (with 18 points)
John N. Staples
Albion W. Tourgée**

1880
William S. Ball**
D. Frank Caldwell
Robert P. Dick**
John Gilmer, Jr.
George H. Gregory
Cyrus P. Mendenhall
James T. Morehead, Jr.
John N. Staples

---

*Prewar Democrats.
**Postwar Republicans.
Remainder were Whigs before the war and Democrats following it.

Notes

✧◦◡◦✧

Abbreviations

DUL: Duke University (Perkins) Library, Durham, North Carolina
NCC: North Carolina Collection, University of North Carolina, Chapel Hill, North Carolina
NCDAH: North Carolina Department of Archives and History, Division of Cultural Resources, Raleigh, North Carolina
SHC: Southern Historical Collection, University of North Carolina, Chapel Hill, North Carolina

Introduction

1. Southern industrial growth following the Civil War is described in many works. These figures are from I. A. Newby, *The South: A History* (New York: Holt, Rinehart, and Winston, 1978), 288.

2. For a useful synopsis of economic analyses in which periodization usually extends from the 1840s to the 1880s, see Ralph Andreano, *The Economic Impact of the American Civil War* (Cambridge, Mass.: Schenckman, 1962). Recent studies of southern planters include Jonathan M. Wiener, *Social Origins of the New South: Alabama, 1860–1885* (Baton Rouge: Louisiana State University Press, 1978), and James L. Roark, *Masters without Slaves: Southern Planters in the Civil War and Reconstruction* (New York: Norton, 1977).

3. Interest in southern social structure began even before the war in novels of plantation life. The prevalent view until the rise of the Owsley school in the 1940s was of a society shaped like a pyramid with wealthy slaveholders at the top, poor whites and slaves at the bottom, and very few persons in between. Frank Owsley and his students at Vanderbilt University challenged this view as they arduously marshaled numerical evidence of a sizable group of small farmers in southern society. Reinforced by students of southern constitutional history, who described the liberalization of southern state constitutions and the participation of propertyless

white males in the political process, the Owsley school argued that small farmers collectively exercised most of the power in the prewar South.

Even before Owsley synthesized his school's findings, he was challenged by Fabian Linden, who did not find small farmers in as strong a position economically as Owsley maintained. Almost thirty years later, in a sophisticated economic treatment, Gavin Wright reached conclusions similar to those of Linden, and Eugene Genovese offered an elaborate exposition on the preeminence of planters in the antebellum South. At this point, the debate shifted from whether planters or small farmers dominated southern society to whether the planter class was capitalist or precapitalist in nature, with Genovese representing the precapitalist position. Most recently William J. Cooper challenged Genovese's interpretation by arguing that the antebellum South constituted "an open, egalitarian, capitalistic, and democratic society." See Clement Eaton, *The Growth of Southern Civilization, 1790–1860* (New York: Harper and Brothers, 1961); James Ford Rhodes, *History of the United States from the Compromise of 1850,* Vol. 1 (New York: Macmillan, 1892); Ulrich B. Phillips, *Life and Labor in the Old South* (Boston: Little, Brown, 1929); Fletcher M. Green, "Democracy in the Old South," *Journal of Southern History* [hereafter cited as JSH] 12 (February 1946): 3–23; Frank L. Owsley, *Plain Folk of the Old South* (Baton Rouge: Louisiana State University Press, 1949); Fabian Linden, "Economic Democracy in the Slave South," *Journal of Negro History* 31 (April 1946): 140–89; Gavin Wright, "Economic Democracy and the Concentration of Agricultural Wealth in the Cotton South, 1850–1860," in William N. Parker, ed., *The Structure of the Cotton Economy of the Antebellum South* (Washington: Agricultural History Society, 1970); Eugene D. Genovese, *Political Economy of Slavery* (New York: Random House, 1961), and *The World the Slaveholders Made* (New York: Pantheon, 1969); and David C. Rankin, "The Politics of Slavery," *Reviews in American History* 12 (June 1984): 223.

The earliest works dealing with the composition of political parties in the antebellum South usually described Whigs, with the exception of those in North Carolina, as the party of slaveholders and large planters and Democrats, in contrast, as self-sufficient, nonslaveholding plain folk. More recent systematic analyses suggested few differences between Whigs and Democrats. Thomas B. Alexander concluded on the basis of extensive quantitative investigations of voters, as well as party leaders, that a socioeconomic interpretation was entirely inadequate for Alabama and that only different world-views separated the two parties, with Democrats being the more provincial. Similarly, Harry Watson discovered important distinctions only in the economic orientation of the two parties, with Whigs oriented toward a positive role for government in economic development, and Burton W. Folsom II emphasized family and friendship connections, along with secessionist attitudes in the 1850s, as the factors distinguishing Whigs from Democrats. Recently, Marc Kruman extended Watson's argument by suggesting that North Carolina Democrats had become like Whigs by the 1850s regarding government's role in the economy. See Arthur C. Cole, *The Whig Party in the South* (Washington: American Historical Association, 1913), and Charles G. Sellers, Jr.,

"Who Were the Southern Whigs?" *American Historical Review* 59 (January 1954): 335–46; Max R. Williams, "The Foundations of the Whig Party in North Carolina: A Synthesis and Modest Proposal," *North Carolina Historical Review* 47 (April 1970): 115–29; Herbert J. Doherty, *The Whigs of Florida, 1845–1854* (Gainesville: University of Florida Press, 1959); Thomas B. Alexander, Kit E. Carter, Jack R. Lister, Jerry C. Oldshue, and Winfred G. Sandlin, "Who Were the Alabama Whigs?" *Alabama Review* 16 (January 1963): 5–19; Harry L. Watson, *Jacksonian Politics and Community Conflict: The Emergence of the Second American Party System in Cumberland County, North Carolina* (Baton Rouge: Louisiana State University Press, 1981); Burton W. Folsom II "The Politics of Elites: Prominence and Party in Davidson County, Tennessee, 1835–1861," *JSH* 39 (August 1973): 359–78; and Marc W. Kruman, *Parties and Politics in North Carolina, 1836–1865* (Baton Rouge: Louisiana State University Press, 1983).

4. Among the few studies related to public officeholding before the war, Richard Beringer assessed Confederate congressmen, and Ralph Wooster investigated members of the secession conventions in one work and important state and county officials in the lower and upper South in two others. In regard to the upper South, Wooster found the number of property- and slaveholders increasing among southern officeholders in the decade before the war, but he maintained that democratic advances had been made in the structures of government, with North Carolina in the upper South and South Carolina in the lower South remaining the most aristocratic. See Richard E. Beringer, "A Profile of the Members of the Confederate Congress," *JSH* 33 (November 1967): 518–41; Ralph A. Wooster, *The Secession Conventions of the South* (Princeton: Princeton University Press, 1962); Wooster, *The People in Power: Courthouse and Statehouse in the Lower South, 1850–1860* (Knoxville: University of Tennessee Press, 1969); and Wooster, *Politicians, Planters, and Plain Folk: Courthouse and Statehouse in the Upper South, 1850–1860* (Knoxville: University of Tennessee Press, 1975).

5. At the turn of the century, William A. Dunning and his students at Columbia University challenged the notion that had prevailed since the war that Radical Republicans had saved the Union by their Reconstruction program, and they characterized southern Republicans in a very negative light. Those writing in the Dunning tradition persisted as late as the early 1940s, but historians throughout the twentieth century slowly chipped away at the negative image established by this school of the various components of the Republican party—blacks, scalawags, and carpetbaggers. Additionally, revisionists assailed Democrats, with C. Vann Woodward leading the attack on the notion that leaders of this party were more honest and less extravagant than their predecessors. For the negative view of Republicans, see William A. Dunning, *Reconstruction, Political and Economic, 1865–1877* (New York: Harper & Row, 1907); Claude Bowers, *The Tragic Era* (Cambridge, Mass.: Houghton, Mifflin, 1929); and E. Merton Coulter, *The South during Reconstruction, 1865–1877* (Baton Rouge: Louisiana State University Press, 1947). A more positive interpretation of the GOP appeared in John R. Lynch, *The Facts of Reconstruction* (New York: Neale, 1913); Alrutheus A. Taylor, *The Negro in South Carolina during*

the Reconstruction (New York: Russell and Russell, 1924); W. E. Burghardt Du-Bois, *Black Reconstruction* (New York: Harcourt, Brace, 1935); Francis B. Simkins, "New Viewpoints of Southern Reconstruction," *JSH* 5 (February 1939): 49–61; and Howard K. Beale, "On Rewriting Reconstruction History," *American Historical Review* 45 (July 1940): 807–27.

Revisionist works following Simkins and Beale are legion; a few include Vernon Lane Wharton, *The Negro in Mississippi, 1865–1890* (Chapel Hill: University of North Carolina Press, 1947); Joel Williamson, *After Slavery: The Negro in South Carolina during Reconstruction, 1861–1877* (Chapel Hill: University of North Carolina Press, 1965); David H. Donald, "The Scalawag in Mississippi Reconstruction," *JSH* 10 (November 1944): 447–60; Richard N. Current, "Carpetbaggers Reconsidered," in David H. Pinkney and Theodore Ropp, eds., *A Festschrift for Frederick B. Artz* (Durham: Duke University Press, 1964); William C. Harris, *Day of the Carpetbagger: Presidential Reconstruction in Mississippi* (Baton Rouge: Louisiana State University Press, 1979); and C. Vann Woodward, *Origins of the New South, 1877–1913* (Baton Rouge: Louisiana State University Press, 1951).

6. The Redeemer view is expressed in Woodward, *Origins,* and Jack P. Maddex, Jr., *The Virginia Conservatives, 1867–1879: A Study in Reconstruction Politics* (Chapel Hill: University of North Carolina Press, 1970). In contrast, a number of recent state studies emphasized the important role played by agrarian elites following the war, and Jonathan Wiener and Dwight Billings carried Genovese's argument forward in time, concluding that precapitalist planters persisted in power. See James Tice Moore, "Redeemers Reconsidered: Change and Continuity in the Democratic South, 1870–1900," *JSH* 44 (August 1978): 357–78; Numan V. Bartley, *The Creation of Modern Georgia* (Athens: University of Georgia Press, 1983); Wiener, *Social Origins;* and Dwight B. Billings, Jr., *Planters and the Making of a "New South": Class, Politics, and Development in North Carolina, 1865–1900* (Chapel Hill: University of North Carolina Press, 1979). Reviews of recent historical literature related to the nature of the postbellum South include Harold D. Woodman, "Sequel to Slavery: The New History Views the Postbellum South," *JSH* 43 (August 1977): 523–54; and Numan V. Bartley, "In Search of the New South: Southern Politics after Reconstruction," *Reviews in American History* 10 (December 1982): 150–63.

7. In a comprehensive study aimed at deriving a definition of community, sociologist George A. Hillery analyzed ninety-four works and determined that ninety-one of them defined communities in these terms ("Definitions of Community: Areas of Agreement," *Rural Sociology* 20 [June 1955]: 111–23).

8. See R. A. MacIver (one of the researchers analyzed by Hillery), *Society: Its Structure and Changes* (New York: Richard R. Smith, 1931), and Dennis E. Poplin (who evaluated Hillery's article), *Communities: A Survey of Theories and Methods of Research* (New York: Macmillan, 1972).

9. In particular, sociologist Robert Redfield underscored the "all-providing self sufficiency" of communities in *The Little Community* (Chicago: University of Chicago Press, 1955).

10. Samuel P. Hays, "Political Parties and the Community-Society Continuum," in William Nisbet Chambers and Walter Dean Burnham, eds., *The American Party Systems* (New York: Oxford University Press, 1967), 154–55.

11. Hays cited two studies which showed that Progressives and Republicans at the state level differed little in such personal attributes as wealth and age, but a study at the local level suggested that Progressives came more frequently from the ranks of blue-collar workers and non-Protestant, immigrant groups than did the Old Guard. Additionally, these Progressives usually had commercial or mercantile interests whereas the Old Guard was connected with banking, lumbering, and railroad groups. Hays's point was that such distinctions would have been missed if state political leaders had been regarded as representative of those at the community level ("Political Parties," 162–64). See also Hays, "Social Analysis of American Political History, 1880–1920," *Political Science Quarterly* 60 (September 1967): 373–94.

12. Hays, "Political Parties," 166–73, and "Social Analysis," 383. See also Roland L. Warren, *The Community in America* (Chicago: Rand McNally, 1963), 153 and Robert O. Schulze, "The Role of Economic Dominants in Community Power Structure," in Michael T. Aiken and Paul E. Mott, eds., *The Structure of Community Power* (New York: Random House, 1970), 67–77.

13. Sociologist Charles Galpin determined early in this century that a trading center and trading tributaries formed the boundary of a rural community. Galpin's work is described in Dwight Sanderson and Robert A. Polson, *Rural Community Organization* (New York: Wiley, 1939).

14. Billings, *Planters and the Making of a "New South,"* 42.

15. Population figures for the entire piedmont are not readily available. Data for North Carolina were compiled recently by the Carolina Population Center, and they indicate that the piedmont in this state was consistently the most populous region from the third census in 1810 through the present (Thomas E. Steahr, *North Carolina's Changing Population* (Chapel Hill: Carolina Population Center, 1973).

Chapter 1

1. Republican newspapers were both scarce and ill-preserved in postwar North Carolina. Their problems are discussed in W. McKee Evans, *Ballots and Fence Rails: Reconstruction on the Lower Cape Fear* (Chapel Hill: University of North Carolina Press, 1966).

2. For a discussion of this issue, see Peter Bachrach and Morton S. Baratz, "Two Faces of Power," *American Political Science Review* 56 (December 1962): 947–52.

3. William H. Chafe, *Civilities and Civil Rights: Greensboro, North Carolina, and the Black Struggle for Freedom* (New York: Oxford University Press, 1980), 64.

4. Settlement patterns are discussed in virtually every history of Guilford, but especially helpful in the construction of this discussion were "Historical Addresses

before the Twenty-First Annual Meeting of the Springfield Memorial Association," August 18, 1928, W. T. Whitsett Papers, SHC, and Blackwell P. Robinson and Alexander R. Stoesen, *The History of Guilford County, North Carolina, U.S.A. to 1980, A.D.* (Greensboro: Guilford County Bicentennial Commission and the Guilford County American Revolution Bicentennial Commission, 1981). For references to the Smith dispute, see Juliana Gilmer's Diary, February 1859, DUL; D. P. Weir to Calvin Wiley, September 28, 1858, January 14, 1859, Calvin Wiley Papers, SHC.

5. *Greensboro Patriot* (hereafter referred to as the *Patriot*), November 4, 1849. Church figures appeared in the Seventh Census of the United States, 1850: Guilford County, North Carolina, Special Schedules, Social Statistics, microfilm of National Archives manuscript copy, NCDAH.

6. For a brief reference to the Methodist colony, see Ethel Stephens Arnett, *Greensboro, North Carolina* (Chapel Hill: University of North Carolina Press, 1955), 129.

7. The economic problems related to poor farming techniques and the significance of the Cape Fear and Yadkin Valley Railroad are discussed in Samuel M. Kipp III, "Urban Growth and Social Change in the South, 1870–1920: Greensboro, North Carolina, as a Case Study" (Ph.D. dissertation, Princeton University, 1974), 12–17, 81, 95.

8. I assigned specific jobs to occupational categories on the basis of supposed commonly shared interests rather than presumed ascribed wealth and status. For example, small farmers, large planters, and overseers, of whom there were few in Guilford, were all placed under the label "Agriculture"; large merchants, as well as small businessmen and shopkeepers, were categorized as businessmen. Although this scheme leaves much to be desired, there are fallacies in classifying occupations on the basis of inferred wealth. Too often, as Edward Pessen pointed out, occupation and wealth are unrelated. Propertyholdings were therefore regarded as better indicators of wealth than occupations, and they were used instead of occupations to gauge an individual's resources. See Pessen, "The Occupations of the Antebellum Rich: A Misleading Clue to the Sources and Extent of Their Wealth," *Historical Methods Newsletter* 5 (March 1972): 49–51.

9. "Autobiography of James Albright," 1:11, James W. Albright Books, SHC.

10. Kipp, "Urban Growth," 9, 11.

11. All of these figures were derived from the Seventh and Tenth Censuses of the United States, 1850 and 1880: Guilford County, North Carolina, Special Schedules, Agriculture, microfilm of National Archives manuscript, NCDAH.

12. This finding is in keeping with that of Gavin Wright but contrary to the Owsley school. See Wright, "Economic Democracy and the Concentration of Agricultural Wealth in the Cotton South, 1850–1860," in William N. Parker, ed., *The Structure of the Cotton Economy of the Antebellum South* (Washington: Agricultural History Society, 1970), 63–93, and Frank L. Owsley, *Plain Folk of the Old South* (Baton Rouge: Louisiana State University Press, 1949). Although not all of the individuals listed in the slave schedules were household heads, so many fit this

category that it seemed more revealing to calculate slaveowners as a proportion of total household heads than as a percentage of the total population. This approach also offered a more realistic assessment of the white families directly involved in the institution.

13. The extent to which county seats also served as centers for social interaction is described in Guion G. Johnson, *Ante-bellum North Carolina: A Social History* (Chapel Hill: University of North Carolina Press, 1937), 139, 148–49.

14. Land assessments for the county were derived from Court of Pleas and Quarter Sessions Minutes, August 1852 and August 1862, NCDAH; *Way of the World,* April 19, 1862; and County Commissioners, Minutes, September 1868 and October 1870, NCDAH.

15. As was done in classifying employed workers by occupation, the categorization of household heads by their real property was accomplished by a hand count. Population schedules rather than agriculture schedules were used in this procedure because a household head's total worth was desired, not simply the cash value of his farm. Since almost all propertyowners were listed in the census records as household heads, the percentage of propertyholders in each cell in Table 2 is calculated on the basis of total households, not total population.

16. W. A. Caldwell to D. F. Caldwell, March 27, 1879, David Frank Caldwell Papers, SHC.

17. Thomas Keogh to Thomas Settle, December 29, 1880, Thomas Settle Papers, SHC.

18. Callie Coble to Louisa Bond, February 11, 1883, and R. F. Fentriss to Louisa Bond, June 12, 1883, Bond and Fentriss Family Papers, SHC.

19. Harriet Garner to Jane Harden, June 4, 1883, Harden Papers, DUL.

20. Albion Tourgée to Emma Tourgée, January 13, February 10, 1879, Albion Winegar Tourgée Papers, SHC.

21. Kipp, "Urban Growth," 1.

22. Thomas Keogh to Emma Tourgée, 1889, Tourgée Papers.

23. Kipp, "Urban Growth," 203–4.

24. Ibid., 202–3.

Chapter 2

1. The terms "power" and "influence" are used interchangeably in this study, although sociologists sometimes make distinctions between the two, considering influence to be more subtle and indirect than power. In recent years, some social scientists have concentrated on political outcomes rather than the attributes of those in power. Carl V. Harris combined the two in an interesting fashion by examining the ability of selected interest groups to place their representatives in positions of power and then assessing the effectiveness of each group in achieving its desired goals (*Political Power in Birmingham, 1871–1921* [Knoxville: University of Tennessee Press, 1977]).

2. In dealing with institutional and extrainstitutional arrangements, the study incorporates the three approaches to power used by most sociologists and political scientists. The scholars usually associated with these approaches include C. Wright Mills (*The Power Elite* [New York: Oxford University Press, 1956]), who identified individuals in positions of power in society's major institutions; Floyd Hunter (*Community Power Structure* [Chapel Hill: University of North Carolina Press, 1953]), who searched for those with a reputation for power; and Robert A. Dahl (*Who Governs? Democracy and Power in an American City* [New Haven: Yale University Press, 1961]), who focused on individuals who participated in certain key community decisions.

All three methods of identifying leaders have been criticized for a variety of shortcomings, most of which could have been eliminated by using the approaches in combination with one another, but Linton C. Freeman et al. ("Locating Leaders in Local Communities: A Comparison of Some Alternative Approaches," *American Sociological Review* 28 [October 1963]: 791–98) made one of the few attempts to combine them. Freeman, who studied leaders in Syracuse, New York, between 1955 and 1960, found that decision makers were members, but not the heads, of local organizations. He theorized, however, that these individuals were one and the same until the early 1930s. Criticisms of the positional approach are expressed in Nelson W. Polsby, "How to Study Community Power: The Pluralist Alternative," *Journal of Politics* 22 (August 1960): 474–84, and T. B. Bottomore, *Elites and Society* (New York: Basic Books, 1964), 27. A few of the many works criticizing the reputational and decision-making approaches include Peter Bachrach and Morton S. Baratz, "Two Faces of Power," *American Political Science Review* 56 (December 1962): 947–52; W. J. M. Mackenzie, *Politics and Social Science* (Baltimore: Penguin Books, 1967); Roderick Bell, David V. Edwards, and R. Harrison Wagner, *Political Power: A Reader in Theory and Research* (New York: Free Press, 1969); and William Spinrad, "Power in Local Communities," *Social Problems* 32 (Winter 1965): 335–56.

3. A lengthy list of those serving on patrol existed only for 1862; therefore, any individual mentioned as serving on patrols during the 1848–52 period was recorded, but only those on the 1862 list were used for the 1858–62 era. Approximately, then, the same number of patrollers appeared in the 1850 power group as in the 1860. Patrols were abolished, along with slavery, and thus were not included in the 1870 and 1880 eras. A similar problem existed for school committeemen. Few names were found in the 1848–52 and 1858–62 periods, longer lists were discovered in 1868 and 1869, and very full lists existed for every year of the 1878–82 time span. Hence all school committeemen in the years preceding the war, only those appearing on the 1868–69 lists, and the first person on each committee of the 1878 and 1882 lists were recorded. Because of this procedure, each power group contained approximately the same proportion of school committeemen. Finally, all pollholders in 1850 and 1860, all in 1869 and 1872, but not those in 1868, 1870, and 1871, and in 1881 and 1882 were recorded. No lists were found for 1878, 1879, or 1880. In none of the preceding cases did more individuals serve in a particular capacity in one period than in another; there were simply more names preserved from one era than an-

other. If the former situation had been the case, all names would have been recorded, possibly resulting in expansion in some power groups. An attempt was therefore intentionally made to prevent one power group from being distinctive from another because of ill-preserved records.

4. As discussed later in this chapter, the power and prestige of the militia had declined considerably in North Carolina by midcentury, but militia captain's districts remained a convenient way of dividing the county until the township system was inaugurated in the constitution in 1868.

5. Insights into the work of the County Court in this area are revealed not only in the Pleas and Quarter Session Minutes but also in the Guilford County Road Papers, 1840–90, both in NCDAH.

6. Pleas and Quarter Session Minutes, May 1861, and John A. Gilmer to Captain William L. Scott, October 2, 20, 1861, William L. Scott Papers, DUL.

7. Pleas and Quarter Session Minutes, May, August, and October 1862.

8. Ibid., May and August 1862; *Patriot,* July 31, 1862.

9. Because the Superior Court concerned itself primarily with judicial rather than administrative duties, the Superior Court Minutes for Guilford consisted largely of names of jurors and the disposition of cases and were therefore not as enlightening about county activities as those of the Pleas and Quarter Sessions and the postwar County Commissioners Board. Guion Johnson, however, offered a helpful overview of this court (*Antebellum North Carolina: A Social Survey* [Chapel Hill: University of North Carolina Press, 1937], 622–25).

10. The latter duty monopolized the minutes of the Board of County Commissioners.

11. County Commissioners Minutes, July 21, 1868, August 1869, NCDAH; *Greensboro Register,* July 17, 1869.

12. The power of the justices to act with the commissioners was repealed in 1895.

13. In anticipation of an expected national grain shortage in the winter of 1881, local attorney and state legislator John N. Staples proposed that the Board of County Commissioners set aside at least $5,000 and possibly $10,000, if it were deemed necessary, to purchase corn in Hyde County, where it was selling at 50 to 60 cents per bushel, which was below the Greensboro rate of $1.00 to $1.10 per bushel and well under the expected winter and spring prices of $1.25 to $1.50 or possibly $1.75 per bushel. Freight rates would be low, Staples argued in his letter to the board, and grain could be sold to the needy at cost. Reluctant to expand their traditional functions and perhaps to undercut local farmers, the commissioners determined they had no legal authority to buy corn for anyone except charges on the county.

14. For a brief recount of the American party in Guilford, see *Patriot and Flag,* March 12, 1858.

15. *Patriot,* June 17, August 12, 1869, August 4, 1870. The postwar labels "Conservative" and "Democrat" are used interchangeably in this study.

16. In Table 3 candidates are categorized on the basis of the local political organization that they represented or came to represent. The national Whig party was

dead long before 1862, for example, but Vance was the candidate of the local Whig organization in that year, even though they were not called Whigs by that time. Similarly, the Republican party did not exist in 1864, but Holden represented the local faction that would constitute the heart of the Republican organization when it was developed. Governors were elected every four years, rather than every two, from 1868 forward.

17. Registered voters in 1868 included 2,783 whites and 1,276 blacks according to figures cited by John H. Wheeler, *The Legislative Manual and Political Register of the State of North Carolina* (Raleigh: Josiah Turner, Jr., State Printer and Binder, 1874).

18. *New North State,* April 25, 1872, July 15, August 26, September 2, 1880.

19. *Patriot,* March 21, 1872.

20. Ibid., June 9, 1880, June 20, 1871.

21. *Patriot and Times,* September 3, July 30, 1868; *Patriot,* July 18, 1872, November 13, 1878, September 22, 1880.

22. *Patriot,* August 18, 1880, June 16, 1870, April 25, 1872, May 1, 1878, March 21, 1872.

23. Ibid., July 12, 1851.

24. The legislature did grant certain towns this privilege, and by 1860 twenty-three towns could prohibit the retailing of liquor within their boundaries (Johnson, *Antebellum North Carolina,* 169, 153).

25. *Patriot,* July 8, 1848; *Weekly Message,* December 18, 1851; Speech by J. L. Gorrell on the First Anniversary of Temperance Division, 1852, Ralph Gorrell Papers, SHC.

26. Robert N. Caldwell to D. F. Caldwell, December 14, 1852, David Frank Caldwell Papers, SHC; Ann Wiley to Calvin Wiley, November 24, 1852, Calvin Wiley Papers, SHC.

27. The temperance resolution was signed by A. Weatherly, M. Cunningham, and A. P. McDonnell. A copy was sent to D. F. Caldwell, July 4, 1854, Caldwell Papers; the licensing of liquor establishments was delineated in Blackwell P. Robinson and Alexander B. Stoesen, *History of Guilford County, North Carolina, U.S.A., to 1980 A.D.* (Greensboro: Guilford County Bicentennial Commission and the Guilford County American Revolution Bicentennial Commission, 1981), 76.

28. The years of the prohibition crisis, 1878–82, saw the most women in public affairs, and even then they numbered only 37 out of a total of 538. Besides prohibition, women participated in public affairs during the thirty-five years of this investigation only in the war effort and social organizations like the monument associations, the Grange, and the county teachers' association. Some women ran their own businesses, including Frances M. Bumpass, an editor, and Susan Dick Weir, an artist and daughter of John M. Dick and wife of the local druggist who managed the Greensboro Mutual Life Insurance Company. Others such as Delphinia Mendenhall pressured prominent public officials through private correspondence and performed individual acts of courage like the continued transportation of slaves to freedom during the war. But formal participation in public affairs remained largely closed to women except on those rare occasions when extraordinary

times permitted uncommon actions. War and prohibition constituted such crises, although even in the case of prohibition the number of female powerholders was minuscule in comparison to males.

29. *Greensboro Times,* February 20, 1858, October 15, 20, 1859.

30. The major difference between charter and regular members seemed to be in the amount of fees paid. Male charter members paid an initiation fee of $3 and female charter members $.50, but once the Grange was formed, men had to pay an initial fee of $5 and women, $3 (D. W. Forbis to Calvin H. Wiley, September 30, 1873, Wiley Papers).

31. *Patriot,* November 27, 1878.

32. J. W. Albright to L. L. Polk, September 16, 1879, Leonidas L. Polk Papers, SHC.

33. James W. Albright, "Guilford County: Its Resources," ca. 1885, NCC, 4.

34. Information concerning both the Co-operative Business Company, designed to help workers purchase homes and to encourage manufacturing, and the tobacco association, created to promote Greensboro as a tobacco market, was limited to brief announcements in the press about the formation of each. Both may have suffered when individuals instrumental to their development left the community. Although a number of blacks and whites, including Albion Tourgée, were involved in the Co-operative Business Company, the company's president, William A. Caldwell, moved to Tennessee in 1873, and Eugene Morehead, instigator of the tobacco association, moved to Durham shortly after launching the tobacco organization (*Patriot,* September 16, 30, 1869, February 8, 1872).

35. Broadside dated December 1, 1875, Caldwell Papers.

36. Ethel Stephens Arnett, *Greensboro, North Carolina* (Chapel Hill: University of North Carolina Press, 1955), 437–38.

37. *Patriot,* June 26, 1878. Wilson & Shober was involved, for example, with Albion Tourgée's N.C. Handle Company, which collapsed in 1874. See Tourgée's Address to the Stockholders, August 10, 1873, Albion Winegar Tourgée Papers, SHC.

38. John B. Wilson, "The Organization, Operation and Demise of the Greensboro Mutual Life Insurance and Trust Company," John B. Wilson Papers, NCDAH.

39. *New North State,* February 1, 1872.

Chapter 3

1. *Greensboro Times,* June 23, 1860.

2. Most of the celebrations were run by whites in honor of whites, but two years after the war, blacks publicly celebrated the Fourth of July in Greensboro, and they did so again in 1871. They also celebrated Emancipation Proclamation Day on at least two occasions, but it was the initial Fourth of July celebration that elicited the most comment. See WCP to William L. Scott, July 5, 1867, and John

Payne to Scott, July 5, 1867, William L. Scott Papers, DUL. Unfortunately, newspapers listed by name only the whites involved in these affairs, although most of the participants were black and some of them undoubtedly served in leadership capacities (Documents 1249 and 1869, Albion Winegar Tourgée Papers, SHC; *Patriot,* July 6, 1871; *New North State,* January 4, 1872).

3. Railroad promotion was classified as a decision until a railroad company was established; a railroad company was categorized as an organization within the economic institution.

4. Unlike modern studies, which use the decision-making approach to identify leaders and must select certain key decisions on which to focus, this investigation included every issue that surfaced in Guilford.

5. In 1850, some newspapers outside the county asked why Wesleyan Methodist minister Jesse McBride was not indicted in Guilford for circulating incendiary material, and in 1860 the *North Carolina Standard* charged that a number of antislavery sympathizers resided around Jamestown and High Point. This same newspaper alleged that Hinton Rowan Helper's book, *The Impending Crisis,* was highly in demand in John Gilmer's congressional district and that most abolitionists arrested in North Carolina were seized in this area. Additionally, the *Goldsboro Rough* claimed that Helper dedicated his *Impending Crisis* to John Morehead, and the *Fayetteville Observer* spoke of a proslavery book that Morehead allegedly wrote (*Patriot,* November 9, 16, 1850, January 1, 1860).

6. After George's accidental drowning in 1860, Delphinia continued to resettle slaves in Ohio, and she even managed to get several through the lines during the war years, removing some as late as the fall of 1864 (Delphinia E. Mendenhall to Judith A. Crenshaw, November 28, 1864, Hobbs and Mendenhall Papers, SHC).

7. *Patriot and Flag,* March 20, 1858.

8. Gilmer to Thurlow Weed, January 12, 1861, Weed Papers, DUL; *Patriot,* November 19, 1858.

9. Wiley objected specifically to the separation of family members, the refusal to permit slaves to learn to read, and the placement of masters above the law, but his objections were voiced in 1865 in response to General Robert E. Lee's proposal that slaves be used in the war effort, which Wiley adamantly opposed. Slaves were already "half-savages," Wiley argued, and to expose them to the evils of army camp life could only result in "robbery, murder, rape and every other crime to which they would be so prone." Wiley's chief concern was to prevent them from serving in the army and bringing "ruin and degradation" in their wake (Thomas Caldwell to D. F. Caldwell, December 8, 1850, David Frank Caldwell Papers, SHC; C. H. Wiley to Zebulon Vance, January 24, 1865, Zebulon B. Vance Papers, NCDAH).

10. Smith, the pastor called to the First Presbyterian Church in 1859, schooled three of his slaves, along with his three sons, all of whom eventually became ministers, but one Sunday early in the war he wished to read a letter that endorsed slavery so strongly that the church elders feared the "large colored audience . . . might misconstrue it," and they ultimately persuaded him to wait until the midweek prayer meeting to read it. James R. McLean, a Democrat and early seces-

sionist, described a war sermon by Smith that he found "a little too ferocious for the pulpit," and D. F. Caldwell, who adamantly opposed the war, became "disgusted" with Smith over his strong war stance (Sketch of Jacob Henry Smith's Life, Charles Van Noppen Papers, DUL; Mrs. J. Henry Smith to Sister Kay, January 18, 1862, Mary Kelly Smith Papers, NCDAH; James R. McLean to William L. Scott, November 17, 1861, and Charles E. Shober to William L. Scott, November 10, 1861, William L. Scott Papers, DUL).

11. Nereus Mendenhall's Diary, March 4, 1851, Hobbs and Mendenhall Papers, SHC.

12. An overview of Wesleyan Methodist ministers and the furor surrounding them appears in Guion G. Johnson, *Ante-bellum North Carolina: A Social History* (Chapel Hill: University of North Carolina Press, 1937), 572–81.

13. Nereus Mendenhall's Diary, April 17, 1851.

14. Nereus Mendenhall believed that the *Patriot,* under the editorship of Lyndon Swaim (no relation to William of earlier years), misrepresented the circumstances of the McBride meeting and appeared "to savor too much of the mob spirit." Swaim maintained that he was just reporting the facts (Mendenhall's Diary, April 20, 26, May 21, 1851).

15. Ibid., May 3, 1851.

16. Ballard's conviction convinced D. Frank Caldwell that law and order could not be preserved at this time (*Patriot,* May 3, 1851; Mendenhall's Diary, May 19, 1851).

17. Mendenhall's Diary, May 20, 25, 1851; *Patriot,* May 24, 1851.

18. J. A. Gilmer to Calvin Wiley, July 19, 1851, Calvin Wiley Papers, SHC; Mendenhall's Diary, July 30, 1851.

19. *Patriot and Flag,* March 20, 1858; *Patriot,* September 3, 1858.

20. Noble J. Tolbert, "Daniel Worth: Tar Heel Abolitionist," *North Carolina Historical Review* 39 (July 1962): 284–304.

21. Tolbert suggested in his article on Worth that the pair was frightened by the news that four other counties in Worth's circuit were seeking his arrest, but this explanation seems implausible because again in the spring Bowman, along with four other individuals, cosigned another bond for Worth, and by this time Worth had already been convicted in both Randolph and Guilford counties.

Bowman, a middle-aged farmer with property valued at $6,000 in 1860 but no slaves, was a magistrate. The twenty-nine-year-old Hodgin came from a modest but respectable farm family who had been in Guilford many years. After the war, the Unionist Hodgin became active in Republican circles at the local level and served for a while as secretary of the state association. He attempted, in conjunction with Albion Tourgée, to found a newspaper in Greensboro shortly after the war and in 1880 became a public school teacher.

22. These remarks, along with other details of Worth's trials in Asheboro and Greensboro appear in Tolbert, "Daniel Worth."

23. Tappan to Gorrell, April 20, 1860, Ralph Gorrell Papers, SHC.

24. Guilford County Superior Court Minutes, Spring Term 1860.

25. Tolbert, "Daniel Worth," 302.

26. J. D. Winslow to Ralph Gorrell, September 11, 1860, Gorrell Papers.

27. Worth to Reverend G. W. Bainum, March 31, 1860, Jonathan Worth Papers, NCDAH.

28. *Times,* November 3, 1860.

29. Worth to Reverend G. W. Bainum, March 31, 1860, Worth Papers, and Vance to Calvin H. Wiley, February 3, 1865, Wiley Papers.

30. *Patriot,* March 21, 7, 1861.

31. William Scott to Levi Scott, March 3, 1861, Scott Papers; "John A. Gilmer," Folder 23, Zeb Vance Walser Papers, SHC; Gilmer to William L. Scott, October 20, 1861, Scott Papers.

32. Smith to Gorrell, May 4, 1861, Gorrell Papers.

33. Ibid. Despite these charges, Murrow, who had served as a tax lister and a pollholder in 1860, managed to qualify as a magistrate three months after Smith's allegations were made. He also served on the local school committee in 1862, 1869, and 1878. By the latter years he had become active in Republican circles, serving as a delegate to the Republican Congressional Convention in 1872 and as vice-president of the County Committee on Permanent Organization in 1880. These activities constituted a departure from the prewar years, when he played no discernible role in politics.

34. *Greensboro Times,* March 9, 1861.

35. *Patriot,* April 25, 1861; *Greensboro Times,* July 27, 1861.

36. *Greensboro Times,* July 20, 1861.

37. Ibid., April 27, 1861.

38. *Semi-Weekly Patriot,* June 1861.

39. *Greensboro Times,* May 8, 1861; *Patriot,* February 3, 1860, March 21, April 25, 1861; *Semi-Weekly Patriot,* June 4, 1861; Pleas and Quarter Session Minutes, August 1861.

40. James R. McLean to William L. Scott, September 18, 1861, Scott Papers.

41. William Scott to Levi Scott, August 22, November 7, 1861; Cousin Cess to William Scott, September 3, 1861; John A. Gilmer to William Scott, September 13, 1861; James R. McLean to William Scott, September 18, 1861; and M. D. Smith to William Scott, November 10, 1861, Scott Papers.

42. McLean to William L. Scott, October 20, November 17, December 26, 1861, Scott Papers; Pinckney Oliver, Guilford County Public School Register, 1857–65, DUL.

43. McLean to Scott, December 26, 1861, Scott Papers; James Sloan to Ralph Gorrell, November 26, 1861, Gorrell Papers.

44. McPherson to N. D. Woody, February 28, 1862, Newton D. Woody Papers, DUL.

45. C. A. Boon to William L. Scott, December 18, 1861, Scott Papers.

46. McPherson to Woody, February 12, 1862, Woody Papers.

47. McLean to William L. Scott, December 26, 1861, Scott Papers.

48. N. J. McLean to William L. Scott, February 24, 1862, Scott Papers. Conscription was not enacted by the Confederate government until April 1862, but the

North Carolina legislature had passed a law apportioning volunteers to be raised among the various counties in the fall of 1861. As the procurement operated in February in Guilford, two militia regiments, one in the northern portion of the county and one in the southern part, met separately and members were given an opportunity to volunteer their services. If the required number was not secured through volunteering, the names of privates were then drawn to meet the quota demanded from the county. Officers were omitted from the draft, as were public officials.

49. Benbow to Albion Tourgée, March 29, 1867, Tourgée Papers.

50. The encounter of the Grays with Yankees in the fall of 1863 probably occurred at Fredericksburg (Mrs. Jacob Henry Smith to Sister Mary, October 26, 1863, Smith Papers; "Autobiography of James W. Albright," Vol. 1, October 24, 1863, July 5, 1864, James W. Albright Books, SHC).

51. F. Memory Mitchell, *Legal Aspects of Conscription and Exemption in North Carolina* (Chapel Hill: University of North Carolina Press, 1965), 59–64, 82, 89.

52. John Gilmer believed this was likely to happen, however, and this possibility explained in part his opposition to a convention plan (Gilmer to Vance, January 5, 1864, Vance Papers).

53. A letter by Mrs. Smith dated February 3, 1864, was reprinted in Blackwell P. Robinson and Alexander R. Stoesen, *History of Guilford County, North Carolina, U.S.A. to 1980, A.D.* (Greensboro: Guilford County Bicentennial Commission and the Guilford County American Revolution Bicentennial Commission, 1981), 96; Long's comment appeared in the *Patriot,* February 4, 1864.

54. Caldwell, Smith noted, sat down "in a perfect fury." Although no names were given in Smith's description in Robinson and Stoesen, *History of Guilford County,* names and actions were pieced together from Smith's letter of February 3 and Long's account in the *Patriot.*

55. Wiley to Jonathan Worth, July 6, 1865, Worth Papers.

56. Caldwell to Hon. John Sherman, March 8, 1867, in James A. Padgett, ed., "Reconstruction Letters from North Carolina," *North Carolina Historical Review* 18 (July 1941): 278–300.

Chapter 4

1. These periods are 1848–52, 1858–62, 1868–72, and 1878–82.

2. Socioeconomic variables incorporated in the analyses were those previous scholars had deemed important in determining the attainment of influence. Not all were available in the census manuscripts in all four periods, however. Those available and used included age, occupation, and place of birth in 1850, 1860, 1870, and 1880; real property in dollar value in 1850, 1860, and 1870; number of slaves in 1850 and 1860; personal property in dollar value in 1860 and 1870; and residence within the county in 1870 and 1880.

3. Among female powerholders, those who participated in wartime organizations such as the ones that distributed food or Bibles derived from a narrower

spectrum of society than prohibitionists. The spouses of the latter included a carriagemaker, a federal government official, and a couple of farmers, although most were professionals and businessmen. In contrast, virtually all of the women who led wartime organizations resided in wealthy slaveholding households over which a male businessman or professional presided. The Quaker origins of some of the prohibitionists explained in part the greater diversity in their socioeconomic attributes, for all resided in either the predominantly Quaker township of Friendship or Greensboro. Like their male counterparts who participated in public affairs, the vast majority were native southerners with only three of thirty-seven born outside the South, and they came from both Republican and Democratic households.

4. The rate of expansion for the population as a whole was particularly slow in the 1850s, when both the white and free black population declined slightly. Only a 6 percent increase in the number of slaves produced an overall growth rate of .08 percent in this decade. Attracted by reports that Guilford offered a less hostile climate toward newly freed persons than many North Carolina counties, blacks contributed significantly to a 4 percent rise in the population in the 1860s; an increase in the white population was primarily responsible for another 4 percent growth rate in the 1870s. In actual numbers, the population expanded from 19,754 in 1850 to 23,585 in 1880. For figures on the participation rates in northern communities, see Stuart M. Blumin, *The Urban Threshold* (Chicago: University of Chicago Press, 1976), 171–72, and Walter S. Glazer, "Participation and Power: Voluntary Associations and Functional Organization of Cincinnati in 1840," *Historical Methods Newsletter* 5 (September 1972): 151–68. Glazer concluded that nineteenth-century voluntary associations were largely vehicles for leadership recruitment rather than catalysts of democracy.

5. The term "natural" is used because scattergrams indicated sharp decreases in the number of individuals earning total scores around the demarcation lines. For example, 50 people scored between 5 and 9 in 1850, and 53 persons obtained points between 10 and 19, but only 20 people earned between 20 and 39 points. Ten then obtained between 40 and 59 and 4 secured 60 or more. Similar circumstances existed at the bottom end of the scale with 184 persons scoring 4 points or less in 1850, and 50, as noted above, earning between 5 and 9. Because these conditions existed in all four periods, 4 was designated the demarcation line between low and medium powerholders and 19 the cutoff point between medium and high powerholders.

6. See, for example, Floyd Hunter, *Community Power Structure* (Chapel Hill: University of North Carolina Press, 1953), and Robert A. Dahl, *Who Governs? Democracy and Power in an American City* (New Haven: Yale University Press, 1961).

7. Gilmer to Z. B. Vance, October 14, 1865, Zebulon B. Vance Papers, NCDAH.

8. F tests (to the 5 percent level) indicated that statistically significant variation occurred in the scores of high powerholders in the categories of public office, partisan activities, prestigious affairs, and decision making during the thirty-five years covered by the investigation.

9. A nonparametric test of independence was applied to each of the contingency tables formed by the cross-tabulation of power and the socioeconomic variables, but Chi-square values obtained from these tests did not weigh heavily in the analysis because the main purpose of tests of statistical significance is to determine the extent to which one's sample is representative of a total population. Such tests were of limited importance at best for this study because, as explained in Chapter 2, samples were used only three times in the entire analysis. Thus the powerholders included in it represented virtually the entire universe of leaders, not a random sample.

10. Samuel M. Kipp III, "Urban Growth and Social Change in the South, 1870–1920: Greensboro, North Carolina, as a Case Study" (Ph.D. dissertation, Princeton University, 1974), 12–17. The number of farms in the community and average farm size were calculated by Kipp.

11. *Patriot*, July 22, 1869.

12. Because some high powerholders either changed occupations during their lifetime or had several occupations simultaneously, categorization in Table 7 was not always clear-cut. John Morehead was listed in the census in 1850 as a manufacturer, but he was described as an attorney in 1860. Both times, he was a large landowner and agrarian as well. Similarly, Jed Harper Lindsay was called a farmer in 1860 and a merchant in 1870. D. W. C. Benbow, also a merchant in 1870, and Julius A. Gray, a banker in the same year, were both labeled farmers in 1880. Individuals were categorized in Table 7 as they were styled in the census within the five-year period in which they were high powerholders, but even if all had been classified as they were in each of the previous censuses in which they appeared with a different occupation, the direction of change observable in Table 7 would not have been altered. If John Morehead had been a manufacturer rather than an attorney in 1860, professionals would still have had a slight edge over businessmen and farmers in that year. Similarly, if Jed Lindsay had been a farmer rather than a merchant in 1870 and Benbow and Gray businessmen instead of farmers in 1880, the preponderance of attorneys among large powerholders in 1870 and 1880 would not have been altered. Regardless, then, of the categorization procedure for Table 7, the most significant change it showed was the declining importance of businessmen and the rising role of professionals in the exercise of a large amount of influence. In 1880, a brickmason, James Deans, and a laborer, Harmon Unthank, became the first black powerholders to join the high power category. Besides Deans and Unthank, those classified in the "Other" category included Frances L. Simpson, whose occupation was unknown, and John Wadington, a surveyor, in 1850, along with Peter Adams, Sr., who was sixty-eight years old and retired by 1870.

13. The "Other" occupational category was omitted from Table 8 because the paucity of people in it rendered averages meaningless. Means for the census year 1880 could not be calculated because real and personal propertyholdings were not included as a part of the population schedules in that year.

14. John D. Scott to William Scott, June 1, 1857, William L. Scott Papers, DUL.

15. Although he later became an editor, Duffy was labeled in 1870 as he was in the census, an attorney, and thus a professional rather than a businessman.

16. Sloan to Gorrell, November 26, 1861, Ralph Gorrell Papers, SHC.

17. Among these families, John Motley Morehead married Ann Elizabeth Lindsay, and John's brother, James Turner Morehead, wed Ann's sister, Mary Teas Lindsay. Ann and Mary were sisters of Jeduthan Harper Lindsay and Jesse Harper Lindsay. The Moreheads and Lindsays were later bound again when Emma Victoria Morehead, the daughter of John M. Morehead and Ann Elizabeth, married Julius A. Gray. Julius's maternal grandfather was Jeduthan Harper, apparently an ancestor of Jeduthan Harper Lindsay. D. F. Caldwell and his four brothers, all of whom were powerholders at one time or another, were also related to the Lindsays by marriage. This occurred when Samuel C. Caldwell, D. F.'s uncle, took as his bride in his second marriage Elizabeth Lindsay, the aunt of Jeduthan, Jesse, Ann Elizabeth, and Mary Teas Lindsay.

Once inaugurated, the trend of intermarriages among wealthy Guilford families continued. The Caldwells, Lindsays, and Moreheads were tied to the Gilmers by the wartime marriage of Sally Lindsay, the daughter of Jesse, and John A. Gilmer, Jr., and another daughter of John Gilmer, Sr., and Juliana Paisley Gilmer, Hattie P., married Peter H. Adams, the eldest son of the affluent, self-made businessman, Peter Adams. In addition to D. F. Caldwell's brothers, Andrew C., Thomas, Robert N., and William Addison, other powerholders related to the Moreheads, Lindsays, Caldwells, Gilmers, and Adamses included Letitia Harper Morehead and Eugene Lindsay Morehead, the children of John M. Morehead and Ann Elizabeth Lindsay Morehead; Robert Lindsay Morehead, James Turner Morehead, Jr., and Joseph Morehead, the sons of James T. Morehead and Mary Teas Lindsay; Robert Lindsay and Robert G. Lindsay, the father and brother, of Jeduthan, Jesse, Ann Elizabeth, and Mary Teas Lindsay; Robert C. Lindsay, the first cousin of Jed and Jesse and their sisters; Joseph W. Gilmer, the brother of John A. Gilmer, Sr.; and James Addison Stewart, Robert M. Sloan, and Robert W. Glenn, the brothers-in-law of John A. Gilmer. Not surprisingly, D. F. Caldwell's niece, whose family moved from Guilford to Tennessee after the war, took for granted that her uncle would be invited to Eugene Morehead's wedding. The elaborate network of kinship ties eventually led D. F. to conclude, "There is too much family favoritism in all our [official] appointments" (Caldwell to Jonathan Worth, September 16, 1866, Jonathan Worth Papers, NCDAH).

18. Levi Scott to William Scott, October 12, 1856, Scott Papers.

19. Nereus Mendenhall's Diary, 1851, Hobbs and Mendenhall Family Papers, SHC; Charles E. Shober to Bryan Grimes, January 30, 1860, Bryan Grimes Papers, NCDAH.

20. This was the case, even though the mean score in decision making was lower for influential leaders in this year than at any other time (see Table 4).

21. In Table 9, the total R Square values indicate the total amount of variation in power scores that a combination of all of the independent variables explained in a given census year. In 1850, for example, 34 percent of the variation in power scores was explained by a combination of real property, age, occupation, and place

of birth. The R Square change shows the percentage of change that is produced in R Square by the addition of each of the independent variables, controlling for the effect of the other independent variables. Thus real property accounted for 31 percent of the variation in power scores in 1850, while age explained an additional 0.9 percent of the variation; occupation, an additional 3 percent, and place of birth, an additional .01 percent. I used a computerized regression program from Norman H. Nie et al., *Statistical Package for the Social Sciences,* 2d ed. (New York: McGraw-Hill, 1975), whereby the variable that caused the most variation in power scores entered first. Since in 1870 occupation accounted for a higher proportion of variation than any of the other variables and was thus entered first, the drop in real property may be slightly exaggerated. The decline in 1860 was also large, however, when real property was entered first. If two of these variables had been highly correlated, the changes contributed by each variable to the total R Square would not necessarily have been accurate because the first of the two highly correlated variables entered into the regression equation would have explained most of the variation in power and the second would have explained very little. This problem of multicollinearity was avoided because none of the independent variables were highly correlated. Personal property and slaveholdings were removed in advance by the researcher from the analysis precisely because they were both highly correlated with real property. Real property also offered the advantage of being available in 1850, 1860, and 1870, whereas slaveholdings existed only for 1850 and 1860 and personal property was available only for 1860 and 1870.

22. As in the case of Table 9, in explaining the amount of power variation produced by a given independent variable, all of the other independent variables were controlled for in Table 10.

Chapter 5

1. It was not just the most influential attorneys who were wealthy. John M. Dick, who at age seventy exercised little power in the 1858–62 years, owned $27,000 in real estate and $45,000 in personal property, including twenty slaves. John Morehead's brother, James T. Morehead, with 9 points on the power scale in 1860, was the largest slaveholder in the county with more than one hundred slaves and $55,000 in real estate.

2. *Patriot,* February 28, 1852.

3. *North State,* July 18, 1881.

4. Morehead's Blandwood was described as a "delightful suburban seat" in retrospect by Judge Kerr and quoted in Bettie D. Caldwell, ed., *Founders and Builders of Greensboro* (Greensboro: Jos. J. Stone, 1925), 50.

5. Morehead's efforts to secure transportation facilities are described in "John M. Morehead," Zeb Vance Walser Papers, SHC. Additionally, Burton Alva Konkle offers a detailed chronicle in *John Motley Morehead and the Development of North Carolina, 1796–1866* (Philadelphia: William J. Campbell, 1922).

6. Speaker Calvin Graves was not an eastern legislator but from the northern

county of Caswell, a community that stood to gain from a north-south line, and it was because the North Carolina Railroad superseded the Danville connection that his constituents were angry.

7. *Patriot,* November 24, 1849.

8. Dick to Reid, June 30, 1851, David S. Reid Papers, NCDAH.

9. Nereus Mendenhall's Diary, 1851, vol. 7, Hobbs and Mendenhall Family Papers, SHC; A. C. Raboteau to D. F. Caldwell, August 18, 1849, David Frank Caldwell Papers, SHC.

10. Levi M. Scott to William L. Scott, November 23, 1856, William L. Scott Papers, DUL.

11. In fact, the Coalfields Road was not completed, and in 1870, Greensboro leaders still struggled to make their town its terminus. Wilmington representatives remained opposed to the plan because of their "hatred of Greensboro," according to one observer (J. M. Morehead to David L. Swain, February 20, 1859, Swain Papers; A. W. Ingold to D. F. Caldwell, May 15, 1870, Caldwell Papers).

12. Morehead to Swain, February 20, 1859, David L. Swain Papers, NCDAH.

13. *Patriot,* February 24, June 30, July 7, July 21, 1849.

14. The estimate that half the initial $60,000 appropriation was in the form of small subscriptions was made in the *Patriot,* November 24, 1850.

15. Hillsboro Coal Mining and Transportation Company, June 14, 1853, Caldwell Papers.

16. Hugh Waddell to D. F. Caldwell, April 30, 1853, Caldwell Papers.

17. Out of a total of 143,970 shares, most stockholders held less than 3,000. Gilmer, in comparison, possessed 20,000 shares. Only he and one other North Carolinian owned enough stock to become directors of the company. Of the remaining seven directors, six were from New York and one from Virginia.

18. Morehead's commercial interests in Morehead City and on the Dan River are mentioned by Dwight Billings in *Planters and the Making of a "New South": Class, Politics, and Development in North Carolina, 1865–1900* (Chapel Hill: University of North Carolina Press, 1979), 79; the Rockingham County operation is discussed in James E. Gardner, *Eden: Past and Present, 1880–1980* (Eden, N.C.: Friends of the Eden Public Library, 1982), 1–7.

19. George C. Mendenhall's Will, dated 1859 and probated 1860, Guilford County Wills, NCDAH.

20. Mendenhall had added several grist mills to one inherited from his father, but one parcel of land was termed the "Cording Machine tract." The "other buildings" probably included a blacksmith shop, harness shop, and tannery mentioned among Mendenhall's taxable property in 1852. See lists of taxable property for 1851 and 1852, George C. Mendenhall's Register Book, vol. 5, as well as his will.

21. Charles M. Haar argues in *The Golden Age of American Law* (New York: George Braziller, 1965), that most U.S. attorneys believed before 1860 that reform had been achieved in the American Revolution and that the task of their profession was to conserve; see pages 11–12 in particular. Some of the social conservatism of Guilford attorneys probably derived from their Whig partisan connections, how-

ever, since Democratic lawyers in antebellum North Carolina favored free suffrage. For the important role played by party politics in influencing the stances of leaders in antebellum North Carolina, see Marc W. Kruman, *Parties and Politics in North Carolina, 1836–1865* (Baton Rouge: Louisiana State University Press, 1983).

22. Weir to Ralph Gorrell, October 2, 1855, Ralph Gorrell Papers, SHC.

23. John B. Wilson, who recently investigated Greensboro Mutual for the Pilot Life Insurance Company, termed the business interests of the company's directors "manifold," and he commented specifically on the advantages of having men like Caldwell and Gilmer in the state legislature ("The Organization, Operation, and Demise of the Greensboro Mutual Life Insurance and Trust Company," John B. Wilson Papers, NCDAH).

24. Jonathan F. Baylin, "An Historical Study of Residential Development in Greensboro, 1808–1965" (Chapel Hill: Department of City and Regional Planning, University of North Carolina, 1968).

25. The construction of the Female College and Edgeworth Seminary south of Market Street enhanced the area west of the city and helped make it into a prestigious residential area before the war (Baylin, "Historical Study of Residential Development," 20).

26. This area provided a "natural" location for freedmen after the war, according to Baylin, but Warnersville, a tract purchased by northern Quaker Yardley Warner for resale to blacks, was built in south Greensboro.

27. Nellie M. Rowe, "Ante-Bellum Homes of Greensboro," ca. 1908, NCC.

28. Baylin, "Historical Study of Residential Development."

29. Rowe, "Ante-Bellum Homes."

30. With two rooms along the front separated from a large center hall by folding doors, Gorrell could readily create "a great reception hall" for large gatherings (ibid.).

31. Baylin, "Historical Study of Residential Development," 17.

32. Rowe, "Ante-Bellum Homes."

33. Haar, *Golden Age*, 331.

34. Warnersville consisted of about thirty acres with plots sold in half-acres to freedmen; Shieldstown, developed by northern investor Joseph Shields, included about fifty acres. Shieldstown was located behind the large estates on Asheboro Street and extended to Warnersville (Baylin, "Historical Study of Residential Development," 38–41).

35. James W. Albright, "Guilford County: Its Resources," ca. 1885, NCC.

36. Although the total area owned by Caldwell was never specified, one tract of a thousand acres was mentioned. A white tenant, Bynum farmed Caldwell's land at least a decade after the war, and scattered references suggested that Bynum's father may have preceded him in the job; see Caldwell Papers. The sale of Mendenhall's nursery to Tourgée is mentioned in Otto H. Olsen, *Carpetbagger's Crusade: The Life of Albion Winegar Tourgée* (Baltimore: Johns Hopkins Press, 1965), 28.

37. Levi Scott to William Scott, October 12, 1856, Scott Papers.

38. John D. Scott to William Scott, June 1, 1856, ibid.

39. Caldwell especially praised Benbow for constructing in Greensboro "the largest and handsomest Hotel in the state" (Caldwell to Calvin Wiley, October 21, 1870, Calvin Wiley Papers, SHC).

40. When Republicans took over as county commissioners in 1869, they asked the public for suggestions as to how to retire the large debt they encountered, and they themselves suggested a special tax for that purpose. The *Patriot* concurred with this suggestion (*Patriot*, November 4, 1869). Although the county owed at least one person from as far back as 1857, the major portion of the debt derived from the war decade; still, the Republican commissioners showed no hesitancy in trying to repay it. In 1870, when Democratic commissioners assumed office, their figures for county indebtedness did not agree with those of the former Republican Board of Commissioners. Rather than attacking the former board, however, the *Patriot* acknowledged in a supplement printed in February 1872 that ascertaining the total indebtedness of the county was not an easy task.

41. These joint efforts occurred both in the years 1868–72 and 1878–82. See *North State,* July 4, 1872, and January 27, 1881.

42. Caldwell's interest in lime quarries and salt mining is indicated in D. H. Starbuck to Caldwell, 1853, and G. W. Swepson to Caldwell, November 14, 1868, Caldwell Papers. The hotel interest is mentioned in George W. May to Caldwell, February 12, 1870, ibid.

43. Julius L. Gorrell informed his brother Henry that Governor Morehead wanted their father, Ralph, to search for iron ore on his property and establish a foundry. As Morehead saw it, there was "an everlasting future" in it (Julius L. Gorrell to Henry Gorrell, June 11, 1862, Ralph Gorrell Papers, SHC). Caldwell indicated an interest in the incorporation of an iron manufacturing company in Guilford in 1870 (John D. Gribble to Caldwell, March 14, 1870, and David Hodgin to Caldwell, January 24, 1870, Caldwell Papers).

44. Gardner, *Eden,* 6–7.

45. A fact that Billings omitted when he drew distinctions between the origins of textile and tobacco manufacturers in his book *Planters and the Making of the "New South."*

46. Eugene Morehead's Diary, SHC, March 7, 18, 1871; *Patriot,* February 8, 1872.

47. Wilson stressed the importance of Weir's death in the company's failure ("Organization, Operation, and Demise").

Chapter 6

1. Gilmer to Wiley, August 30, September 5, 1856; Caldwell to Wiley, October 21, 1870, Calvin Wiley Papers, SHC. The evidence of Wiley's ghostwriting for Cunningham is unmistakable. Wiley not only composed but also offered suggestions on delivery of the remarks, and he drafted personal, as well as public, statements. Even an inquiry by Cunningham to the owner of a neighboring plantation asking about the quality of work performed by Cunningham's overseers was

in Wiley's handwriting. See John Wilson Cunningham Papers, SHC, for the quantity and range of Wiley's work.

2. Wiley to John Gilmer, April 27, 1865, Wiley Papers. In writing in search of a job before the war, Wiley, who, as Caldwell phrased it, had had "a hard scuffle *for life* or rather *bread*," still insisted, "I will not consent to be made a laborious drudge in some office requiring no intellect, seeing political asses appointed over me." "I must be," he continued, "a free agent and a free thinker" (Wiley to D. M. Barringer, December 16, 1848, Daniel M. Barringer Papers, SHC).

3. *Raleigh Standard,* June 14, May 24, 1865.

4. Although leaders at the Union meetings were not included in the power scale and thus were not analyzed systematically because these affairs did not occur in the 1868–72 time period, a cursory investigation suggested that the meetings held in opposition to the one at Greensboro were not led by the poor and inarticulate. Dr. Robert C. Lindsay, a cousin of Jed and Jesse Lindsay of Greensboro, guided the High Point assembly, and Dr. William P. Pugh, a High Point physician who lost approximately $10,000 as a result of the war, played a key role in both the High Point and Bloomington affairs. Reverend George W. Welker, the pastor of Brick Church for more than twenty years at the time of the war, was very involved in the Pleasant Union meeting, and he was assisted by such Unionists as John Corsbie, a blacksmith, who officiated as superintendent of common schools in 1849 and served on the Board of Superintendents from 1858 through 1862. Corsbie was among the wealthiest 15 percent of the community in 1860.

5. *Raleigh Standard,* June 12, 1865.

6. Presumably, the latter clause meant that they could support politicians such as Holden, who withdrew support for the war as the conflict progressed.

7. *Raleigh Standard,* June 12, 1865.

8. McPherson to Woody, June 25, 1865; Corsbie to Woody, June 23, 1865, Newton D. Woody Papers, DUL.

9. D. M. Corsbie to P. W. Corsbie, July 24, 1865; McPherson to Woody, September 3, 1865, ibid.

10. Mendenhall to Worth, March 31, 1866, in J. G. de Roulhac Hamilton, *The Correspondence of Jonathan Worth,* 2 vols. (Raleigh: Edwards & Broughton, 1909), 1:523–24; Sherwood to B. S. Hedrick, March 31, 1866, Benjamin Sherwood Hedrick Papers, SHC; Worth to Gilmer, September 4, 1866, Jonathan Worth Papers, NCDAH.

11. Notes from a speech in Pennsylvania, 1866, Document 686, Albion Winegar Tourgée Papers, SHC.

12. Otto H. Olsen, *Carpetbagger's Crusade: The Life of Albion Winegar Tourgée* (Baltimore: Johns Hopkins Press, 1965), 50.

13. Worth to Mendenhall, September 30, 1866; Worth to Gilmer, September 4, 1866; and Worth to editor of *Patriot,* September 10, 1866, Worth Papers.

14. Worth to Mendenhall, Dick, Gilmer, Settle, and Hiram C. Worth, December 14, 1867, in Hamilton, *Worth Correspondence,* 2:1085–86. Worth could not countenance a continued military presence in North Carolina because it implied

that officials like him were not managing affairs well enough to be kept in office and because he believed it made it more difficult to place the state on a sound financial footing.

15. Causey to Newton D. Woody, April 2, 17, 1865, Woody Papers.

16. Corsbie to Woody, May 13, 1868, Woody Papers; testimony of J. B. Summers, Alamance County, December 20, 1871, Tourgée Papers.

17. He was not responsible for the "ultra war tendency of Gov. Vance," Wiley insisted, but, instead, he had defended Holden when the "destructives" began to delude the wartime governor (Wiley to Worth, July 6, 1865, Worth Papers).

18. William L. Scott is discussed in this chapter and the following one along with other attorneys in the high power group in 1870, although his score of 18 was 2 points below the cutoff point of 20 for a high powerholder. Although Scott was not included among the eleven lawyers who emerged as large powerholders during the 1868–72 years in the previous chapter, he is included here because, as the only native Republican whose papers were available, the Scott data reveal a great deal about lawyers and politics in the community that cannot be found anywhere else, and a shortage of 2 points on the power scale was deemed insignificant in comparison to the insights to be gained from Scott's actions. Additionally, Scott was well on the way toward becoming a high powerholder when he became ill in the summer of 1871 and died a year later. Besides participating in numerous Republican affairs, Scott was active in the commemoration for John Gilmer and ran as an anticonvention candidate in 1871. He had also served as provisional mayor of Greensboro immediately following war, that is, before 1868–72, when his activities would have counted toward his power score. As indicated early in this work, the power scale was designed as a way of ascertaining the relative strength of various groups within the community; it was not intended to impose such a rigid mechanistic quality on the data that insights would be missed.

19. Gilmer to Vance, November 23, 1863, Vance Papers.

20. In July 1868, Republican Judge Thomas Settle informed fellow Republican R. M. Pearson that Scott had endorsed the Grant-Colfax ticket, and the following month he was admitted to inner Republican circles in Guilford. At that time, constitutional convention delegate and state legislator G. W. Welker indicated to Scott that he or fellow legislator Albion Tourgée would keep him informed on new legislative actions. He also urged Scott to take steps to secure a "strong hold" on local Republicans (Pearson to Scott, July 16, 1868; Welker to Scott, August 4, 1868, William L. Scott Papers, DUL).

21. Wiley to Worth, March 30, 1866, Worth Papers.

22. Gilmer to Worth, June 26, 1866; J. J. Jackson to Worth, August 4, 1866; Caldwell to Worth, August 4, 1866, Worth Papers.

23. Hugh Talmage Lefler and Albert Ray Newsome, *The History of a Southern State: North Carolina,* 3d ed. (Chapel Hill: University of North Carolina Press, 1973), 488.

24. Caldwell to Hon. John Sherman, March 8, 1867, in James A. Padgett, ed., "Reconstruction Letters from North Carolina," *North Carolina Historical Review* 18 (July 1941): 294–97.

25. Caldwell to Worth, July 31, August 4, 1866; J. J. Jackson to Worth, August 9, 1866, Worth Papers.

26. Thomas Settle and D. H. Starbuck, members of the Executive Committee on the Question of Another 5th Congressional Republican Convention, n.d., Tourgée Papers.

27. Caldwell to Worth, September 16, 1866, Worth Papers.

28. Many Unionists felt they should have been permitted to keep their slaves following the war, and Unionist-Republican John Corsbie explained to fellow Republican Newton Woody three years after the conflict that all of Woody's financial woes derived from black equality. Even white Republicans with the best of intentions sometimes behaved in a high-handed fashion toward their black allies. Thomas Settle's brother-in-law, R. M. Douglas, signed the name of black leader George M. Arnold on a petition without Arnold's knowledge, and Albion Tourgée developed a temporary "coolness" toward Afro-American Harmon Unthank when the attorney failed in his bid to secure the Fifth District congressional nomination in 1868 and determined that Unthank had not worked hard enough for him (Thomas B. Keogh to William L. Scott, January 16, 1872, Scott Papers; Unthank to Tourgée, July 22, 27, 1868, Tourgée Papers).

29. John Clapp to Woody, May 27, 1865, Woody Papers; Blackwell P. Robinson and Alexander R. Stoesen, *The History of Guilford County, North Carolina, U.S.A. to 1980 A.D.* (Greensboro: Guilford County Bicentennial Commission and the Guilford County American Revolution Bicentennial Commission, 1981), 119; A. Y. Headen to Ralph Gorrell, May 11, 1870, Gorrell Papers.

30. Dick's wife, a Virginia native, was reputedly the only woman in town to wear the latest style hats fashionable among the wives of northern officers following the conflict, and she was so delighted "with the kindness shown her and the general prosperity" that she experienced on a trip to the North that she was cured of all of her " 'rebel sympathies' " and wished to move to some northern state, according to her husband (Dick to Gov. T. D. Cox, July 6, 1867, in Padgett, ed., "Reconstruction Letters," 373–75).

31. Caldwell to Worth, September 16, 1866, Worth Papers; Hodgin to Tourgée, October 8, 1866, Tourgée Papers.

32. Worth to Caldwell, January 6, May 6, 1867, Caldwell Papers; Caldwell to Graham, March 7, 1871, August 25, 1868, William Alexander Graham Papers, SHC; *Patriot,* August 13, October 19, 1868, August 12, 1869.

33. William C. Harris makes this point in a forthcoming biography of William Woods Holden.

34. Caldwell to Worth, July 31, August 4, 9, 1866, Worth Papers.

35. Worth to Gilmer, September 8, 1866; Caldwell to Worth, September 16, November 2, 1866, Worth Papers.

36. Scott had had problems during his tenure in the army with an unruly local physician, A. P. McDaniel, who had attempted to attach himself to Scott's unit, and with Colonel W. W. Kirkland, who replaced Scott's first commander, Colonel J. M. Leach, when Leach resigned and returned home, but his decision to leave the Confederate ranks apparently stemmed from his dissatisfaction and that of his men

with conscription. As John Gilmer explained the situation to his brother, Colonel J. F. Gilmer, the various military companies were composed of "12 months men," who were in "a state of great disorganization & demoralization" and who elected captains and other officers who had little or no qualifications for their positions. Becoming convinced that he could not bring credit to himself and command his regiment, Scott resigned. In Scott's own words, he quit his post "by reason of the dissatisfaction of my regiment with the Conscript Act." Much to Gilmer's chagrin, his nephew John C. Gilmer elected to follow his colonel's example and resigned also (John A. Gilmer to Colonel J. F. Gilmer, August 24, 1862, Jeremy Francis Gilmer Papers, SHC).

37. For an indication of Scott's efforts to secure a position in the military, see Scott to Cole, May 29, 1862; Scott to Brigadier-General Gardner July 8, 1862; and A. J. Stafford to Scott, July 11, 1862, Scott Papers.

38. Scott acted in behalf of the petitioner in thirty of thirty-seven cases, but there was no way of knowing the total number of such cases prosecuted in his district, for only a fragment of the official records remained. Significantly, however, it was John Gilmer who defended a young miller and millwright in one of two cases that were always cited when exemptions were granted on account of trade. In the precedent-setting case, Scott prosecuted in behalf of the Confederacy (Guilford County, Civil War Papers, 1862–65, NCDAH).

Efforts to procure exemptions were far more common than oral tradition would have one believe. A report issued by the *Raleigh Register* for the year ending July 1863 showed that North Carolina supplied about 15,000 troops for the year (11,874 conscripts and between 3,000 and 4,000 volunteers) and that exemptions totaled 21,558. Indeed, efforts to procure exemptions were so commonplace and the liberality of North Carolina courts in granting them so great that F. Memory Mitchell, a former judge and attorney as well as a historian and editor, concluded that "the lack of wholehearted support is apparent throughout the legal opinions, and the backing by the Court of many citizens who appealed to its judges to support citizens in their thinking makes clearly evident the weakness of the Confederacy as a government" (Mitchell, *Legal Aspects of Conscription and Exemption in North Carolina* [Chapel Hill: University of North Carolina Press, 1965], 34–35).

Mrs. Smith, wife of the local Presbyterian minister, mentioned Scott as one of those involved in the peace meeting of February 1864, but he was not included in James A. Long's account in the *Patriot*. Smith's letter of February 3, 1864, was reprinted in Robinson and Stoesen, *History of Guilford County,* and Long's editorial appeared in the *Patriot* about February 3, 1864.

39. William Scott to Ella Scott, July 21, 1870, Scott Papers.

40. Scott, "Life of Lieutenant Colonel C. C. Cole," October 2, 1865, Scott Papers.

41. Scott, "Our Duties and Our Hopes," an address delivered at Low's Church, July 4, 1866; Colored men of Salem to W. L. Scott, Esq., May 31, 1870; Scott to Alexander Gates and the colored men of Salem, July 6, 1870; and G. M. Arnold to Scott December 28, 1871, Scott Papers.

42. John W. Payne to William L. Scott, July 27, 1871, Scott Papers.

43. Ibid.

44. Payne to Scott, August 4, July 29, 1871, Scott Papers.

45. Despite the success of proconventionists in Guilford County, the measure was defeated statewide. Ironically, two years later, when a similar effort was successful throughout the state, Guilford defeated it and chose anticonvention delegates. Thus the county was represented in the conservative constitutional convention of 1875 by the same individual who represented it in the convention of 1868, Albion Tourgée. A. S. Holton, peace member of the 1864 legislature, accompanied Tourgée to Raleigh as Guilford's other delegate.

Chapter 7

1. The preaching of a tract on infant salvation at the funeral of D. P. Weir's child was apparently the bone of contention against Smith. The issue was finally resolved when Smith departed for Indiana and Reverend J. Henry Smith (no relation to J. J.) arrived from Virginia to accept the pastorship (Juliana Gilmer's Diary, February 1859, DUL; D. P. Weir to Wiley, September 28, 1858, January 14, 1859, Calvin Wiley Papers, SHC).

2. "He will soon find out how popular he is," Levi Scott chortled when Gorrell decisively lost in his bid for commander of the North Regiment. James McLean, Scott's cousin, was particularly incensed by the appearance of the civilian Gorrell with a sword at his side during a women's wartime fundraising event and commented, "That part was tolerable disgusting to me" (Levi Scott to William L. Scott, February 24, 1862; McLean to William Scott, December 26, 1861, William L. Scott Papers, DUL).

3. Levi Scott to William Scott, October 31, 1861, Scott Papers.

4. Mary Eliza Scott to William L. Scott, November 31, 1861; Levi Scott to William Scott, February 7, 1862, Scott Papers.

5. Mendenhall to Gorrell, December 29, 1866, Ralph Gorrell Papers, SHC; N. L. Stick of Thomasville to Caldwell, March 28, 1870, February 21, 1871; Robert N. Caldwell to D. F. Caldwell, August 12, 1875, David Frank Caldwell Papers, SHC.

6. Tourgée described Dick as "not worth a wet dish cloth" after Dick did not do all Tourgée thought he should have to aid Tourgée in his bid for the nomination for the Fifth District congressional seat, and the Ohio native allegedly refused to assist when Scott and Dick, among others, tried to establish a newspaper in 1870 (Tourgée to Reverend G. W. Welker, March 23, 1868, Albion Winegar Tourgée Papers, SHC; George M. Mathes to D. F. Caldwell, January 3, 1870, Caldwell Papers). The Keogh-Tourgée hostilities are mentioned in Albion to Emma Tourgée, March 1, 1868, Tourgée Papers; Otto H. Olsen, *Carpetbagger's Crusade: The Life of Albion Winegar Tourgée* (Baltimore: Johns Hopkins Press, 1965), 117; and Keogh to Settle, March 19, 1869, Thomas Settle Papers, SHC.

7. Ball to Settle, June 24, 1874, Settle Papers. Ball also referred to animosities between himself and Tourgée in earlier days in a communication with the former judge, dated April 19, 1892, Tourgée Papers.

8. *Greensboro Times,* April 2, 1868.

9. *Patriot and Times,* October 8, 1868.

10. *Patriot,* July 29, 1869, April 17, 1868; Olsen, *Carpetbagger's Crusade,* 73.

11. *Patriot and Times,* September 24, 1868; *Patriot,* July 28, 1869, July 14, 1870.

12. Editorial prepared by Tourgée for the *Raleigh Standard,* Document 1467, Tourgée Papers.

13. *North State,* June 13, July 11, 1878.

14. Ibid., June 20, July 4, 18, 25, 1878.

15. Ibid., July 4, 18, 25, 1878.

16. Tourgée to David Hodgin, April 4, 1868, Tourgée Papers; *New North State,* September 19, 1872.

17. Tourgée to Thomas Settle, September 7, 1872, Thomas Settle Papers, SHC.

18. Tourgée, "In Contempt of the People," ca. 1875, Document 1886A, Tourgée Papers.

19. Scales, who claimed that the woman's brother-in-law committed the seduction, refused to fight when the pair arrived from the Deep South, choosing instead to post guards around his house for a week, Tourgée uproariously reported (Tourgée to Emma Tourgée, February 4, 1879, August 21, 1878, Tourgée Papers).

20. Tourgée, "Resolutions & Indictments Vindicating the Truth of History," September 9, 1875, and unidentified letter to Tourgée, May 8, 1871, Tourgée Papers; R. P. Dick to Settle, September 7, 1876, Settle Papers.

21. Tourgée to editor of the *Standard,* November 12, 1869; Tourgée to Captain A. G. Wilcox, April 2, 1868; Tourgée to Emma Tourgée, September 23, 1875, Tourgée Papers.

22. Letter by Gilmer to William H. Bagley, August 8, 1865, *Raleigh Daily Progress,* August 16, 1865.

23. Eugene Morehead's Diary, February 5, 1870, SHC.

24. Emma Tourgée to Albion Tourgée, September 8, 25, 1875; Tourgée to Angie, September 5, 1870; Tourgée to Dr. Sunderland, April 15, 1877, Tourgée Papers.

25. The letter to Emma urged her to try to persuade her husband to remain in the North for a while because if he returned, he would be "made way with some how." Even ladies were claiming that Tourgée needed a suit of tar and feathers, the writer continued, and "we who have always lived in the South know what such hints precede" ("The friend of all loyal people" to Mrs. Tourgée, n. d., Document 669, ibid.).

The letter to Albion was even less friendly: "It is about time that your lying tong [sic] was stopped—and if you ever show your ugly face in Guilford County again I will take care with some of my friends that you find the bottom of that *niger* pond you have been ranting so much about—I warn you never to show yourself in this county again" (unsigned letter to Tourgée, September 1866, ibid.).

26. In a letter to R. M. Tuttle, Tourgée commented that he had visited Stephens just before his murder (Tourgée to Tuttle, May 26, 1869 [1870?], ibid.).

27. Albion Tourgée to Emma Tourgée, March 20, 1872, ibid.

28. William Scott to Ella Scott, July 18, 1870, Scott Papers.

29. The press did not always distinguish between the names of the organizations, but once confessions began to come in 1871, the White Brotherhood was mentioned more frequently than the Klan, although their activities differed little (Tourgée, "Address to Grand Jury," ca. 1871, Tourgée Papers).

30. *Patriot and Times,* June 10, 1869.

31. *Greensboro Register,* October 20, 1869; *Republican Gazette,* October 28, 1869.

32. *Patriot,* October 28, November 4, 1869. Interestingly, the Democratic paper had only praise for black troops stationed for thirty days in Guilford during the election in November 1868 (*Patriot and Times,* November 12, 1868).

33. Albion Tourgée to B. B. Bulla, May 20, 1870, Tourgée Papers.

34. A. Dockery to Caldwell, April 14, 1870; Jas. A. Graham to Caldwell, July 30, 1870, Caldwell Papers.

35. Tourgée to Settle, August 30, 1870; Tourgée to J. C. Abbott, January 27, 1871, Tourgée Papers. Tourgée's persistence in pursuing Klan leaders is discussed in Olsen, *Carpetbagger's Crusade,* 184–87. The confessions obtained by Tourgée provided a profile of Guilford powerholders involved in organized violence because several Alamance confessors were members of White Brotherhood "camps" in Guilford. Especially useful was a detailed description by Julius B. Summers of "Apple's Camp," located in the Gibsonville vicinity in eastern Guilford and named for Macon Apple, who may have been the same individual as powerholder M. V. Apple (testimony of J. B. Summers, Alamance County, December 20, 1871, ibid.).

Among the seventy-six members of Apple's Camp identified by Summers were eleven members of the 1870 power group and two young men who were the sons of 1870 leaders. The latter two were John Boon, the son of Caleb, the former sheriff, who complained bitterly to Scott during the war about its unfairness, and Abner Apple II, the son of small farmer Abner Apple, who served as a tax lister, justice of the peace, and school committee member in 1868 and participated in Democratic politics in Washington Township as chairman of a nominating meeting in 1869 and chairman of a township meeting to choose delegates to the county convention as well as serving as a delegate in 1870. Like Apple's father, nine of the eleven powerholders who were members of the White Brotherhood were public officials, and three of these nine also participated in Democratic partisan efforts. Additionally, the two leaders who were not public officials secured power through Democratic activities. The most publicly active member of the group, James M. Sutton, was involved in decision making as secretary of a meeting to nominate candidates for the proposed constitutional convention in 1871 and as a delegate from Rock Creek Township to a county convention regarding this matter. Additionally, the forty-year-old deputy sheriff served as a delegate to the state Democratic convention in 1868, secretary of the Rock Creek Township nominating meeting in 1869, a delegate to the county convention in 1870, and a member of the Resolutions Committee of the county convention in 1872.

The most striking feature of the leaders who belonged to an association dedicated to the perpetration of violence and intimidation was their similarity to other powerholders. Seventy-five-year-old Ludwick Summers, with $20,000 in real estate and $10,000 in personal property, was by far the wealthiest member of the group, but all were well-to-do propertyowners, with James M. Sutton and William Love, each owning real property worth $1,000, having the smallest amount. The vast majority were middle-aged farmers who dwelled in the eastern townships of Washington and Rock Creek, although three hailed from the western townships of Oak Ridge and Friendship.

36. William Scott to Ella Scott, July 21, 1870, Scott Papers; Tourgée, "Ku Klux War in North Carolina," for the *National Standard,* August 1870, Tourgée Papers.

37. Tourgée, "Ku Klux War."

38. J. Morgan Kousser, *The Shaping of Southern Politics* (New Haven: Yale University Press, 1974), 14–15.

39. In keeping with Kousser's argument concerning the viability of Republicans in the South until the turn of the century, the Republican vote in Guilford did not decline dramatically until after disfranchisement in 1900. In the election of 1900, 3,343 voters participated; in 1904, voters totaled only 1,718.

40. William Scott to Ella Scott, July 21, 1870, Scott Papers.

41. Tourgée to E. S. Clark, August 1870, Tourgée Papers.

42. Glenn to Wiley, August 8, 1870, Calvin Wiley Papers, SHC.

43. *Greensboro Times,* February 27, 1868; *Patriot,* July 22, 1869. Warner purchased thirty-five acres of property on the outskirts of Greensboro, subdivided the land into half-acre lots, and transferred ownership to the Philadelphia Association of Friends, which over the next twenty years sold the plots to freedmen.

44. A forty-two-year-old cabinetmaker with $2,000 in real property and $700 in personal property in 1870, John A. Pritchett was elected coroner in 1868. He also served as a justice of the peace, registrar, and assessor in 1868–69, as well as chairman of the Resolutions Committee of the Republican county convention in 1872. Pritchett remained faithful to the GOP in the years 1878–82, serving in several partisan as well as official capacities. His most important office during this era was that of state legislator, a position to which he was elected in 1880.

Robert M. Stafford, the forty-year-old sheriff, managed to keep his political options open in 1870 by convincing both sides that he was sympathetic to them and thereby running as the only candidate in the election. Stafford subsequently beat Republican candidates in 1872, 1874, and 1876, did not run in 1878, and then lost as a member of the Coalition ticket in 1882 to a Democratic opponent.

45. Albion Tourgée to Emma Tourgée, March 1, 4, 6, 1868, Tourgée Papers. Despite his previous servitude, there was no evidence that Unthank was ever intimidated by Tourgée, even when the white attorney lost in his efforts to secure the Republican nomination for Congress and developed a "coolness" toward his black ally. Unthank, in fact, informed Tourgée that he preferred Thomas B. Keogh to William F. Henderson, although he knew that Tourgée did not like Keogh, and when chastised by Tourgée for not working hard enough in his congressional bid, Unthank replied unhappily but certainly not condescendingly: "I understood that the principle of the republican party was liberty, freedom of speech, etc. but by the

way you write, I do not think *freedom* of *speech* is *allowed*" (Unthank to Tourgée, July 22, 27, 1868, ibid.).

46. Almost thirty years after the partisan campaigns of the late 1860s, Arnold recalled having heard Tourgée speak at the opera house in Wilmington in 1868, but there was no other indication of the black leader's origins.

47. This assemblage, reputedly the first of its kind ever held in the community, resolved to support Grant and the National Union Republican party and urged that federal executive officials not discriminate on the basis of race. The group expressed fear that if Democrats came to power, the Thirteenth, Fourteenth, and Fifteenth amendments would be abrogated (*New North State,* April 4, 1872).

48. Of the nine black leaders in 1870, four were located in the population schedules and all four were artisans. Of eleven black powerholders in 1880, nine were found in the population schedules. Of these nine, four were laborers and one a farmer; the remaining four were in a trade. That all of the black leaders found in the census records in the years 1868–72 were skilled workers, whereas a majority of those located in the 1878–82 era were unskilled, may have resulted from the inadequacy of the census data, but it also raises the possibility that economic conditions were worsening for Afro-Americans generally in Guilford either because of the depression of the late 1870s or because the increased white population of those years resulted in blacks being pushed out of skilled work.

49. *Patriot,* August 11, 1870.

50. A few black leaders were nonpartisan officeholders, but they fared no better than their Republican counterparts. Joseph Wharton was a member of the school committee from the "colored district" of Gilmer Township; James Deans, a Holden appointee as justice of the peace in 1868, served in 1882 as a pollholder in Gilmer Township.

51. "COLORED MEN: Who rents you lands? Is it Radicals or Democrats? Look out for your interests," the *Patriot and Times* declared in September 1868.

52. The numbers of blacks in positions of influence are in all probability understated. It seems certain that there were black leaders in organizations like the Benevolent Society, an all-black association whose activities the *Patriot* chose to ridicule rather than report, but probably most of the Afro-Americans who were influential in the community as a whole are included since black officeholders were religiously reported by the Democratic press and partisan workers were included in Republican newspapers. Blacks who were involved in economic institutions such as the building and loan associations were also mentioned by both presses.

53. *Patriot and Times,* September 10, 1868; *North State,* July 18, 1878.

54. Caldwell to Worth's neighbor, August 5, 1845, Caldwell Papers.

55. Caldwell to Graham, August 25, 1868, William Alexander Graham Papers, SHC.

56. *Patriot and Times,* August 13, October 29, 1868, August 12, 1869. The extent to which the crime rate rose just after the war was difficult to determine, but there well may have been some increase. This did not necessarily mean that all of the

crimes were attributable to blacks, however, for there was a reported increase in crimes just after the Mexican War as well, and certainly Afro-Americans were not responsible at that time. For comments linking an increase in local crime and the Mexican War, see Nereus Mendenhall's Diary, March 26, 1851, Hobbs and Mendenhall Family Papers, SHC.

57. Payne to Scott, July 29, 1871, Scott Papers.

58. For the very important role of constitutional issues and political procedures in North Carolina politics before the war, see Marc W. Kruman, *Parties and Politics in North Carolina, 1836–1865* (Baton Rouge: Louisiana State University Press, 1983), esp. chap. 4.

59. Shober to Bryan Grimes, January 30, 1860, Bryan Grimes Papers, NCDAH.

60. Leach to Scott, November 21, 1865, Scott Papers; A. W. Ingold to Caldwell, May 15, 1870, Caldwell Papers.

61. C. B. Evans to D. F. Caldwell, June 4, 1870, Caldwell Papers; Leach to Scott, April 13, 1870, Scott Papers.

62. Albion Tourgée to Emma Tourgée, August 21, 1878, Tourgée Papers.

63. Gray to Vance, June 4, 1878, Zebulon B. Vance Papers, NCDAH.

64. Caldwell supported A. S. Merrimon in part because of their longtime friendship but also because he like Merrimon's soft money policy. Like Caldwell, Merrimon believed that the reauthorization of silver was "but a step in the right direction" (Merrimon to Caldwell, February 6, 1878, Caldwell Papers).

65. Pool to Scott, October 25, 1871; William Scott to Ella Scott's mother, November 9, 1871; W. W. Wheeler to Scott, November 9, 1871; Scott to Thomas Settle, December 22, 1871, Scott Papers.

66. Albion Tourgée to Emma Tourgée, March 19, 1868; Sophronia Winegar to Albion Tourgée, December 2, 1869; Albion Tourgée to Doctor Anderson, n.d., Document 1716; Emma Tourgée to Albion Tourgée, September 29, 1873; Albion to Emma Tourgée, February 4, 1875; Emma to Albion Tourgée, December 18, 1875; Tourgée to Honorable Third Auditor, Washington, June 19, 1876, Tourgée Papers; Olsen, *Carpetbagger's Crusade*, 208, 221.

67. Robert M. Douglas to Settle, February 9, 1881; Keogh to Settle, June 9, 1878, March 19, 1879, June 2, 1882, Settle Papers.

68. The relatively poor position of Democrats in comparison to Whigs was not noticeable in the more general analysis of powerholders in the preceding chapter because relative to all leaders, Democrats were not dissimilar. It was only in relation to Whigs that they appeared less affluent.

69. Democrats and Republicans also appeared at about the same rates in occupations outside of agriculture, with 19 percent of the Democrats engaging in business and 9 percent in a profession; comparable figures for Republicans were 14 percent and 8 percent.

70. Borrowing a quotation from Parson Brownlow, *On Village Aristocracy,* the editor of the *Carolina Watchman* of Salisbury prayed in his newspaper at midcentury, "God deliver us from the *bastard* aristocracy of our little villages, and the *cod fish* aristocracy of our larger towns" (*Carolina Watchman,* May 16, 1850, quoted in

Guion G. Johnson, *Ante-bellum North Carolina: A Social History* [Chapel Hill: University of North Carolina Press, 1937], 61).

71. James Willard Hurst, *The Growth of American Law: The Law Makers* (Boston: Little, Brown, 1950), 256; Judith N. Shklar, *Legalism* (Cambridge, Mass.: Harvard University Press, 1964), see esp. p. 9; Charles M. Haar, *The Golden Age of American Law* (New York: George Braziller, 1965), 7.

72. According to Hurst, law schools of this nature "were little more than an extension of the office-apprenticeship type of training, more systematized, and made available to more men by use of lectures" (*Growth of American Law*, 258).

73. Ibid., 257.

74. Ibid., 277.

75. Ibid., 286.

76. Juliana Gilmer's Diary, January, June 1848 and April 26, 1859; Robert P. Dick to Col. J. T. Morehead, May 27, 1865, James T. Morehead Papers, DUL; Dick to Settle, March 2, 1872, Thomas Settle Papers, SHC.

77. William Scott to Ella Scott, August 4, 1867, Scott Papers.

78. Morehead's Diary, February 5, 1870; J. M. Worth to D. F. Caldwell, September 10, 1873, Caldwell Papers; poem by Tourgée read by Gilmer, May 10, 1872, and Memorial Day Speech by Tourgée delivered at Wilmington, May 3, 1874; Albion Tourgée to Emma Tourgée, February 13, March 2, 1879, Tourgée Papers.

79. Tourgée purchased a house and lot from Julius A. Gray, and he sold property to Junius I. Scales. Lyndon Swaim designed the Tourgées' house, and Peter H. Adams loaned them money (Tourgée to Gray, May 1869; Tourgée to Emma Tourgée May 10, 1869; Swaim to Tourgée, October 13, 1869; Adams to Tourgée, August 11, 1870, Tourgée Papers).

80. Albion Tourgée to Emma Tourgée, September 10, 1875; Tourgée to Mendenhall, April 28, 1868; memos between Caldwell and Tourgée, October 13, 1868; Tourgée to Settle, October 14, 1873; J. M. Leach to Tourgée, October 23, 1873; and Dillard to Tourgée, September 5, 1879, ibid.

81. Tourgée's response to the Guilford Bar, August 16, 1870, ibid.

82. Tourgée to Joe, September 5, 17, 1870, ibid.

83. *Raleigh Standard*, December 29, 1868, quoted in Olsen, *Carpetbagger's Crusade*, 146.

84. Gorrell to Settle, July 16, 1873, and R. P. Dick to Settle, Settle Papers; Dick to Vance, October 22, 1865, Vance Papers.

85. Speech by Calvin Wiley in Greensboro for the Fourth of July celebration, July 4, 1876, Wiley Papers; Dick to Settle, January 21, 1878, Settle Papers; Judge Dick to Caldwell, January 9, 1879, Caldwell Papers.

86. William Scott to Ella Scott, September 16, 1868, Scott Papers.

87. Ibid., April 12, 21, May 12, 1867.

88. Scott to Leach, November 1865 (?) ibid.

89. Leach to Scott, June 2, 1870; Scott to Leach, June 29, July 6, 1870; Scott to Ella Scott, July 12, 1870, ibid.

90. William Scott to Ella Scott, July 18, 1870, ibid.

91. Ibid., October 12, 1870.
92. Ibid., October 16, 1870.

Conclusion

1. The literature surrounding these positions is discussed in the Introduction, note 3.

2. Eugene D. Genovese, *Political Economy of Slavery* (New York: Random House, 1961), and *The World the Slaveholders Made* (New York: Pantheon, 1969); Jonathan Wiener, *Social Origins of the New South: Alabama, 1860–1885* (Baton Rouge: Louisiana State University Press, 1978); Dwight B. Billings, Jr., *Planters and the Making of a "New South": Class, Politics, and Development in North Carolina, 1865–1900* (Chapel Hill: University of North Carolina Press, 1979).

3. In 1900, in another of their conservative solutions to political challenges, Democrats broke the back of the Republican party by eliminating most blacks from politics and discouraging many whites from participating through the addition of a suffrage amendment to the state constitution. Two-party politics would not return to North Carolina until the 1970s, when a much more conservative Republican party challenged more progressive Democrats.

4. J. Mills Thornton III, *Politics and Power in a Slave Society: Alabama, 1800–1860* (Baton Rouge: Louisiana State University Press, 1978), 64, 121–22. Thornton did note, however, that attorneys were especially prominent in the secession convention in Alabama, where they advocated immediate withdrawal from the Union (ibid., 426).

5. Wooster reported a decreasing percentage of lawyer-legislators in South Carolina, Mississippi, Louisiana, and Alabama, although the proportion of lawyers in the Alabama legislature remained at a constant 26 percent according to Thornton (Wooster, *Politicians, Planters, and Plain Folk: Courthouse and Statehouse in the Upper South, 1850–1860* (Knoxville: University of Tennessee Press, 1975), 119, 149; Thornton, *Politics and Power*, 64, 121–22). Wooster's upper South states included Virginia, Maryland, North Carolina, Kentucky, Tennessee, Missouri, and Arkansas. Wooster never explained his statement on page 33 that the number of lawyers increased among legislators in all upper South states except Missouri, but his Table 5f on page 152 indicated that the occupations of Missouri state senators in 1860 were not determined. Wooster, *Politicians*, 119, 149.

6. Others too mentioned increased participation in postwar affairs by young men, but it was Maddex who stressed this group as a key one among Virginia Conservatives (*The Virginia Conservatives, 1867–1879: A Study in Reconstruction Politics* [Chapel Hill: University of North Carolina Press, 1970], esp. 287–92. See also William C. Harris, *Day of the Carpetbagger: Republican Presidential Reconstruction in Mississippi* [Baton Rouge: Louisiana State University Press, 1979], and Wiener, *Social Origins*).

7. Twenty-four percent of the Republican voters in Tennessee were white in

the 1880 presidential election and 21 percent in North Carolina (Kousser, *The Shaping of Southern Politics* [New Haven: Yale University Press, 1974], 11–44, esp. 15).

8. Thornton observed that lawyers were always important in the Alabama Whig party, although some moved toward the Democracy in the 1850s because the latter party consistently controlled state offices (*Politics and Power*, 120). Wooster discovered that attorneys were much more likely to be Whig legislators than Democratic ones in all of the upper South states and that the percentage of lawyers among Whig legislators was almost twice as high as that among Democratic lawmakers in North Carolina, 33 percent compared to 18 percent (*Politicians*, 49).

9. Maddex strongly emphasized the involvement of former Whigs in postbellum Virginia, and Woodward cited their importance in Tennessee and North Carolina. Roger Hart also found Whigs in ascendancy in Tennessee, although his Redeemers included some old-line Democrats as well (Maddex, *Virginia Conservatives;* C. Vann Woodward, *Origins of the New South, 1877–1913* [Baton Rouge: Louisiana State University Press, 1951], esp. 103; and Hart, *Redeemers, Bourbons, and Populists: Tennessee, 1870–1896* [Baton Rouge: Louisiana State University Press, 1975]).

10. Billings, *Planters and the Making of a "New South,"* 213.

11. V. O. Key, Jr., *Southern Politics in State and Nation* (New York: Knopf, 1949), 211; emphasis added.

12. William H. Chafe, *Civilities and Civil Rights: Greensboro, North Carolina, and the Black Struggle for Freedom* (New York: Oxford University Press, 1980), 4–5.

13. Fusing with Republicans, North Carolina Populists enjoyed greater success than those in any other southern state, capturing all three branches of state government, legislative, judicial, and executive, by the mid-1890s. The extent of attorneys in their ranks is unclear.

14. Thornton, *Politics and Power*, 120.

15. Charles M. Haar, *The Golden Age of American Law* (New York: George Braziller, 1965), 3–4.

16. Marc Kruman carefully documented the resuscitation of the Whig party in North Carolina before the war and its lasting triumph over Democrats in 1862 in his work *Politics and Parties in North Carolina, 1836–1865* (Baton Rouge: Louisiana State University Press, 1983). The fortunes of the Whig party in Tennessee paralleled those in North Carolina. See Robert E. Corlew, *Tennessee: A Short History* (Knoxville: University of Tennessee Press, 1981), 275–82. No detailed information concerning prewar Virginia Whigs was located, but the strong emphasis placed by historian Jack Maddex on the important role played by former Whigs in postbellum politics leads one to suspect that, as in North Carolina and Tennessee, Whigs of Virginia may have begun to revive before the war. (*Virginia Conservatives*, esp. 283–87).

17. This unique feature of the second party system in North Carolina derived from exceedingly poor port facilities. Unlike other southern states with good harbors, a commercial, Whig-oriented elite did not arise in the coastal regions of North Carolina, for good ports were virtually nonexistent and planters, mainly

Democratic, tended to rely on commercialists in Norfolk or Charleston. (Only the Cape Fear River dumped directly into the Atlantic Ocean at Wilmington, North Carolina, and at the mouth of this harbor stood the treacherous Frying Pan Shoals.) Thus Whiggery emanated, in opposition to coastal Democrats, from North Carolina's uplands.

18. Morton Keller, *Affairs of State: Public Life in Late Nineteenth Century America* (Cambridge, Mass.: Belknap Press of Harvard University Press, 1977), 349, 351.

19. This point is made by both Keller, *Affairs of State*, 350, and Joel F. Handler, *The Lawyer and His Community: The Practicing Bar in a Middle-Sized City* (Madison: University of Wisconsin Press, 1967), 4.

20. Keller, *Affairs of State*, 350.

21. James Tice Moore commented on the preeminence of agrarian elites in recent studies of South Carolina, Alabama, Texas, Louisiana, Mississippi, and Florida, but he acknowledged that a similar group did not return to power in Tennessee until the early 1880s and that Maddex reached very different conclusions in his study of Virginia (Moore, "Redeemers Reconsidered: Change and Continuity in the Democratic South 1870–1900," *JSH* 44 [August 1978]:367–68). The important role played by the agrarian elite in Georgia is discussed in Numan V. Bartley, *The Creation of Modern Georgia* (Athens: University of Georgia Press, 1983).

22. Hart, *Redeemers*, 26.

23. Maddex, *Virginia Conservatives*, 276, and Hugh Talmage Lefler and Albert Ray Newsome, *The History of a Southern State: North Carolina*, 3d ed. (Chapel Hill: University of North Carolina Press, 1973), 542. Billings also discussed the involvement of North Carolina leaders in industrial development in his *Planters and the Making of a "New South,"* esp. 70–90.

24. Both these points are made by Kousser, *Shaping of Southern Politics*, 16–17. There were also additional factors that mitigated against social revolution in the lower, as well as the upper, South. These included Congress's lack of interest in land redistribution; the decision of the Reconstruction governments—and soon Congress—not to proscribe Confederate leaders; and the centrist strategy of Republicans and Democrats.

25. James L. Roark, *Masters without Slaves: Southern Planters in the Civil War and Reconstruction* (New York: Norton, 1977).

26. It should be emphasized that North Carolina's successes occurred relative to other southern states. Even as the state led others in the number of workers in manufacturing in 1940, for example, the proportion of industrial workers to the total working population was only 26.9 percent. Today, North Carolina remains one of the most rural states in the nation (Billings, *Planters and the Making of a "New South,"* 4–5, and Key, *Southern Politics*, 206).

27. Billings, *Planters and the Making of a "New South."*

28. Key, *Southern Politics*, 211.

29. Jack Bass and Walter DeVries, *The Transformation of Southern Politics: Social Change and Political Consequence since 1945* (New York: New American Library, 1976), 218–47, quote on p. 227.

Appendix 2

1. Floyd Hunter, *Community Power Structure* (Chapel Hill: University of North Carolina Press, 1953).

2. John Gilmer to Calvin Wiley, March 28, 1852, August 30, 1856, September 5, 1856, Calvin Wiley Papers, SHC.

3. September 1, 6, 1858, *Greensboro Daily News,* October 22, 1922, in Ralph Gorrell Papers, SHC, and Gorrell's will, dated and probated 1873, Guilford County Wills, NCDAH.

4. John M. Dick's will, probated 1861, Guilford County Wills, NCDAH; William D. Valentine Diary, June 2, 1855, SHC.

5. Bettie D. Caldwell, ed., *Founders and Builders of Greensboro, 1808–1908* (Greensboro: Jos. J. Stone, 1925), 39–41, 189–93.

6. Folders 34 and 35, William Calvin Rankin Papers, SHC.

Appendix 3

1. *Patriot and Times,* January 7, 1869, and *Patriot,* January 6, 1870. For municipal election results in the 1878–82 period, see *Patriot,* May 8, 1878, May 7, 1879, May 6, 1880, May 5, 1881, and May 4, 1882.

2. Additional insights into the workings of county conventions appear in *Patriot,* June 20, 1872, and June 26, 1878, as well as in *North State,* September 2, 1880.

3. *Patriot and Times,* September 3, 1868.

4. Ibid., October 8, 1868.

Bibliography

∽∽∽

Primary Sources

MANUSCRIPTS

Duke University Library, Durham,
N.C.
  Robert P. Dick to Democracy of
    Fifth Congressional District,
    Broadside Collection
  Juliana P. Gilmer Diary
  Guilford County Public School
    Register, 1857–65
  William D. Harden Papers
  Elias Hurley Letter
  James T. Morehead Letters
  William L. Scott Papers
  Charles Van Noppen Papers
  Thurlow Weed Papers
  Newton D. Woody Papers
North Carolina Department of
  Archives and History, Raleigh,
  N.C.
  Bryan Grimes Papers
  David S. Reid Papers
  Charles E. Shober Papers
  Mrs. Mary Kelly Smith Papers
  David L. Swaim Papers
  George W. Swepson Papers
  Zebulon B. Vance Papers
  John B. Wilson Papers
  Jonathan Worth Papers

MANUSCRIPTS (*continued*)

Southern Historical Collection,
  University of North Carolina,
  Chapel Hill, N.C.
  James W. Albright Books
  Daniel M. Barringer Papers
  Battle Family Papers
  Bond and Fentriss Family Papers
  Thomas Bragg Diary
  Addison Gorgas Brenizer Papers
  Bumpass Family Papers
  David Frank Caldwell Papers
  John Wilson Cunningham Papers
  Joseph Gibson Papers
  Jeremy Francis Gilmer Papers
  Ralph Gorrell Papers
  William Alexander Graham Papers
  Guilford Militia Book, 1806–54
  Benjamin Sherwood Hedrick Papers
  Hobbs and Mendenhall Family
    Papers
  Charles Lanman Papers
  Miscellaneous Papers
  Morehead Family Papers
  Eugene Lindsay Morehead Diary
  Leonidas L. Polk Papers
  William Calvin Rankin Papers
  Thomas Settle Papers

MANUSCRIPTS *(continued)*
Albion Winegar Tourgée Papers,
  microfilm, 60 rolls
William D. Valentine Diary
Abraham W. Venable Papers
Zeb Vance Walser Papers
W. T. Whitsett Papers
Calvin Wiley Papers

GOVERNMENT DOCUMENTS
North Carolina Department of
  Archives and History, Raleigh,
  N.C.
Guilford County, Board of
  Education, Minutes, 1878–82
Guilford County, Civil War Papers,
  1862–65
Guilford County, Common School
  Reports, 1847–52, 1858–62
Guilford County, County
  Commissioners, Minutes,
  1868–72
Guilford County, Court of Pleas and
  Quarter Sessions, Minutes,
  1848–52, 1858–62, 1868
Guilford County, Road Papers,
  1840–90
Guilford County, Superior Court
  Minutes, 1850–68
Guilford County, Wardens of the
  Poor, Minutes, 1848–52, 1858–62

GOVERNMENT DOCUMENTS
  (continued)
Guilford County, Wills, 1771–1925
U.S., Bureau of Census, Seventh,
  Eighth, Ninth, and Tenth
  Censuses of the United States,
  1850, 1860, 1870, 1880: Guilford
  County, North Carolina,
  Population and Slave Schedules,
  originals in NCDAH; Special
  Schedules, microfilm of National
  Archives manuscript copies,
  NCDAH.

NEWSPAPERS
Carolina Beacon, 1880
Daily Battleground (Greensboro),
  scattered issues, 1881
Greensboro Patriot, 1848–52, 1858–62,
  1878–82
Greensboro Register, 1869
Little Ad (Greensboro), May–July 1860
New North State (Greensboro), 1871–
  72; *North State,* 1878–84
Patriot and Times (Greensboro),
  1868–72
Raleigh Standard, 1865
Republican (Greensboro), 1870–71
Republican Gazette (Greensboro), 1869
Times (Greensboro), 1858–62
Way of the World (Greensboro), 1862
Weekly Message (Greensboro), 1851

UNPUBLISHED SOURCES
North Carolina Collection, University of North Carolina, Chapel Hill, N.C.
Albright, James W. "Guilford County: Its Resources." Ca. 1885.
"Greensborough: Its Population, Schools, Health, Etc." Ca. 1846.
Troxler, George. "Eli Washington Caruthers." 1865.

PUBLISHED SOURCES
Hamilton, J. G. deRoulhac. *The Correspondence of Jonathan Worth.* 2 vols. Raleigh:
  Edwards & Broughton, 1909.
Moore, Bartholomew, and Biggs, Asa. *Revised Code of North Carolina of 1854.*
  Boston: Little, Brown, 1855.

Padgett, James A., ed. "Reconstruction Letters from North Carolina." *North Carolina Historical Review* 18 (July 1941): 278–300; (October 1941): 373–92.

Parsons, C. G. *Inside View of Slavery: A Tour among the Planters.* Boston: John P. Jewett, 1855.

Secondary Sources

BOOKS

Aiken, Michael, and Mott, Paul A., eds. *The Structure of Community Power.* New York: Random House, 1970.

Arnett, Ethel Stephens. *Greensboro, North Carolina.* Chapel Hill: University of North Carolina Press, 1955.

Bartley, Numan V. *The Creation of Modern Georgia.* Athens: University of Georgia Press, 1983.

Bass, Jack, and DeVries, Walter. *The Transformation of Southern Politics: Social Change and Political Consequences since 1945.* New York: New American Library, 1976.

Bell, Roderick; Edwards, David V.; and Wagner, R. Harrison. *Political Power: A Reader in Theory and Research.* New York: Free Press, 1969.

Berle, Adolf. *Power.* New York: Harcourt, Brace, and World, 1967.

Billings, Dwight B., Jr. *Planters and the Making of a "New South": Class, Politics, and Development in North Carolina, 1865–1900.* Chapel Hill: University of North Carolina Press, 1979.

Blumin, Stuart M. *The Urban Threshold.* Chicago: University of Chicago Press, 1976.

Bottomore, T. B. *Elites and Society.* New York: Basic Books, 1964.

Caldwell, Bettie D., ed. *Founders and Builders of Greensboro, 1808–1908.* Greensboro: Jos. J. Stone, 1925.

Chafe, William H. *Civilities and Civil Rights: Greensboro, North Carolina, and the Black Struggle for Freedom.* New York: Oxford University Press, 1980.

Cheney, John L., Jr., ed. *North Carolina Government, 1585–1974: A Narrative and Statistical History.* Winston Salem: Hunter, 1975.

Clark, Terry N., ed. *Community Structure and Decision-Making: Comparative Analyses.* San Francisco: Chandler, 1968.

Cole, Arthur Charles. *The Whig Party in the South.* Washington: American Historical Association, 1913.

Corlew, Robert E. *Tennessee: A Short History.* Knoxville: University of Tennessee Press, 1981.

Coulter, E. Merton. *The South during Reconstruction, 1865–1877.* Vol. 8 of A History of the South. Edited by Wendell Holmes Stephenson and E. Merton Coulter. Baton Rouge: Louisiana State University Press, 1947.

Dahl, Robert A. *Who Governs? Democracy and Power in an American City.* New Haven: Yale University Press, 1961.

Davies, Ioan. *Social Mobility and Political Change*. New York: Praeger, 1970.

DuBois, W. E. Burghardt. *Black Reconstruction*. New York: Harcourt, Brace, 1935.

Dunning, William A. *Reconstruction, Political and Economic, 1865–1877*. New York: Harper & Row, 1907.

Eaton, Clement. *The Growth of Southern Civilization, 1790–1860*. New York: Harper and Brothers, 1961.

Edmonds, Helen G. *The Negro and Fusion Politics, 1884–1901*. Chapel Hill: University of North Carolina Press, 1951.

Evans, W. McKee. *Ballots and Fence Rails: Reconstruction on the Lower Cape Fear*. Chapel Hill: University of North Carolina Press, 1966.

Franklin, John Hope. *Reconstruction: After the Civil War*. Chicago: University of Chicago Press, 1961.

Gardner, James. E. *Eden: Past and Present, 1880–1980*. Eden, N.C.: Friends of the Eden Public Library, 1982.

Genovese, Eugene D. *Political Economy of Slavery*. New York: Random House, 1961.

——. *The World the Slaveholders Made*. New York: Pantheon, 1969.

Girvetz, Harry K. *Democracy and Elitism*. New York: Charles Scribner's Sons, 1967.

Green, Fletcher M. *Constitutional Development in the South Atlantic States, 1776–1860*. 1930. Reprint. New York: Norton, 1966.

Haar, Charles M. *The Golden Age of American Law*. New York: George Braziller, 1965.

Hamilton, J. G. de Roulhac. *Party Politics in North Carolina, 1835–1860*. Vol. 15 of The James Sprunt Historical Publications. Edited by J. G. De Roulhac Hamilton and Henry Wagstaff. Durham: James Sprunt Publications, 1916.

——. *Reconstruction in North Carolina*. New York: Columbia University Press, 1914.

Handler, Joel F. *The Lawyer and His Community: The Practicing Bar in a Middle-Sized City*. Madison: University of Wisconsin Press, 1967.

Harris, Carl V. *Political Power in Birmingham, 1871–1921*. Knoxville: University of Tennessee Press, 1977.

Harris, William C. *Day of the Carpetbagger: Presidential Reconstruction in Mississippi*. Baton Rouge: Louisiana State University Press, 1979.

Hesseltine, William B. *Confederate Leaders in the New South*. Baton Rouge: Louisiana State University Press, 1950.

Holmes, R. H. *Rural Sociology*. New York: McGraw-Hill, 1932.

Hunter, Floyd. *Community Power Structure*. Chapel Hill: University of North Carolina Press, 1953.

Hurst, James Willard. *The Growth of American Law: The Law Makers*. Boston: Little, Brown, 1950.

Johnson, Guion Griffis. *Ante-bellum North Carolina: A Social History*. Chapel Hill: University of North Carolina Press, 1937.

Jordan, Paula Stauls. *Women of Guilford County, North Carolina*. Greensboro: Greensboro Printing Company, 1979.

Keller, Morton. *Affairs of State: Public Life in Late Nineteenth Century America.* Cambridge, Mass.: Belknap Press of Harvard University Press, 1977.

Keller, Suzanne. *Beyond the Ruling Class.* New York: Random House, 1963.

Key, V. O., Jr. *Southern Politics in State and Nation.* New York: Knopf, 1949.

Konkle, Burton Alva. *John Motley Morehead and the Development of North Carolina, 1796–1866.* Philadelphia: William J. Campbell, 1922.

Kousser, J. Morgan. *The Shaping of Southern Politics.* New Haven: Yale University Press, 1974.

Kruman, Marc W. *Parties and Politics in North Carolina, 1836–1865.* Baton Rouge: Louisiana State University Press, 1983.

Lefler, Hugh Talmage, and Newsome, Albert Ray. *The History of a Southern State: North Carolina.* 3d ed. Chapel Hill: University of North Carolina Press, 1973.

Lipset, Seymour Martin. *Political Man: The Social Bases of Politics.* Garden City, N.Y.: Doubleday, 1960.

Lynch, John R. *The Facts of Reconstruction.* New York: Neale, 1913.

MacIver, R. A. *Society: Its Structure and Changes.* New York: Richard R. Smith, 1931.

Mackenzie, W. J. M. *Politics and Social Science.* Baltimore: Penguin Books, 1962.

Maddex, Jack P., Jr. *The Virginia Conservatives, 1867–1879: A Study in Reconstruction Politics.* Chapel Hill: University of North Carolina Press, 1970.

Mills, C. Wright. *The Power Elite.* New York: Oxford University Press, 1956.

Minar, David W., and Greer, Scott. *The Concept of Community.* Chicago: Aldine, 1969.

Mitchell, F. Memory. *Legal Aspects of Conscription and Exemption in North Carolina.* Vol. 47 of The James Sprunt Studies in History and Political Science. Chapel Hill: University of North Carolina Press, 1965.

Moore, Barrington, Jr. *Political Power and Social Theory: Six Studies.* Cambridge, Mass.: Harvard University Press, 1958.

Moore, John W. *History of North Carolina.* Raleigh: Charles C. McDonald, 1900.

Newby, I. A. *The South: A History.* New York: Holt, Rinehart, and Winston, 1978.

Nie, Norman H., et al. *Statistical Package for the Social Sciences.* 2d ed. New York: McGraw-Hill, 1975.

Nordlinger, Eric A. *Politics and Society: Studies in Comparative Political Sociology.* Englewood Cliffs, N.J.: Prentice-Hall, 1970.

Norton, Clarence Clifford. *The Democratic Party in Ante-Bellum North Carolina, 1835–1841.* Vol. 21 in The James Sprunt Historical Studies. Edited by R. D. W. Connor, W. W. Pierson, Jr., and Mitchell B. Garrett. Chapel Hill: University of North Carolina Press, 1930.

Olsen, Otto H. *Carpetbagger's Crusade: The Life of Albion Winegar Tourgée.* Baltimore: Johns Hopkins Press, 1965.

Owsley, Frank Lawrence. *Plain Folk of the Old South.* Baton Rouge: Louisiana State University Press, 1949.

Parker, William N., ed. *The Structure of the Cotton Economy of the Antebellum South.* Washington: Agricultural History Society, 1970.

Parry, Gerant. *Political Elites*. New York: Frederick A. Praeger, 1969.

Parsons, Talcott. *Politics and Social Structure*. New York: Free Press, 1962.

————. *The Social System*. New York: Free Press, 1951.

Pegg, Herbert Dale. *The Whig Party in North Carolina*. Chapel Hill: Colonial Press, 1969.

Phillips, Ulrich B. *Life and Labor in the Old South*. Boston: Little, Brown, 1929.

Polsby, Nelson W. *Community Power and Political Theory*. New Haven: Yale University Press, 1963.

Poplin, Dennis E. *Communities: A Survey of Theories and Methods of Research*. New York: Macmillan, 1972.

Press, Charles. *Main Street Politics: Policy-Making at the Local Level*. East Lansing, Mich.: Board of Trustees, Michigan State University, 1962.

Presthus, Robert. *Men at the Top: A Study in Community Power*. New York: Oxford University Press, 1964.

Redfield, Robert. *The Little Community*. Chicago: University of Chicago Press, 1955.

Rhodes, James Ford. *History of the United States from the Compromise of 1850*. Vol. 1. New York: Macmillan, 1892.

Roark, James L. *Masters without Slaves: Southern Planters in the Civil War and Reconstruction*. New York: Norton, 1977.

Robinson, Blackwell P., and Stoesen, Alexander R. *The History of Guilford County, North Carolina, U.S.A. to 1980, A.D.* Greensboro: Guilford County Bicentennial Commission and the Guilford County American Revolution Bicentennial Commission, 1981.

Sanderson, Dwight, and Polson, Robert A. *Rural Community Organization*. New York: Wiley, 1939.

Shklar, Judith N. *Legalism*. Cambridge, Mass.: Harvard University Press, 1964.

Siegel, Sidney. *Non-Parametric Statistics for the Behavioral Sciences*. Cambridge, Mass.: Harvard University Press, 1958.

Stampp, Kenneth M. *The Era of Reconstruction, 1865–1877*. New York: Knopf, 1965.

Stockard, Sallie W. *The History of Guilford County, North Carolina*. Knoxville, Tenn.: Gaut-Ogden, 1902.

Taylor, Alrutheus A. *The Negro in South Carolina during the Reconstruction*. New York: Russell and Russell, 1924.

Thornton, J. Mills III. *Politics and Power in a Slave Society: Alabama, 1800–1860*. Baton Rouge: Louisiana State University Press, 1978.

Thorpe, Francis N., ed. and comp. *The Federal and State Constitutions*. Washington: U.S. Government Printing Office, 1909.

Tourgée, Albion W. *A Fool's Errand*. New York: Fords, Howard, & Hulbert, 1879.

Wager, Paul. *County Government and Administration in North Carolina*. Chapel Hill: University of North Carolina Press, 1928.

Warren, Roland L. *The Community in America*. Chicago: Rand McNally, 1963.

Watson, Harry L. *Jacksonian Politics and Community Conflict: The Emergence of the Second American Party System in Cumberland County, North Carolina*. Baton Rouge: Louisiana State University Press, 1981.

Wharton, Vernon Lane. *The Negro in Mississippi, 1865–1890.* Vol. 28 of The James Sprunt Studies in History and Political Science. Edited by Albert Ray Newsome. Chapel Hill: University of North Carolina Press, 1947.

Wiener, Jonathan M. *Social Origins of the New South: Alabama, 1860–1885.* Baton Rouge: Louisiana State University Press, 1978.

Woodward, C. Vann. *Origins of the New South, 1877–1913.* Baton Rouge: Louisiana State University Press, 1951.

Wooster, Ralph A. *The People in Power: Courthouse and Statehouse in the Lower South, 1850–1860.* Knoxville: University of Tennessee Press, 1969.

————. *Politicians, Planters, and Plain Folk: Courthouse and Statehouse in the Upper South, 1850–1860.* Knoxville: University of Tennessee Press, 1975.

————. *The Secession Conventions of the South.* Princeton: Princeton University Press, 1962.

ARTICLES

Alexander, Thomas B. "Persistent Whiggery in the Confederate South, 1860–1877." *Journal of Southern History* 27 (August 1961): 305–29.

————. "Whiggery and Reconstruction in Tennessee." *Journal of Southern History* 16 (August 1950): 291–305.

Alexander, Thomas B.; Carter, Kit E.; Lister, Jack R.; Oldshue, Jerry C.; and Sandlin, Winfred G. "Who Were the Alabama Whigs?" *Alabama Review* 16 (January 1963): 5–19.

Alexander, Thomas B.; Elmore, Peggy Duckworth; Lowrey, Frank M.; and Skinner, Mary Jane Pickens. "The Basis of Alabama's Ante-Bellum Two-Party System." *Alabama Review* 19 (October 1966): 243–76.

Bachrach, Peter, and Morton S. Baratz. "Two Faces of Power." *American Political Science Review* 56 (December 1962): 947–52.

Bartley, Numan V. "In Search of the New South: Southern Politics after Reconstruction." *Reviews in American History* (December 1982); 150–63.

Beale, Howard K. "On Rewriting Reconstruction History." *American Historical Review* 45 (July 1940): 807–27.

Beringer, Richard E. "A Profile of the Members of the Confederate Congress." *Journal of Southern History* 33 (November 1967): 518–41.

Bonner, James C. "Profile of a Late Ante-Bellum Community." *American Historical Review* 49 (July 1944): 663–80.

Current, Richard N. "Carpetbaggers Reconsidered." In *A Festschrift for Frederick B. Artz,* edited by David H. Pinkney and Theodore Ropp. Durham: Duke University Press, 1964.

Donald, David H. "The Scalawag in Mississippi Reconstruction." *Journal of Southern History* 10 (November 1944): 447–60.

DuBois, W. E. Burghardt. "Reconstruction and Its Benefits." *American Historical Review* 15 (July 1910): 781–99.

Eutsler, Roland B. "The Cape Fear and Yadkin Valley Railway." *North Carolina Historical Review* 2 (October 1925): 427–41.

Folsom, Burton W. II. "The Politics of Elites: Prominence and Party in Davidson

County, Tennessee, 1835–1861." *Journal of Southern History* 39 (August 1973): 359–78.

Franklin, John Hope. "Reconstruction and the Negro." In *New Frontiers of the American Reconstruction,* edited by Harold M. Hyman. Urbana: University of Illinois Press, 1966.

――――. "Whither Reconstruction Historiography?" *Journal of Negro Education* 17 (1948): 446–61.

Freeman, Linton C.; Fararo, Thomas J.; Bloomberg, Warner, Jr.; and Sunshine, Morris H. "Locating Leaders in Local Communities: A Comparison of Some Alternative Appproaches." *American Sociological Review* 28 (October 1963): 791–98.

Glazer, Walter S. "Participation and Power: Voluntary Associations and the Functional Organization of Cincinnati in 1840." *Historical Methods Newsletter* 5 (September 1972): 151–68.

Green, Fletcher M. "Democracy in the Old South." *Journal of Southern History* 12 (February 1946): 3–23.

Hays, Samuel P. "Political Parties and the Community-Society Continuum." In *The American Party Systems,* edited by William Nisbet Chambers and Walter Dean Burnham. New York: Oxford University Press, 1967.

――――. "The Politics of Reform in Municipal Government in the Progressive Era." *Pacific Northwest Quarterly* 4 (October 1964): 157–69.

――――. "Social Analysis of American Political History, 1880–1920." *Political Science Quarterly* 60 (September 1967): 373–94.

――――. "A Systematic Social History." In *American History: Retrospect and Prospect,* edited by George Athan Billias and Gerald N. Grob. New York: Free Press, 1971.

Hillery, George A. "Definitions of Community: Areas of Agreement." *Rural Sociology* 20 (June 1955): 111–23.

Hollingshead, August B. "Community Research: Development and Present Condition." *American Sociological Review* 13 (April 1948): 136–56.

Jeffrey, Thomas E. "The Progressive Paradigm of Antebellum North Carolina Politics." *Carolina Comments* 30 (May 1982): 66–75.

Jones, Robert R. "James L. Kemper and the Virginia Redeemers Face the Race Question: A Reconsideration." *Journal of Southern History* 38 (August 1972): 393–414.

Linden, Fabian. "Economic Democracy in the Slave South." *Journal of Negro History* 31 (April 1946): 140–89.

McWhiney, Grady. "Were the Whigs a Class Party in Alabama?" *Journal of Southern History* 23 (November 1957): 510–22.

Moore, James Tice. "Redeemers Reconsidered: Change and Continuity in the Democratic South, 1870–1900." *Journal of Southern History* 44 (August 1978): 357–78.

Parenti, Michael. "Power and Pluralism: A View from the Bottom." *Journal of Politics* 22 (August 1970): 501–30.

Parsons, Talcott. "The Principal Structures of Community: A Sociological View." In *Community,* edited by Carl J. Friedrich. New York: Liberal Arts Press, 1959.

Polsby, Nelson W. "How to Study Community Power: The Pluralist Alternative." *Journal of Politics* 22 (August 1960): 474–84.

Sellers, Charles Grier, Jr. "Who Were the Southern Whigs?" *American Historical Review* 59 (January 1954): 335–46.

Simkins, Francis B. "New Viewpoints of Southern Reconstruction." *Journal of Southern History* 5 (February 1939): 49–61.

Tolbert, Noble J. "Daniel Worth: Tar Heel Abolitionist." *North Carolina Historical Review* 39 (July 1962): 284–304.

Trelease, Allen W. "Who Were the Scalawags?" *Journal of Southern History* 29 (November 1963): 445–68.

Weisberger, Bernard A. "The Dark and Bloody Ground of Reconstruction Historiography." *Journal of Southern History* 25 (November 1959): 427–47.

Wharton, Vernon L. "Reconstruction." In *Writing Southern History: Essays in Historiography,* edited by Arthur S. Link and Rembert W. Patrick. Baton Rouge: Louisiana State University Press, 1965.

Williams, Max R. "The Foundations of the Whig Party in North Carolina: A Synthesis and a Modest Proposal." *North Carolina Historical Review* 47 (April 1970): 115–29.

Woodman, Harold D. "Sequel to Slavery: The New History Views the Postbellum South." *Journal of Southern History* 18 (August 1977): 523–54.

Woodward, C. Vann. "The Political Legacy of Reconstruction." In *The Burden of Southern History.* Baton Rouge: Louisiana State University Press, 1960.

UNPUBLISHED SOURCES

Baylin, Jonathan F. "An Historical Study of Residential Development in Greensboro, 1808–1965." Chapel Hill: Department of City and Regional Planning, University of North Carolina, 1968.

Doherty, Robert. "Power and Society in New England." University of Pittsburgh, 1975.

Kipp, Samuel M. III. "Urban Growth and Social Change in the South, 1870–1920: Greensboro, North Carolina, as a Case Study." Ph.D. dissertation, Princeton University, 1974.

Rowe, Nellie M. "Ante-bellum Homes of Greensboro." Chapel Hill: North Carolina Collection, ca. 1908.

Index